FREEHAND DRAWING a primer

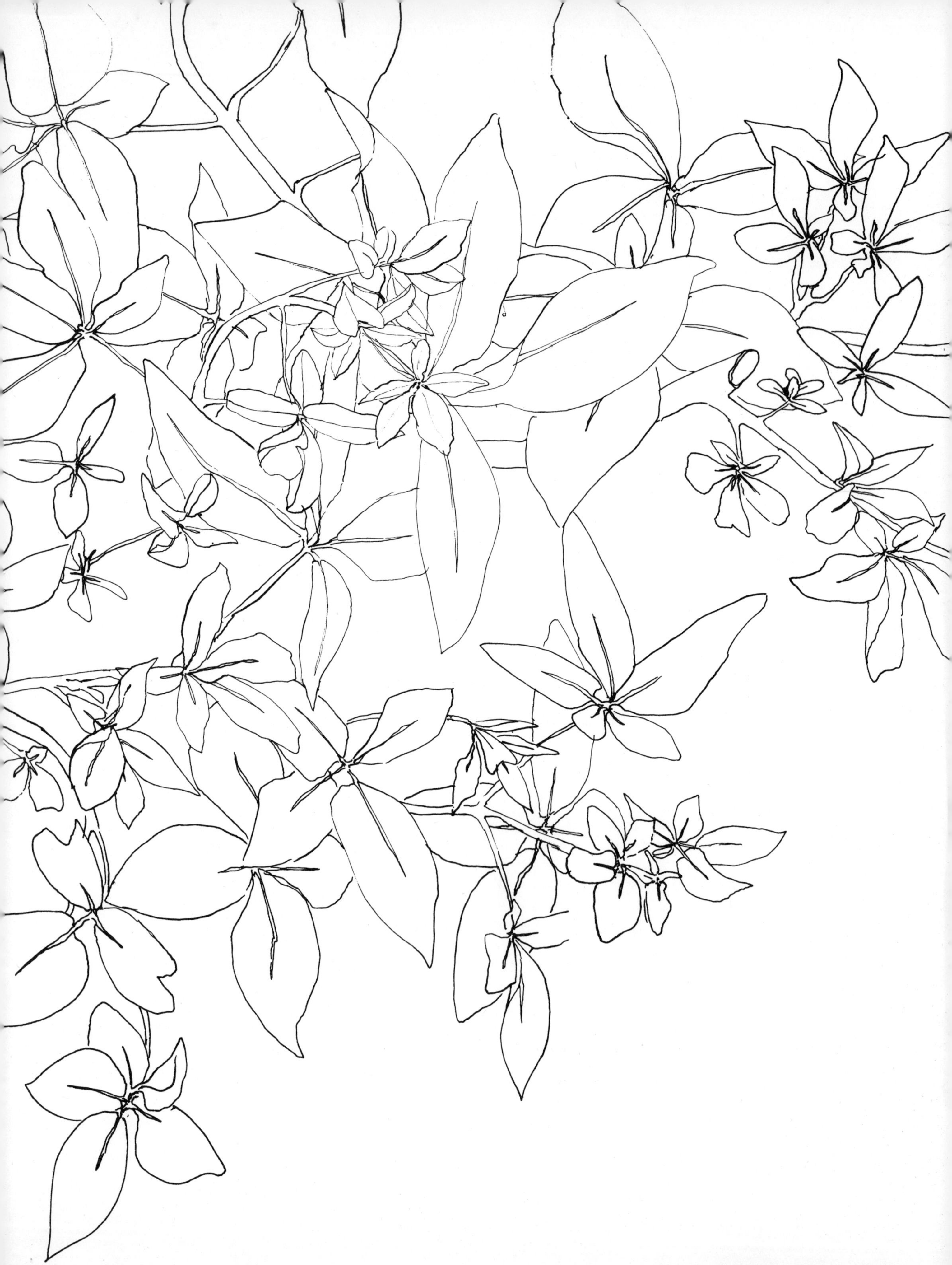

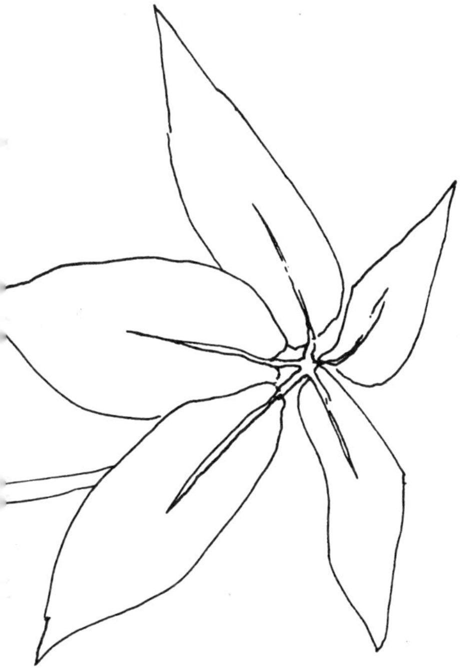

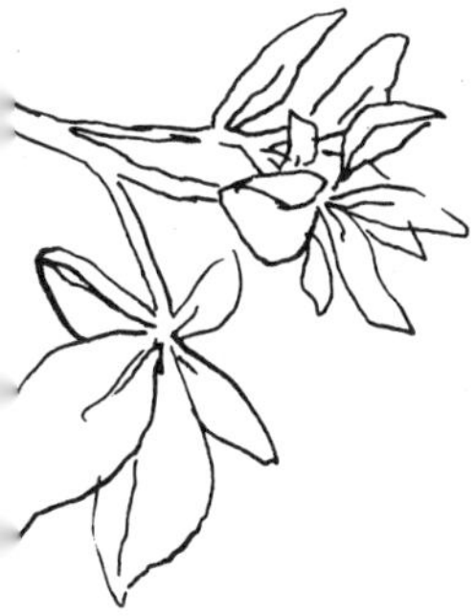

PHILIP THIEL

FREEHAND DRAWING

VAN NOSTRAND REINHOLD COMPANY
NEW YORK CINCINNATI TORONTO LONDON MELBOURNE

The author wishes to acknowledge the contributions of several teachers and many students to the development of the method of approach of this primer. He also wishes to thank the Louvre Museum for permission to reproduce the self-portrait of Hokusai.

First published in paperback in 1981

Library of Congress Catalog Card Number 81-51119
ISBN 0-442-28296-6

Printed in the United States of America

Van Nostrand Reinhold Company Inc.
135 West 50th Street, New York, NY 10020

Van Nostrand Reinhold Australia Pty. Ltd.
480 Latrobe Street, Melbourne, Victoria 3000

Van Nostrand Reinhold Company Ltd.
Molly Millars Lane, Wokingham, Berkshire, England RG11 2PY

Cloth edition published 1965 by the University of Washington Press
Seventh cloth impression 1978

16 15 14 13 12 11 10 9 8 7 6 5 4 3 2

CONTENTS

WHO CAN DRAW?

Experience indicates that anyone who can freely make a mark on paper can learn to draw very well indeed. The major requirements (other than determination) seem to be principally the virtues of responsibility and self-respect. Time, of course, is another factor; and as Hokusai suggests, a lifetime is hardly long enough. But a three-hour session once a week, for about thirty weeks, has been shown to be enough to develop the latent potentialities we all possess.

This is a primer for those who are interested in learning how to draw. More specifically, it presents a series of studies by means of which one may gradually and confidently develop a greater awareness of visual form relationships, a greater sensitivity to form qualities, and competence in clear and coherent freehand graphic representation. In its role as a freehand drawing primer this book is not directly con-

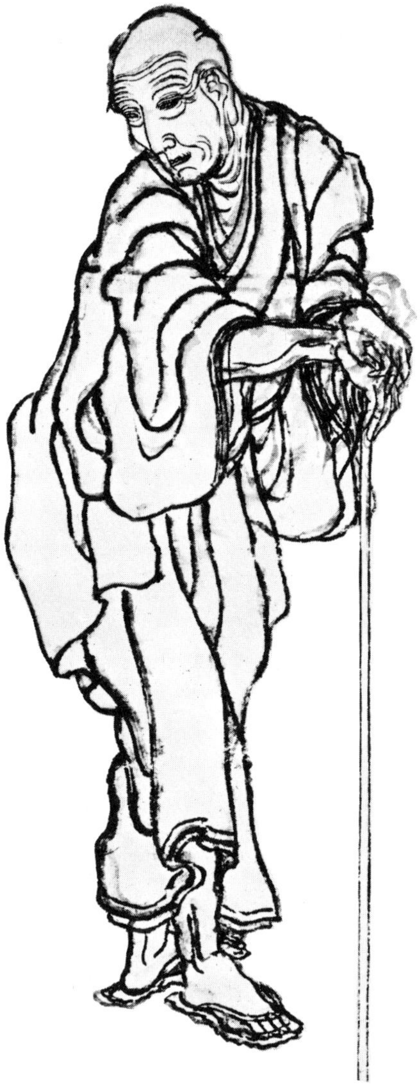

From the age of six I had a mania for drawing forms of things. By the time I was fifty I had published an infinity of drawings, but all I have produced before the age of seventy is not worth taking into account. At seventy-five I learned a little about the structure of nature—of animals, plants, and bees, birds, fishes and insects. In consequence when I am eighty I shall have made a little more progress. At ninety I shall certainly have reached a marvelous stage, and when I am a hundred and ten, everything I do—be it but a line or a dot—will be alive.
Hokusai, The Manga

cerned with drawing as "Art," in terms of personal expressions of feelings or attitudes, but it is concerned with representational drawing as the art of the successful graphic communication of visual form data. Thus it is an academic text, concerned with the development of basic, fundamental skills in objective observation and representation. Having established this foundation of competence one is then in a position to launch more successfully into richer, more complex, and more subjective forms of visual expression.

But note that this work will cost you effort, time, and trouble. This is a major skill you are developing, and it will not suddenly blossom in you, a full-blown rose. You may confidently expect to shed blood, sweat, and tears if you persevere in these studies, as the inevitable price of any worthwhile achievement.

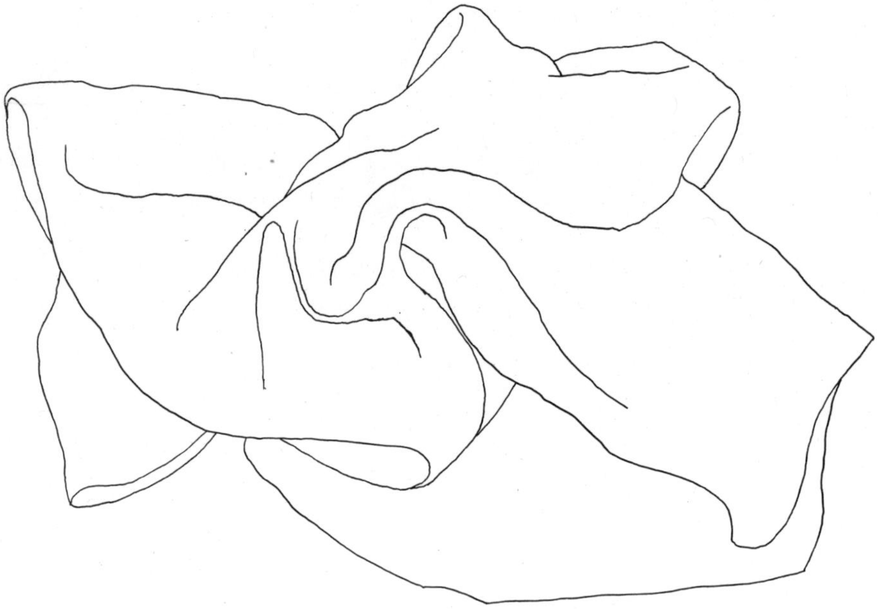

ON OBSERVATION AND REPRESENTATION

The discipline of observation involves a heightened level of awareness and the appreciation of uniqueness; the discipline of representation involves the graphic communication of what has been seen and understood. As you will discover later, it may also unconsciously include what has been felt about what has been seen.

Observation means more than merely looking: it implies the discernment of significant form relationships. The clarity of these observed relationships is tested in the fact of your representation, just as in written communication the clarity of the ideas expressed is tested by the coherence of what is written.

The processes of observation and representation interact on each other. The discovery of a particular form quality (such as the softly modulated fold of a piece of cloth, or the flaky, crusty quality of a bit of tree bark) will demand the invention of a specific mode of representation; the process of devising and evaluating suitable ways to do this will heighten your form sensitivity. Thus, representational drawing is a potent means of developing form sensitivity, a deeper awareness of visual relationships, and of strengthening your ability to make coherent graphic statements.

You will understand that you must make your own explorations, and thus your own form discoveries and descriptive inventions. These will be your own contributions to the art of communication and are a result of your personal growth and development.

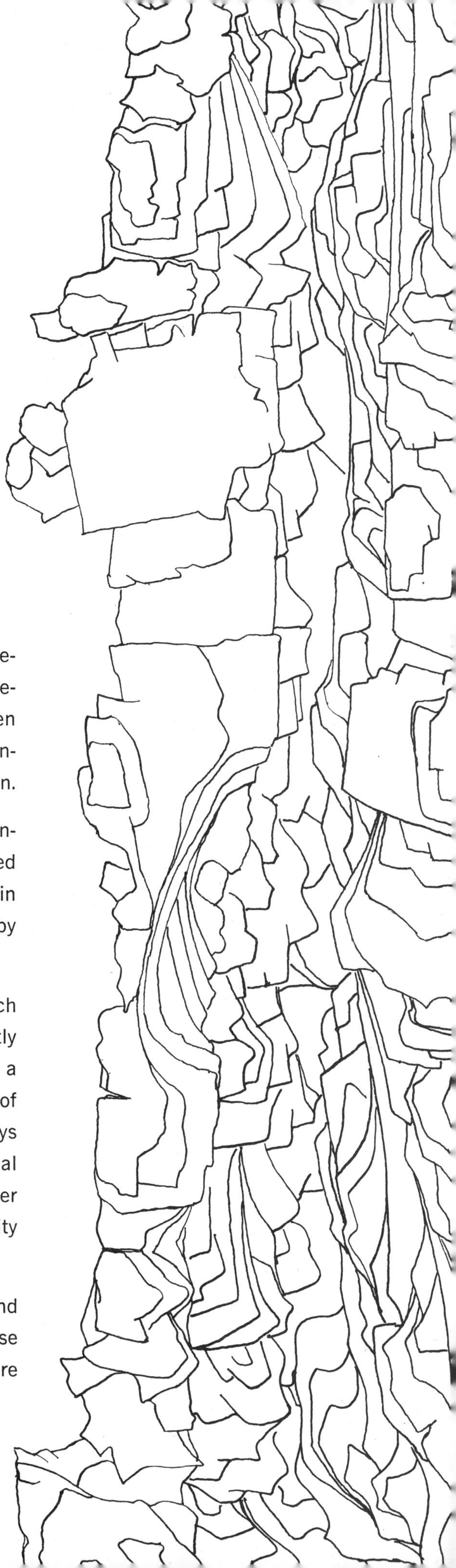

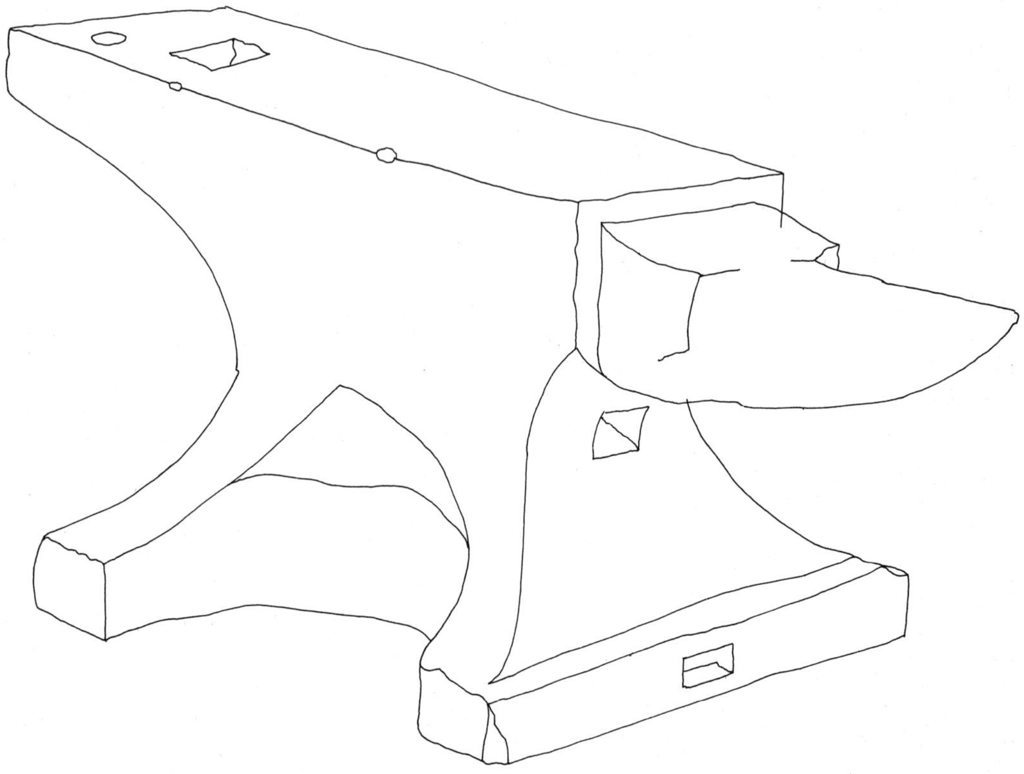

WHAT TO USE

If drawing is the art of representing form by means of marks on a surface, then anything that will make a mark may be used for drawing. Your toe in the sand, your finger on the frosted windowpane; a stick in clay, a brush on rice paper, and a quill on parchment; a grease crayon on stone, a steel needle on a copper plate; a pencil on the tablecloth, or a ball-point pen on the back of an envelope—these and many more are all legitimate and valid tools, and, like every instrument in an orchestra, each possesses its own characteristic "color."

For the special purposes of this primer, however, we shall use two specific sets of tools and surfaces. The first set consists of the soft velvety lead pencils known by the trade names of "Ebony" or "Draughting," and newsprint paper. The pencils should be sharpened (and kept sharpened) to a fine conical point. The newsprint is available in pads or blocks: the size should be no smaller than 18 inches by 24 inches; and the paper with the smoother, less textured surface is preferable. These pencils and the newsprint are inexpensive and humble things, and you will use them freely and without intimidation.

When the block of newsprint is used up you will be ready for the second set of tools and surfaces. These are the delicate steel pens known as "Crowquill," and they should be used with black India ink on white or buff "detail" paper. The inexpensive pens come in a variety of degrees of flexibility, and you should try them all to find which ones are best suited to you. The detail paper is about the most inexpensive paper that will work well with the pen: the color is immaterial, but the sheet should be no smaller than 18 inches by 24 inches in size.

In addition to the above you should have a lightweight drawing board a little larger than 18 inches by 24 inches and a wallet-type envelope portfolio to hold all your work without folding. You need nothing more.

These tools are suggested because they can be used to produce precise, incisive lines. The method of this primer is based on this incisiveness. But even at this you will discover that each of these tools is capable of a range of "weight," or width and blackness of line, depending on the pressure applied. This "palette," or range, may be consciously or unconsciously exploited in drawing for expressive purposes. But for our purpose of developing control we require that attention shall be concentrated on achieving a lightweight, uniform line.

What is the correct way to use these tools? The answer is, any way you discover that will enable you to do what you want to with them. This suggests that you should experiment with the tool to see what it (and you) are capable of. Go ahead; try them out on a piece of paper; put them through their paces, and see how many different effects you can devise.

THE PROCEDURE

The method of this primer is indicated by the series of studies described in the following pages. They are in a specifically arranged order: each one depends and builds on the preceding ones. The subjects have been selected to provide a wide range of form qualities.

The following notes describe the procedure:

1. All drawing is to be directly from life, **in line only,** slowly and deliberately, with no preliminary "sketching" or "blocking-out." There should be no alterations, additions, changes, or corrections to the line once it is down; like a spoken word, it can never be recalled. If it is not satisfactory, you have learned something; but then start over again, on a new sheet or on the other side of the sheet. **This is most important and is the essence of the method.** This procedure concentrates all creative effort on the heart of the problem: the development of judgment of size, position, direction, and shape. To "sketch," or to approximate, is to shirk this basic problem and thus waste your time. The problems are so graduated that it is easily possible to achieve a good measure of success on each in turn, and thus build an increasing store of confidence.

2. Start drawing at any point of what you see; go very slowly, draw very lightly, and try to imagine you are lightly touching the object as you draw it. Do not worry about "proportion" or "perspective" or "composition." These matters will take care of themselves, automatically (you probably will not believe this), but if you are concerned over them as "problems" they will inhibit your exploration and discovery of form. This is not to say that "proportion" and "perspective" and "composition" are not important, but only that preoccupation with them will stand in the way of your learning to see, at this time.

3. You will encounter many problems in representing particular form qualities. This is your individual problem, and if your drawing is to have any meaning and value to you (and others), it must be solved individually. It is for you to find a way by a series of experimental trials. In a very real sense your studies represent original research.

4. The criterion for evaluating your work is whether it is coherent, explicit, complete, and clear enough to enable a sculptor who is unfamiliar with the object to reconstruct it on the basis of your drawing alone, without supplementary verbal explanation.

Associated with this is the matter of economy. If your work conveys the clearest indication of the form with a minimum use of means, you have penetrated to the heart of the matter. By eliminating the nonessential you have made visible the quintessence.

Since your individual struggles in solving the following problems are indispensable to your development, and since your individual achievements are significant in their own right, the drawings shown here—all student work—should be used not as guides to solutions, but as indications of possible and preferred levels of responsibility. They are intended only as yardsticks of achievement which your own solutions should equal, and could exceed.

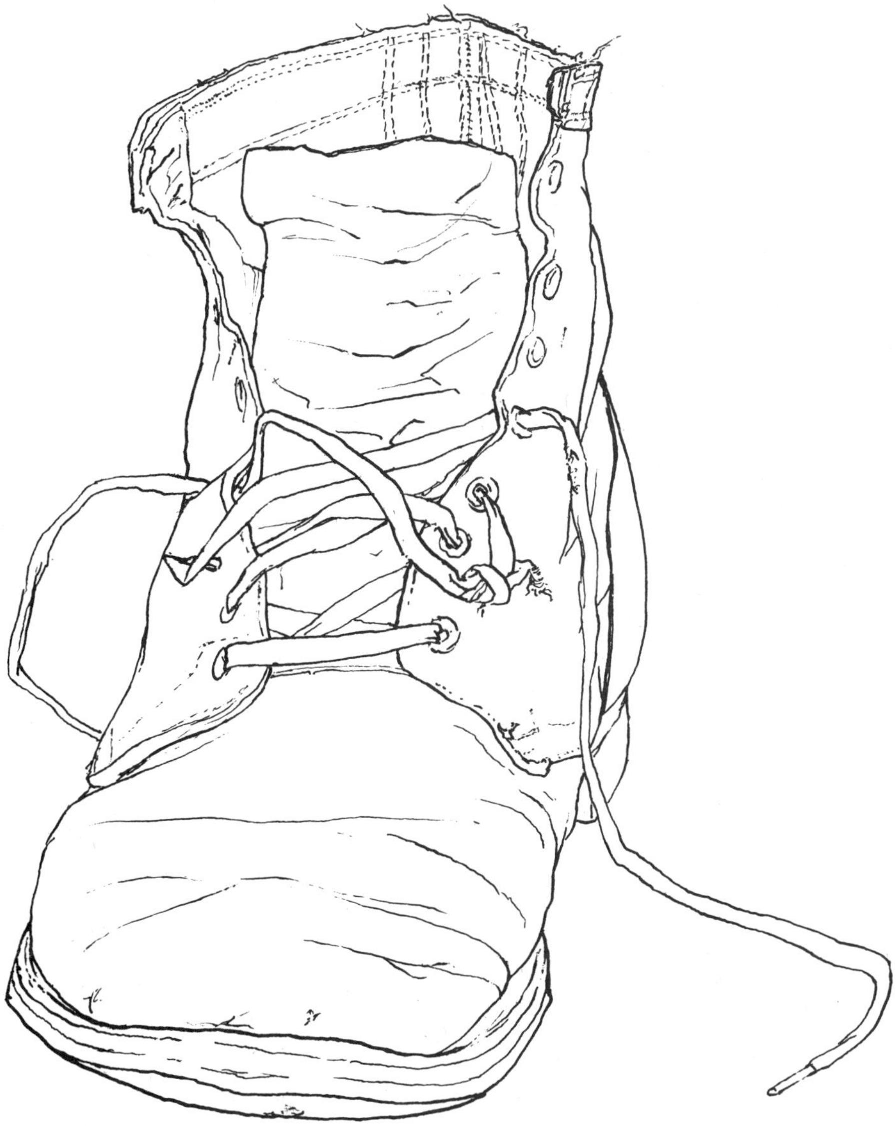

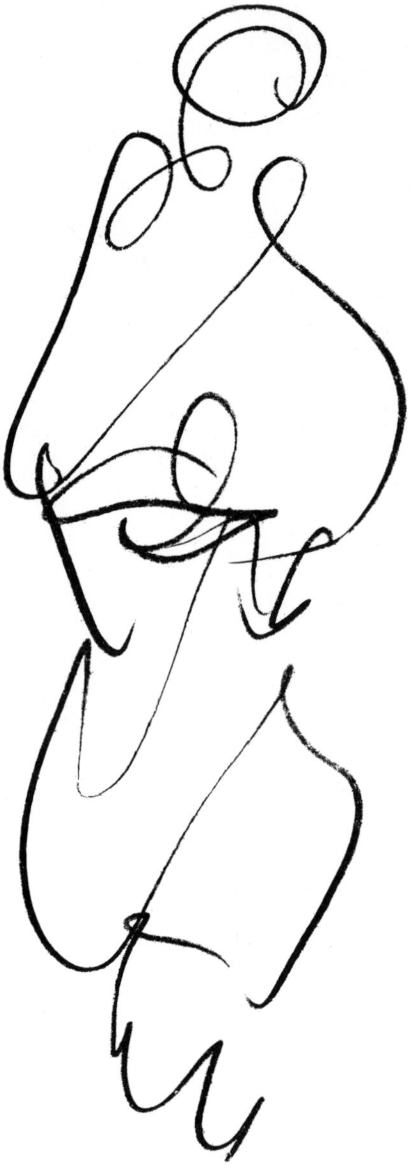

OUTLINE AND CONTOUR *Visual contour dominates visual space. Perceptually a contour is a line. When we hear that Nature has no such thing as a line, vision answers that all contours are lines. That every contact of fields of light or color is sharpened and stressed into a line—a psychological line. "Contrast" develops a "line" at every contact between abruptly distinguishable areas. If the mind did not deal in "lines" an outline drawing could hardly be the magical thing it can be. Simple outline diagrams, serving to illustrate clearly by the thousands. The mind dealt in "lines"? The so-called rivalry of contours is a master key to "meaning" in visual perception. As far as the mind thinks spatially its thinking largely accepts "lines" and manufactures them.*

Sir Charles Sherrington, Man on His Nature
(New York: Cambridge University Press, 1953)

Outline is used abstractly in the earliest human record of graphic communication. In perception, the figure contained by its own boundary line is part of a larger visual field, is colored, rounded, soft or hard, and exists in deep space. In early cave drawings, the outline is all—there are no interior details to complete the figure, no background to orient it in space. A three-dimensional object has been converted to a two-dimensional pattern. Many different experiences of an animal have been combined and reconciled; a composite experience is communicated. The creative faculties of early man have constructed what was clearly regarded as the animal's permanent, most characteristic aspect. We are given a symbol. . . .

. . . We approach abstract thinking as we sharpen our perception and learn by observation to distill invariant aspects of nature from shifting, complicated visual events. We distinguish the moon, animals, trees as figures—sensed forms—against the background of what they are not. Physiologically, we receive our strongest visual impression at the contour line, the boundary line between figure and background. Thus, our visual images of objects are defined by the contours.

When a figure is an irregular three-dimensional form—like the body of a human being—we are not confused or led astray by the shifting contour that never remains the same for a moment. We are made to see these endlessly changing aspects as persistent forms. In our heads, we build images of the moon, of animals, of trees, choosing from our remembered perceptions the contours which are significant to us. Perception of the boundary line enables man to populate his inner world with the forms and patterns which correspond to the outer world's objects. He begins to understand relations with greater clarity, developing his capacity to control his environment.

Defining objects by shape was only one aspect of the role of line, just as separating a thing from its metamorphoses is only one aspect of perception. Once invented, the graphic line could assume a kind of independent life. The movement of the graphic tool across a surface could convey experience of movement and change, abstracting from perception of process and transformation. In the life of the stroke there was more than shape—motion and change were there as well. The growth of the line—its emergence from nothing, its speed, rhythm, length and directional changes—presented another key to the understanding of the world. . . .

Gyorgy Kepes, The New Landscape in Art and Science
(Chicago: Paul Theobald and Co., 1956)

Gestures often describe the shape of objects by their outlines, and it is for this reason that representation by outline seems to be the simplest psychologically and most natural technique for making an image by hand. The filling of the surface with paint or the modeling or carving of an object involves movements that may lead to the desired shape but are not in themselves an imitation of that shape. They serve visual representation more indirectly than recorded gesture.

Line, the prime element of the child's work, must be considered a tremendous abstraction by the realist. "There are no lines in nature," he points out. Lines are indeed highly abstract if we view drawings merely in comparison to "photographic" reality. However, if we understand representation to be the creation of a structural equivalent rather than a mechanical duplication, and if we remember that line is produced by a motor act in a pictorial medium, we find that the one-dimensional trace is the eminently concrete and direct rendering of perceived shape.

Rudolf Arnheim, Art and Visual Perception
(Berkeley: University of California Press, 1954)

The great and golden rule of art, as well as of life, is this: That the more distinct, sharp, and wirey the bounding line, the more perfect the work of art, and the less keen and sharp, the greater is the evidence of weak imitation, plagiarism, and bungling. . . . The want of this determinate and bounding form evidences the want of idea in the artist's mind, and the pretence of the plagiary in all its branches. How do we distinguish the oak from the beech, the horse from the ox, but by the bounding outline? How do we distinguish one face or countenance from another, but by the bounding line and its infinite inflexions and movements? What is it that builds a house and plants a garden, but the definite and determinate? What is it that distinguishes honesty from knavery, but the hard and wirey line of rectitude and certainty in the actions and intentions? Leave out this line and you leave out life itself; all is chaos again, and the line of the almighty must be drawn out upon it before man or beast can exist. . . .

William Blake, "A Descriptive Catalogue," 1809

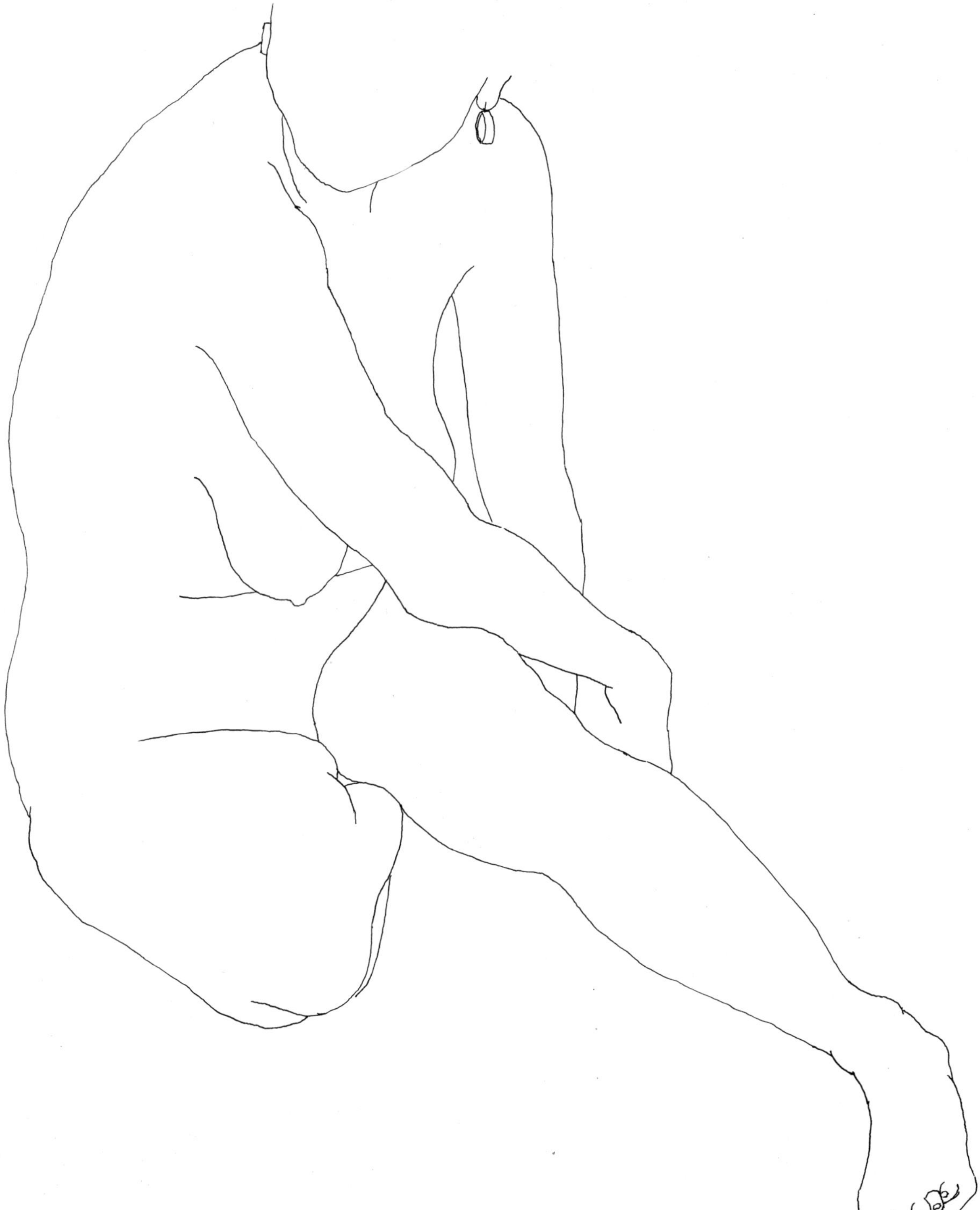

1

EXPLORATIONS *three hours*

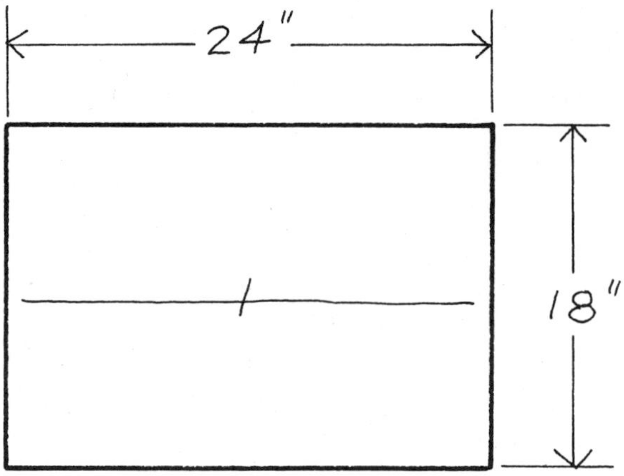

Our purpose here is to introduce you to the pencil and paper—and to yourself, as indicated by your responses to the problems set. Another purpose is to establish and objectify such basic matters as control, and the evaluation of performance.

Start by arranging your 18-by-24-inch newsprint pad in a horizontal format. Using the point (not the side!) of your well-sharpened pencil, **slowly** draw a **light, even,** continuous **straight** horizontal line across the middle of the sheet, the full 24 inches in length. Hold your hand any way that is comfortable and either use a single continuous motion or stop and rest at intervals. The line itself should look continuous, and it should be straight. To check on the straightness, "sight" the line by looking at it endwise, along its length, with your eye near the plane of the paper. In this way you can more readily check on the unevenness of the line.

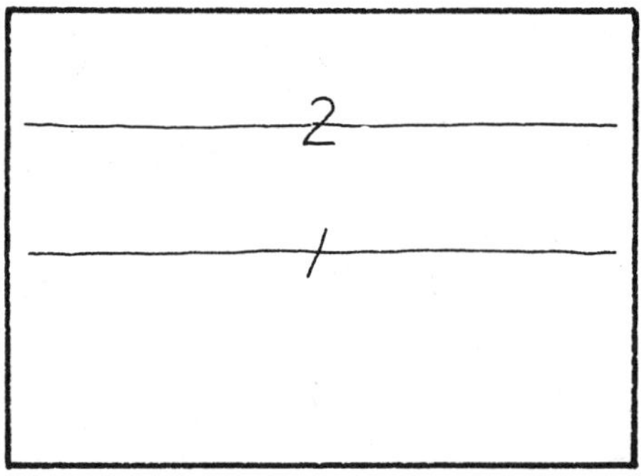

Now, draw a **straighter** horizontal line the same way through the middle of one of the remaining two spaces; sight it again, and repeat once more. Each time consciously correct as you go along any tendencies you noted in sighting the previous line. Relax, and remember to draw evenly and lightly. Repeat this procedure once again, on a new sheet.

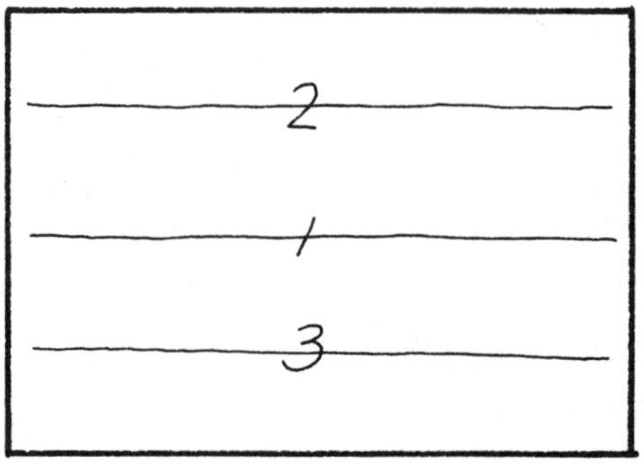

Next, arrange your pad vertically and, working either from top to bottom or from bottom to top, slowly draw light, even, **straight** vertical lines following the same procedure. Be sure to keep the pad vertically in front of you; do not change your orientation to the pad.

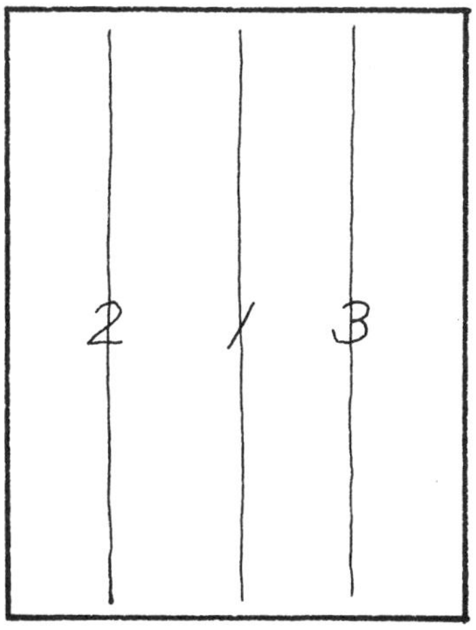

Going fast will smooth out local irregularities but will tend to increase the over-all curvature. Go slowly and keep the **total** line straight. Do not be concerned over the inevitable small irregularities; they only prove that you are a human being, and not a machine.

It may be desirable consciously to overcorrect a tendency you may discover. Keep the pencil point sharp, and use it quite lightly; think of it as an extension of your own body. Put all you have into each line; fall in love with the very idea of straightness! There is no virtue in filling up the sheet quickly with imperfectly straight lines. Remember that this is a work sheet and you are exploring a problem.

Now, on a fresh sheet, locate a point near the center and, without altering your relation to the pad, slowly draw light, even-weight straight lines radiating out from the center to the edges of the sheet. This exercise is designed to objectify the problem of drawing straight lines in any direction, without changing your body position in relation to the paper.

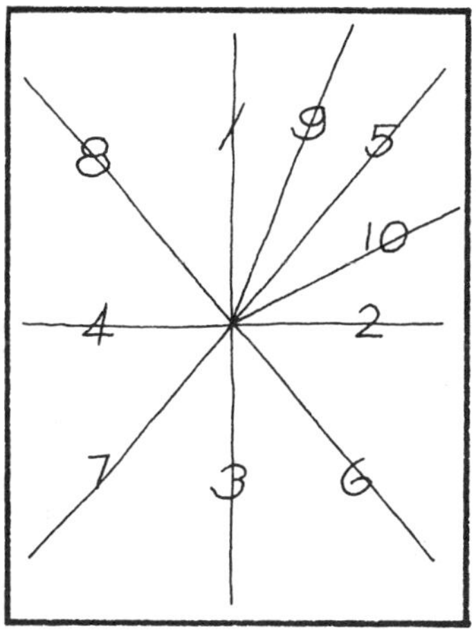

As a suggestion, first draw a straight line upward to twelve o'clock, next out to three o'clock, then down to six o'clock, and finally over to nine o'clock. **Sight each line after you draw it.**

Then go around again, this time bisecting (more or less) each of the four quadrants, and then around once more. Do not hurry; remember that the objective is to develop your ability to produce good **straight** lines, drawn in any direction, **without** changing your body position.

Now try a variation on this by drawing a square spiral. Start again at the center of the sheet and, moving either clockwise or counterclockwise, with a single continuous line draw alternately horizontal and vertical lines in an expanding square spiral. Here the new challenge is not only in making the lines straight and uniform in weight, as drawn in any direction, but in keeping them parallel and a constant distance—say ¼ inch—apart. Do this out to the edge of the paper, and resist the tendency to increase the space between the lines as you grow out from the center.

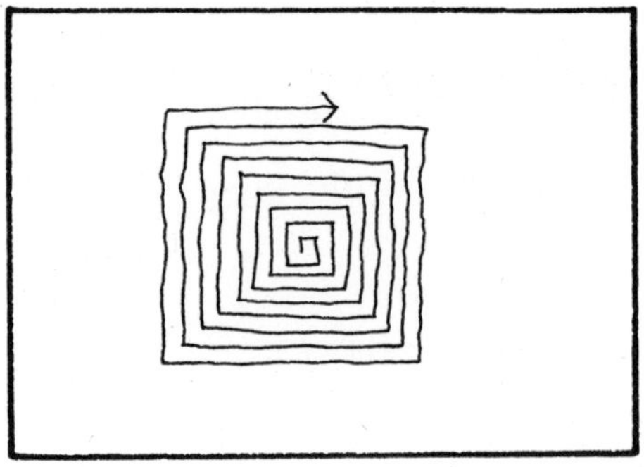

Expect to have trouble. If you are not having difficulties, either you are already a master or your standards are too low. Trouble is a symptom of growth. Get used to it, for you will always have it with you. As you master certain problems, new ones will arise. Each time you shift the problem to a new level.

Next, take a fresh sheet of paper and using the entire area locate on it at random fifteen or twenty small precise dots. Call one of these near one edge of the sheet M (for Minsk), and from it draw a **straight,** light, even line all the way across the continent toward another dot, called P (for Pinsk). Perhaps your straight line will end at Pinsk; more likely it will end in a suburb. Do not curve it! (And do not make a new Pinsk at the end of your line!) Now make some more transcontinental trips—slow, long, straight ones from one dot toward another distant one. Travel in all directions; you are already used to doing this. Be honest about your misses, let them show, and just do better on the next trip.

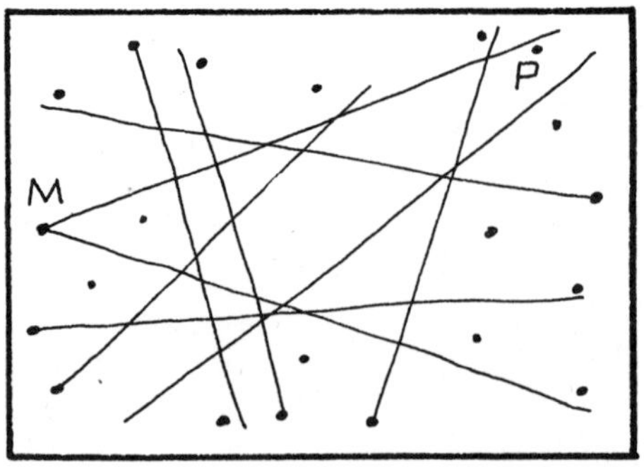

Now draw a circular spiral. As before, start at the center of a new sheet. Circle outward with a light, even line, a constant distance from the previous line, maintaining a **circular** form. Avoid the ovoid. Go right out to the edge of the paper, and be sure that you are not increasing the distance between lines in a rush to get done. Speed comes later—about forty years later.

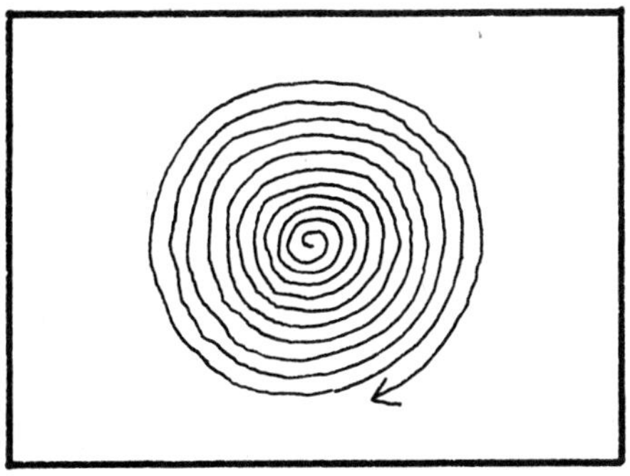

Next draw a row of circles between imaginary horizontal guidelines about 2 inches apart. Keep your hand moving slowly and evenly in a circular motion, and go right on to the next circle as you finish the one before. Become a circle yourself. Make each circle more circular than the one before. Be sure you are making circles; do not lay eggs.

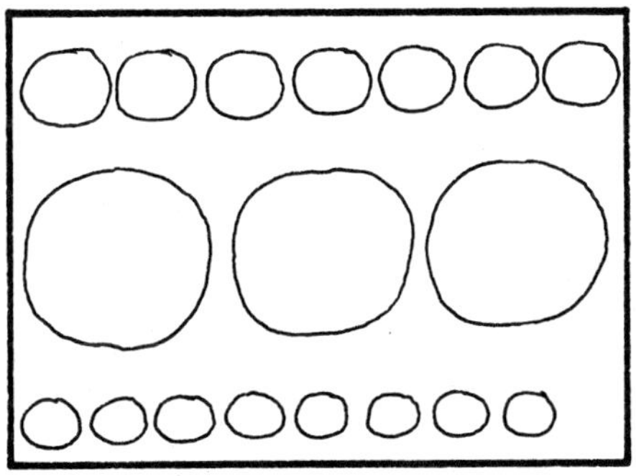

Then do a continuous scroll, working as before between imaginary guidelines about 2 inches apart. You will discover that a definite rhythm of motion is involved: the scroll should pour out of your hand in a slow, easy motion. Make the scrolls circular in form, and work to achieve a uniform distance between the lines.

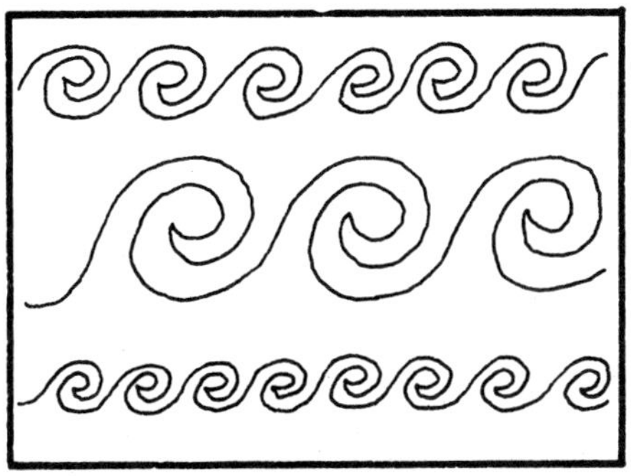

By way of variation do a square scroll, using a continuous motion and striving to achieve a really square form with the lines a uniform distance apart. These two exercises involve you in instantaneous decisions on distances and proportions.

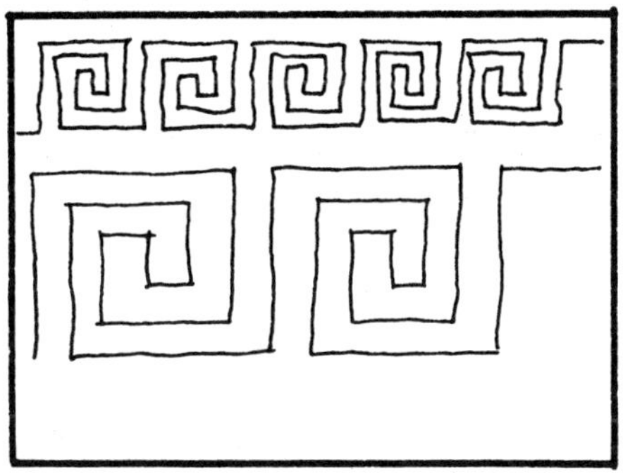

When you have conscientiously done all these exercises you will have discovered many things, many of them about yourself. Save these studies—put them on your wall for a while. You may want to invent new ones for yourself. For example, try them all again, but this time, instead of using a uniform even line, do them with a line that varies uniformly from light to dark each inch of length; or try drawing them from right to left, or with your other hand.

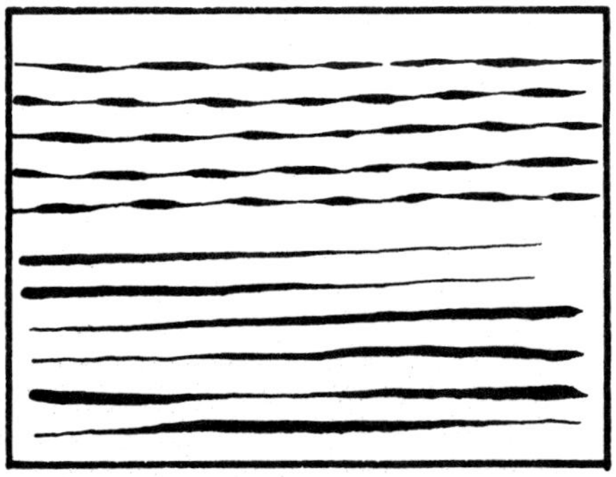

Above all, **do not hurry.**

2

BOXES *three hours*

Collect half a dozen empty cardboard cartons of varied sizes ranging from 1 to 4 feet in any dimension. By making a jumbled pile of them on the floor, you have, in their edges, a wonderful array of straight lines in space.

For this study you should idealize these cartons as pure geometric forms: parallelepipeds, with smooth rectangular planes intersecting in straight lines. Disregard the incidental blemishes and details of construction, and do not draw shadows or surface patterns or textures. In looking at these edges you will note that you have already drawn similar things: straight lines, of different lengths extending in different directions. You may find this collection of lines very exciting: just as in the case of human facial features, they show a wonderful range of variations on the same basic elements.

Adjust your pad either horizontally or vertically so as to permit the largest drawing of the complete pile of cartons. Start to draw the straight lines you see at any point; a suggestion is to begin at the point nearest to you and work outward from there.

You should make a large drawing; use up the whole sheet of paper. Avoid postage-stamp-sized drawings because they give you no exercise in control. Remember you have already drawn long straight lines in any direction. Draw very slowly, and imagine that your pencil point is just touching the edge of

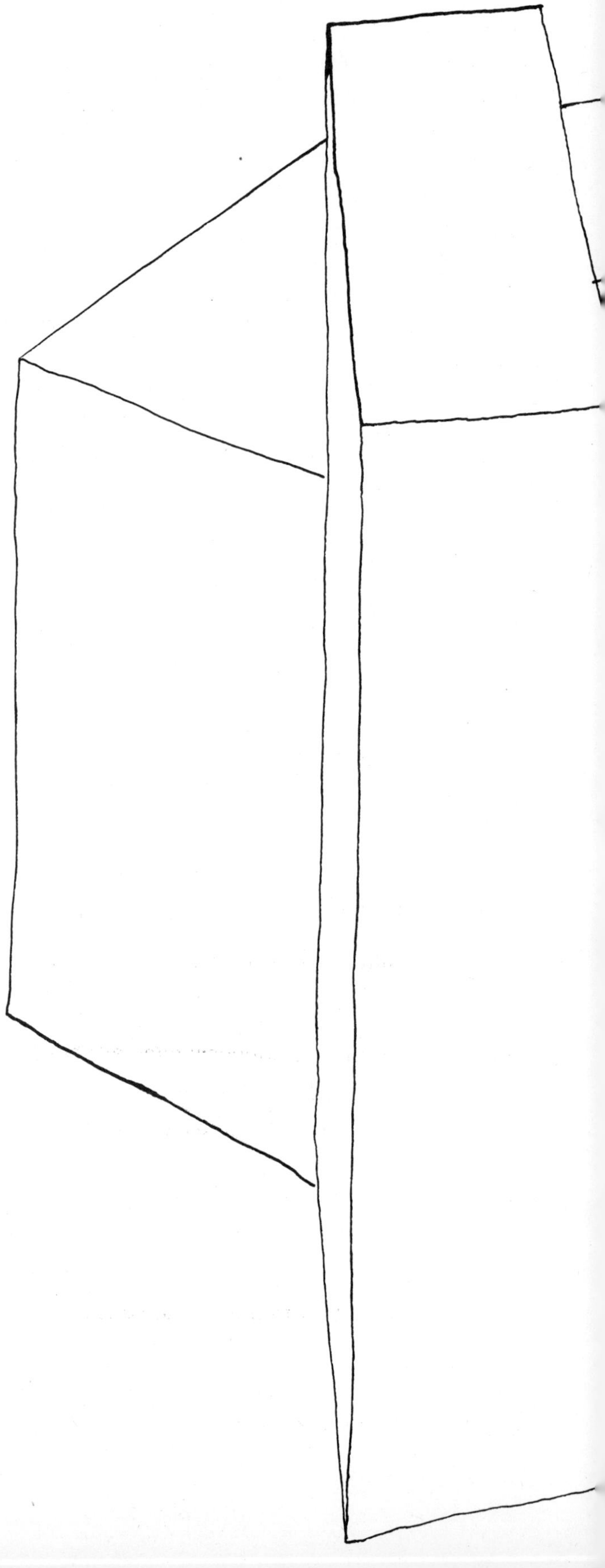

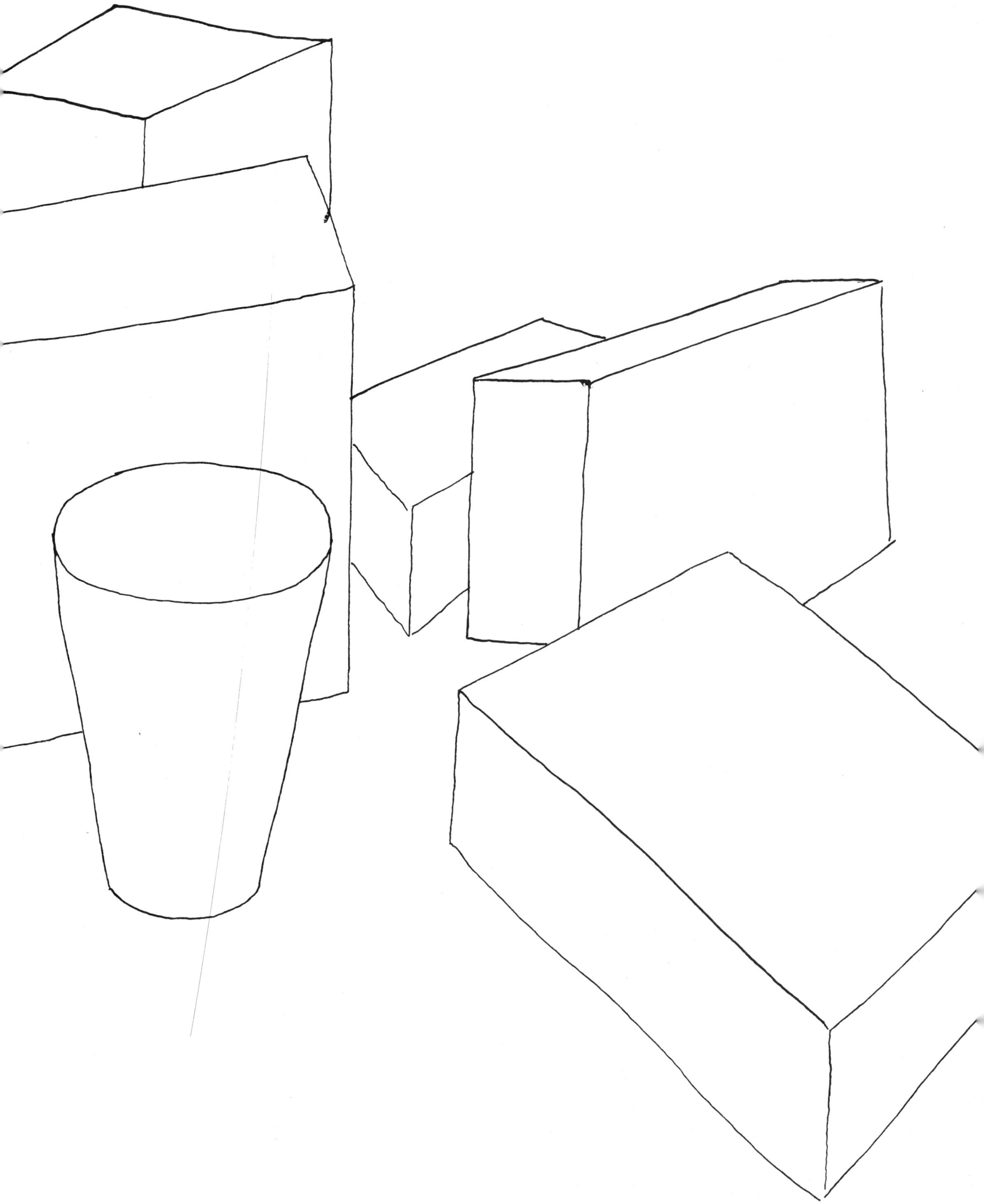

the box you are drawing. Do not press too hard; draw lightly, or you will push the box over.

Decide on the line before you draw it: once it is down, leave it. Do not change it. Concentrate on getting it right the first time. In this act lies the essence of drawing, and if you shirk this—by approximating, by "sketching" and "correcting" the line—you may be making marks on paper, but you will not be learning to draw. If you are not satisfied with a line, rejoice, for this means that you have **seen**, have evaluated, and have found a difference between what there is and what there should be. This means that you are developing in skill. Exult!

Start over, then, on a new sheet of paper. Don't "correct" the work you have already done. It can only be improved in a new drawing on a new sheet. The paper is cheap, and you will realize the most benefit from your time if you do not try to economize on it.

Your biggest problem may be in a misplaced concern for "perspective," "proportion," or "composition." Experience has shown that these matters will gradually take care of themselves; to bother about them now will do you no good at all. Forget about these issues and concentrate instead on producing light, uniform, straight lines that meet precisely. Be conscientious about corners: do not be timid and leave air gaps or, on the other hand, play it oversafe and overrun the intersections. Come to a precise, definite conclusion.

Do several large drawings of this pile of boxes, each one from a different viewpoint. After this introduce one or two circular forms, such as a wastebasket or a large ball. You will be delighted to see how all these simple lines you have drawn will magically evoke splendid impressions of space and object.

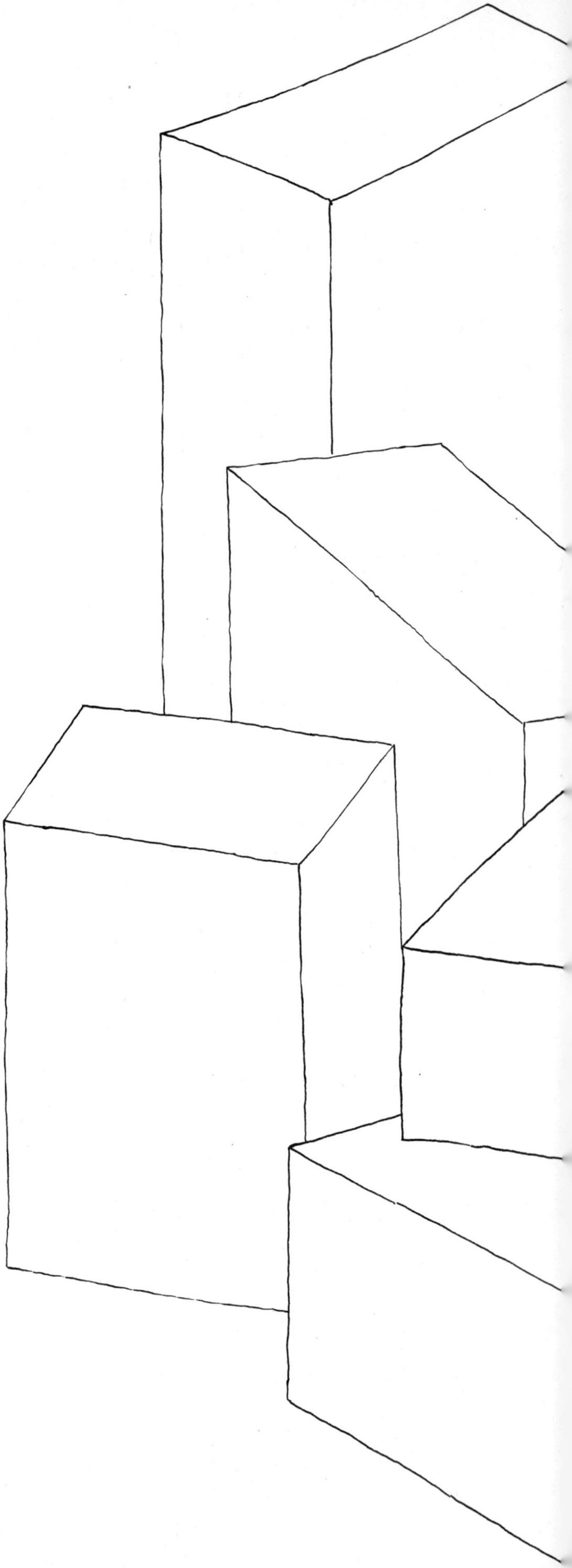

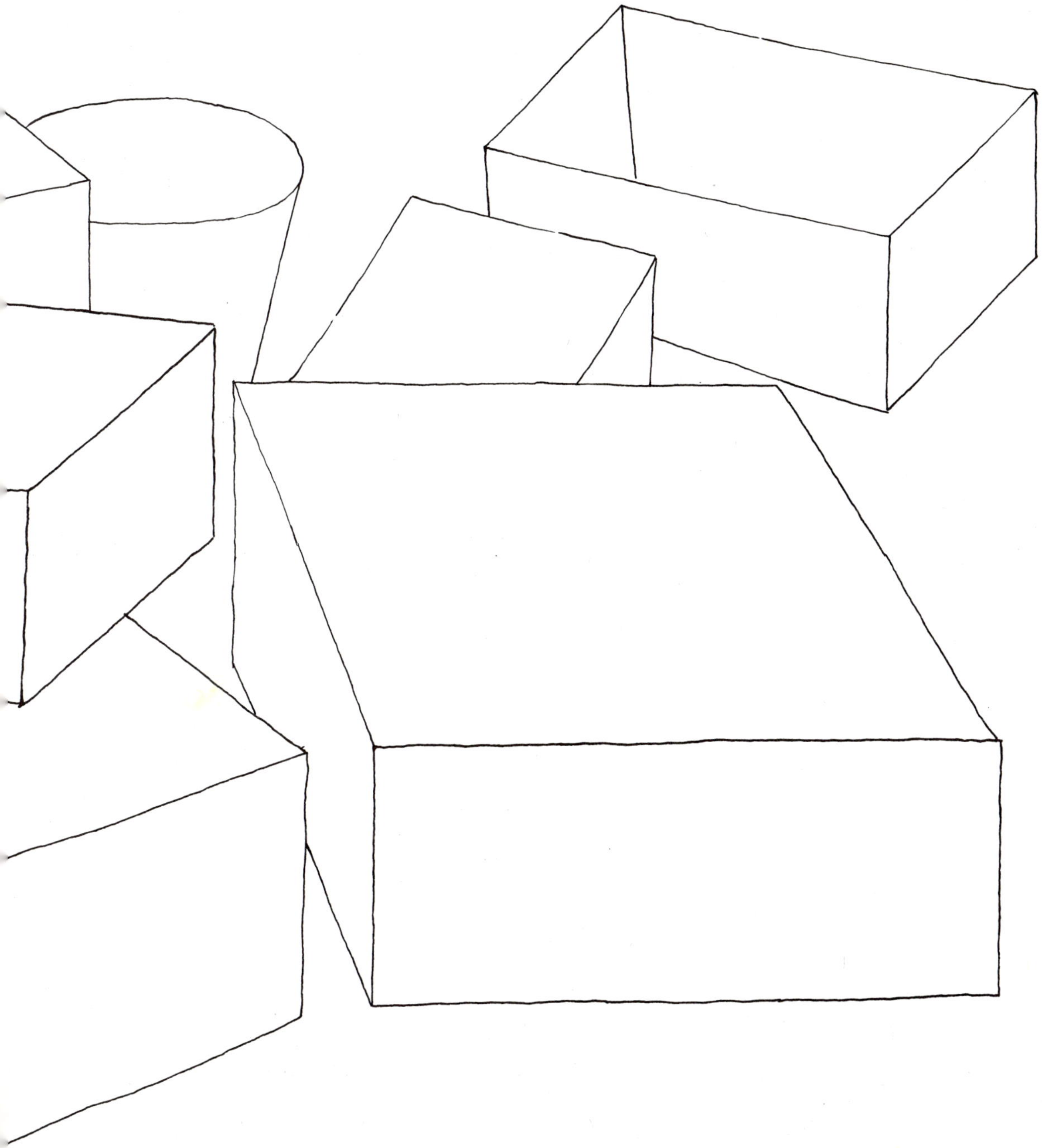

3

THREAD, ROPE, WIRE *optional, three hours*

Take a piece of black button thread about 12 inches long and drop it on one end of a new sheet of paper. Do not try to "arrange" the form it takes; it will naturally arrange itself each time in a wonderfully sinuous pattern of loops and curls. Now copy this linear form, the same size, on the other end of the sheet. Use a single, light, even pencil line and, again, imagine that you are lightly touching the thread as you draw it. Do not push too hard! It is of course not necessary to draw the thread in one continuous motion, but take pains to make your "joints" inconspicuous. Pick up the thread and drop it again for each drawing, so you will not be mechanically repeating the same form each time.

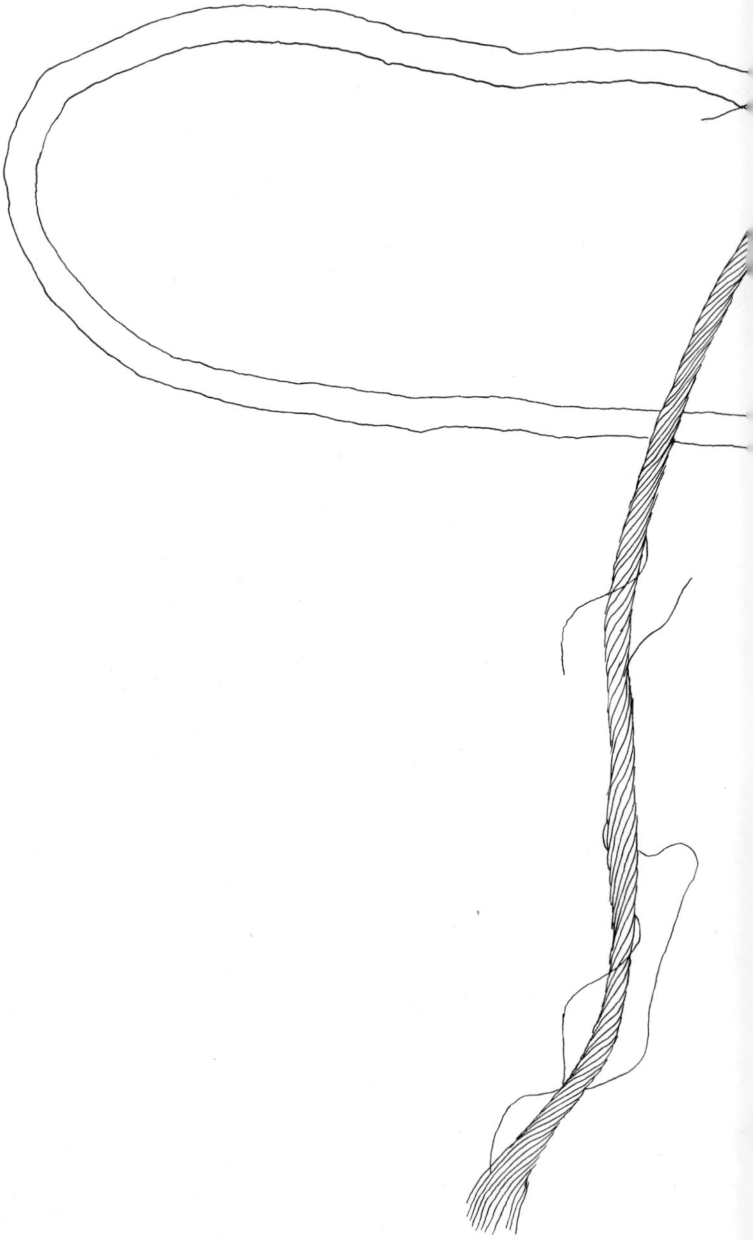

Now make two drawings of the same thread pattern: one drawing half the size of the original, and the other **double** size. Measure them after you have drawn them to be sure you have done just this. Note how the character of the drawing changes with the changed size.

After this, procure a piece of crumpled bare steel or copper wire, a length of coarse, hairy rope or twine, and some slender splintered pieces of wood. All these items exhibit similar varieties of threadlike curved lines, but in drawing them at one time you will be challenged with the necessity of closely observing their subtle but significant differences. Draw them at least twice life-size.

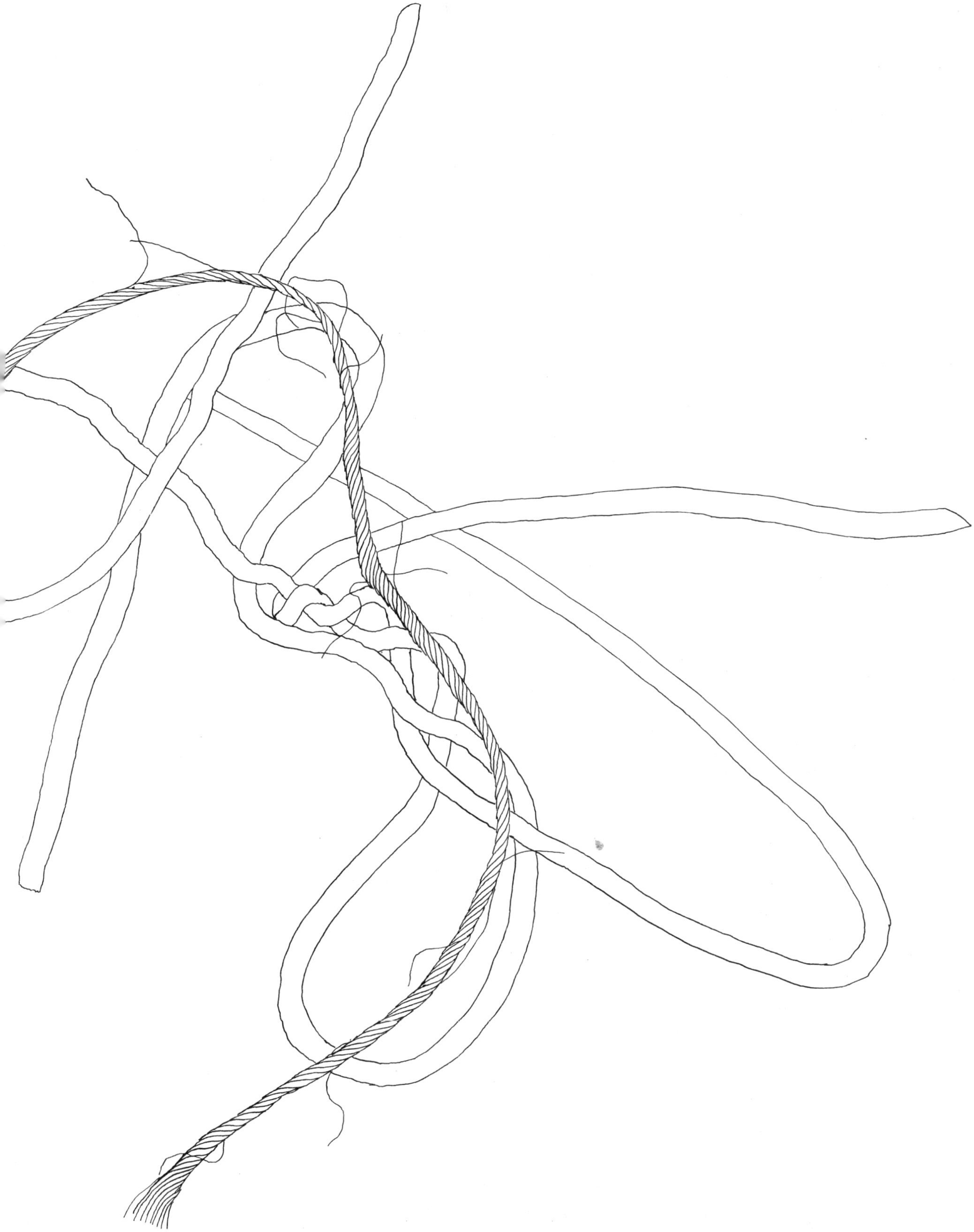

4

CHAIRS *three hours*

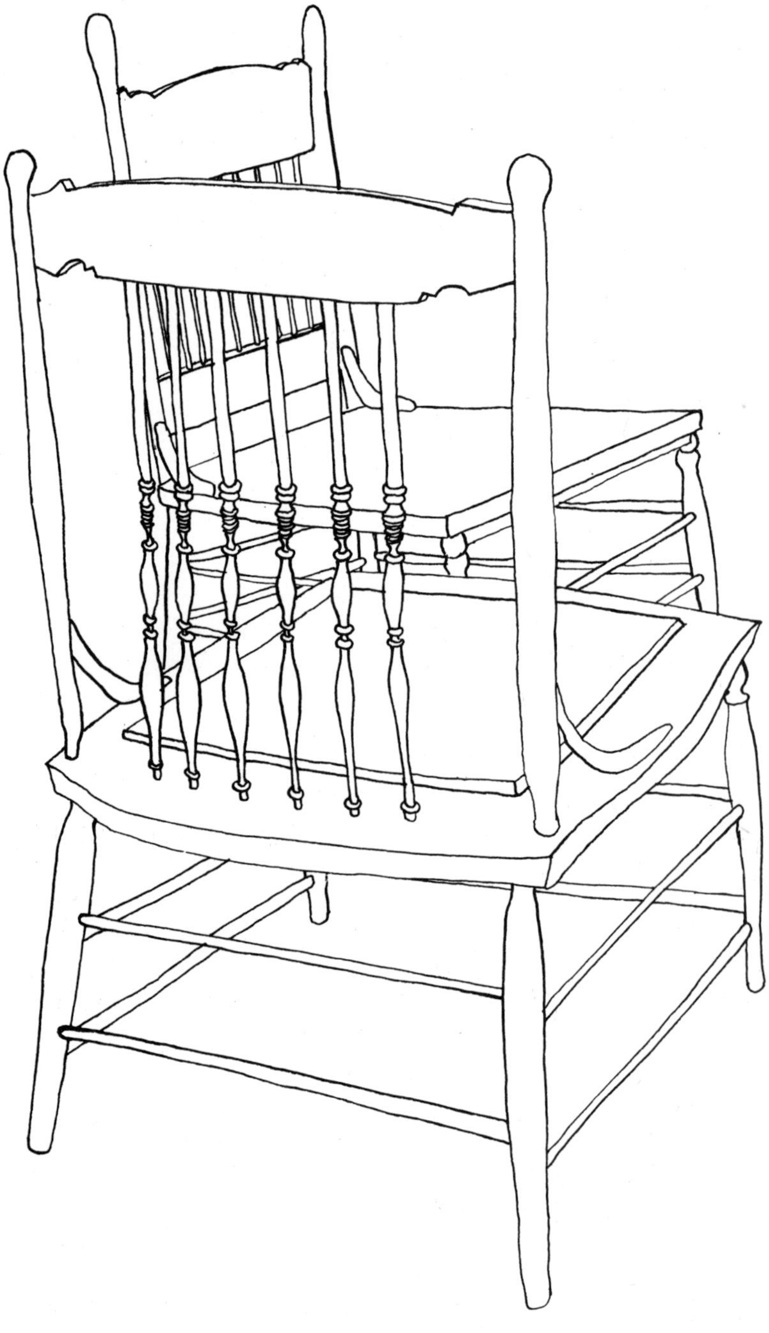

Unupholstered chairs, benches, or stools—in wood, metal, or plastic—are the next subject. You might start with simple school or office furniture. A variety of three or four such objects, arranged casually in a group so that some are partly hidden by others, is best. One or two of the chairs might be lying on their sides, or upside down.

You will note that the above objects are again composed chiefly of simple geometric forms: cylinders, parallelepipeds, cones, and so forth. Thus the problem is really quite similar to those preceding in that it presents an array of lines—edges—in space.

Hold your paper in the position that will permit the largest drawing of the group as you see it from a given position. Start drawing at any point: just where does not really matter, but you will probably find it easiest to start with some edge or intersection near you. As before, do not do any preliminary layout or studies. Look carefully; visualize what you will do before you put a mark on the paper; and then, when you are sure, slowly and carefully draw the first light, even line where it should be. Then add the next line, and continue until you run out of paper, time, or subject matter. Do not worry if you cannot get all of the subject on your sheet; draw too large rather than too small.

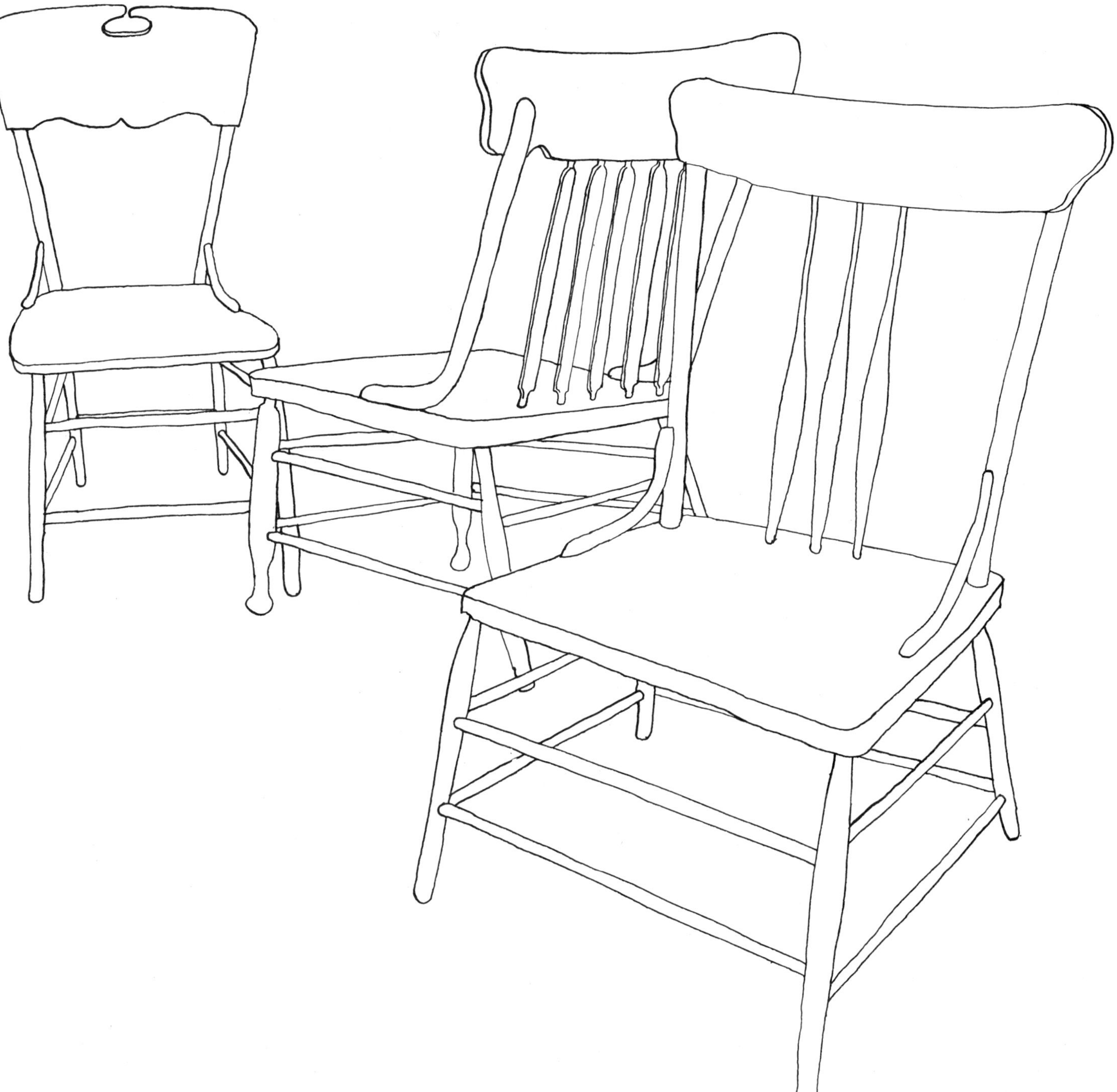

The special new condition to observe here will be the understanding and representation of the thickness of the material. Wood, metal, and plastic all have thickness: you do not see any paper used in the construction of the chairs before you and should therefore take care to communicate this fact in your drawing. The joints or connections usually provide the best opportunity to explain the form. Draw every part with equal care and understanding: if you are not interested in a particular form, or do not understand it, either do not draw it or examine it from a closer viewpoint. You should explain and define what you have seen and understood.

You will probably want to start over two or three times. You should do this rather than "correct" your work if it does not satisfy you. Turn the sheet over or start a new sheet: in any case, either select a new viewpoint or make a slight rearrangement of the subject for each new drawing. But do not worry about proportion or perspective. Draw what you see carefully and slowly; concentrate on understanding and explaining the forms and their connections. The results will in all probability be very good, although you will not think so at this time. Take care to get even lines of uniform weight, and exact intersections, and be sure to indicate the thickness of the materials.

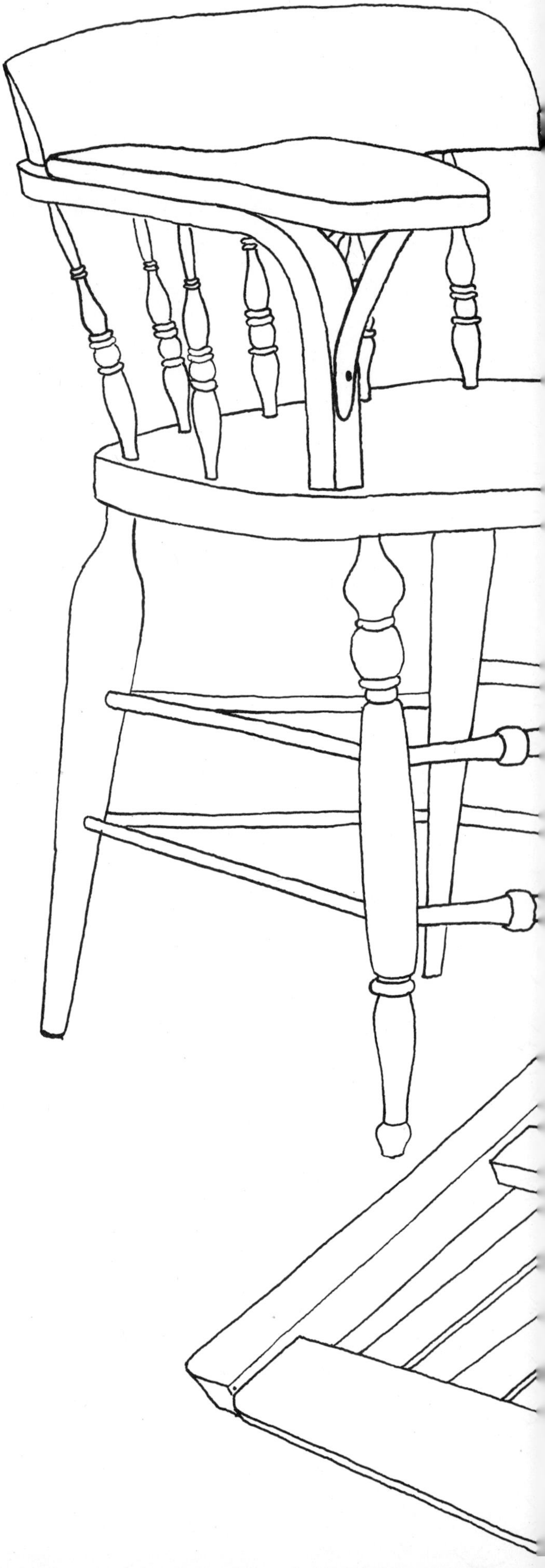

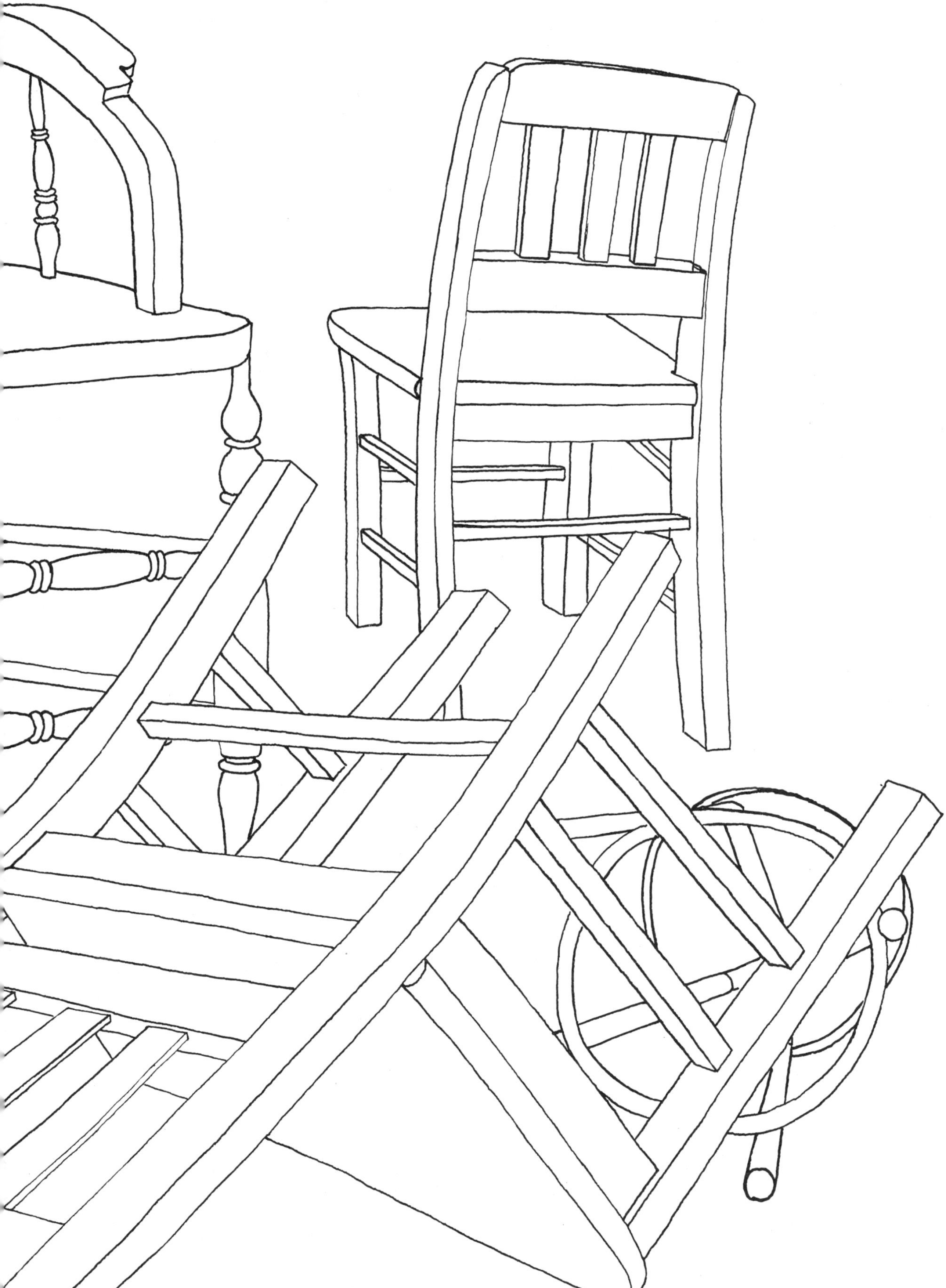

5

HANDS *three hours*

Imagine the hands of a little baby—small, soft, supple, and pudgy. Then imagine the hands of a manual laborer—large, hard, knotty, and workworn. Much of our contact with reality is through our hands, and each person's hands tell us something about that person and his life. Look at your own: your hands, like a dancer, produce a different gesture and a new expression with each slight movement.

Thus, you have with you always a very versatile model. Drop the hand you do not draw with on one end of your drawing paper. Then draw it, life-size, on the other half of the sheet. Try to imagine that you are touching the skin as you go along; do not press too hard, for then you will distort the flesh. But be sure to "maintain contact" with the contour you see, for otherwise you will gloss over the nuances of form.

Be careful to note the differences in character of the various parts of the hand. Some of the flesh is soft and loose; some is drawn and tense; some may be hard and calloused. Note particularly the nails—of a very different material, of a definite thickness (they are not made of paper!), and showing a complicated relationship at the junction with the skin at the base of the nail. It is important that you draw large enough to be able to explain this. (It will be worthwhile to make several studies double life-size of just this part, so that you will really be able to see and understand it through the process of explaining it adequately in your drawings.)

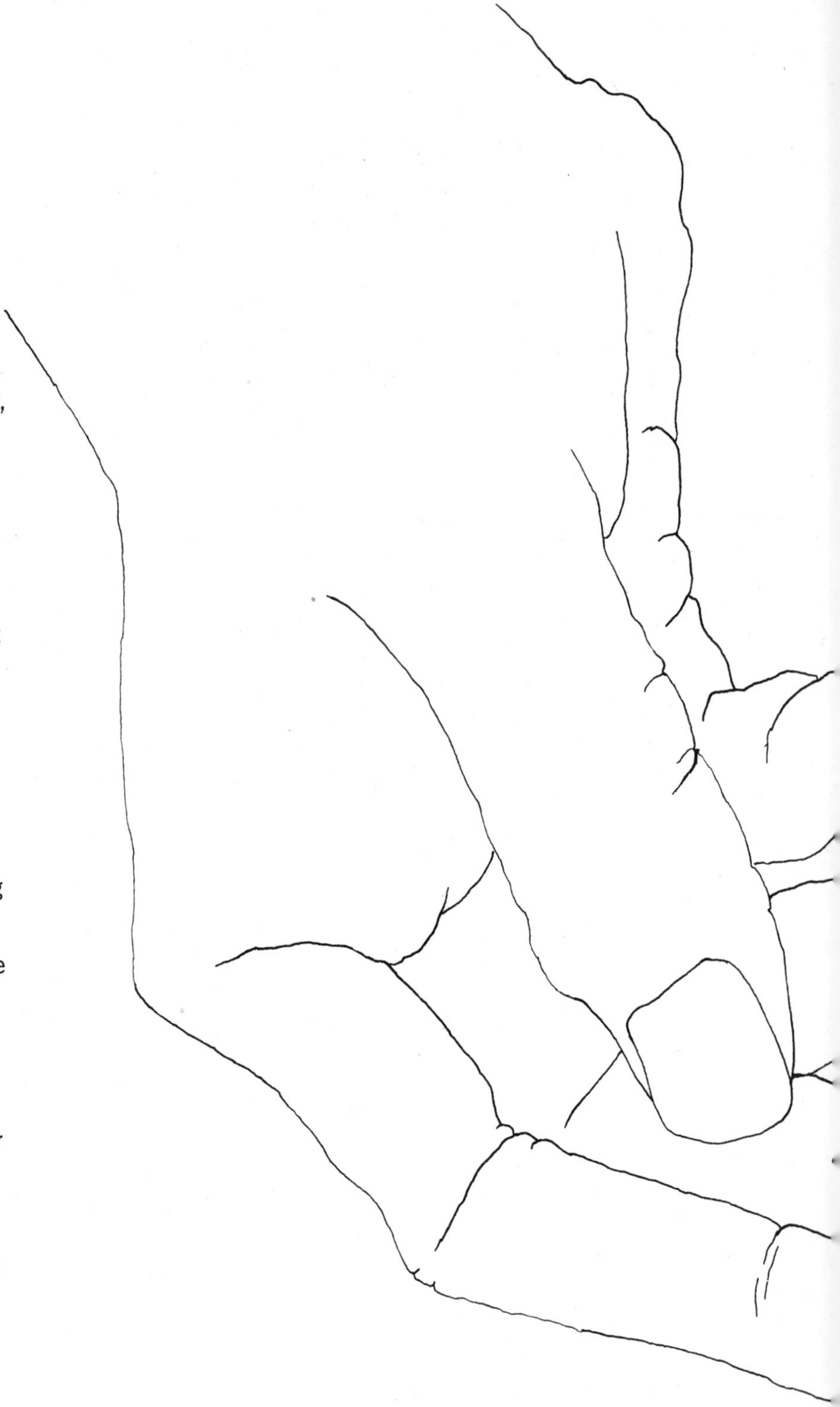

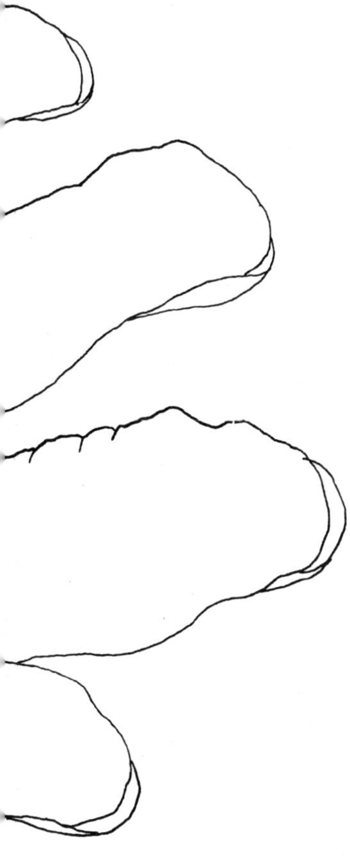

Note carefully the following. In many cases you will see and draw a groove or a fold of flesh that goes across a contour, around to the opposite side of the finger, palm, or wrist. Note what happens to the contour at this point. It is not continuous. If you draw it as continuous, the line that is supposed to represent a groove will appear as a line **on** the surface, rather than a groove **in** the surface, as in A:

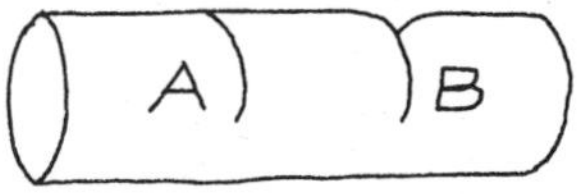

To represent a groove, you must carefully note what happens at the contour. It will probably be something like B.

A new problem you will encounter here is that of significance of detail. You may find yourself recording every minute crease, wrinkle, hair, or fold—all the new details that you are beginning to see. A question you should now ask yourself is, "How little can one show and still represent a hand with differing flesh and nail qualities?" To do the most with the least requires the greatest art, for it demonstrates that one has grasped the essence of the situation.

There is another aspect of this matter. If you grant that the line representing the edge of a finger, for example, is more basic to the representation of the hand than the line denoting a minor wrinkle, you will understand that if you use the same weight line for each you will be giving unequal elements equal importance. And we are still drawing with a uniform weight line.

Draw your hand, at least life-size, in several different positions. Draw it holding different objects, and draw the objects themselves (as well as any rings, watches, shirtcuffs, and so forth) with as much care as you draw the hand itself. After you have drawn a number of hands, try drawing with your other hand. The results may very well surprise you.

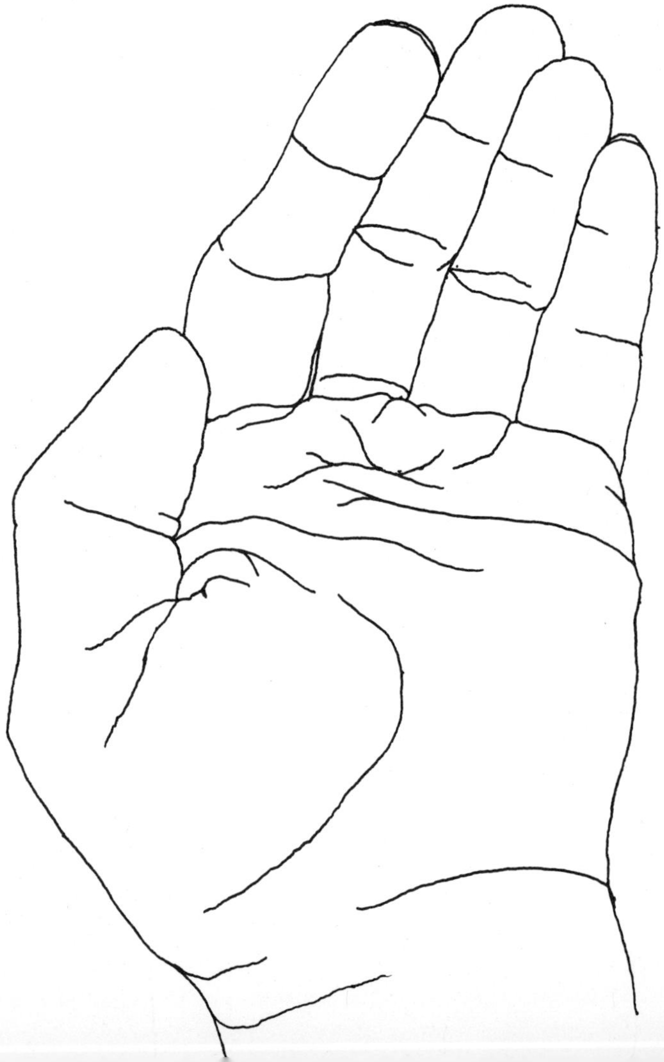

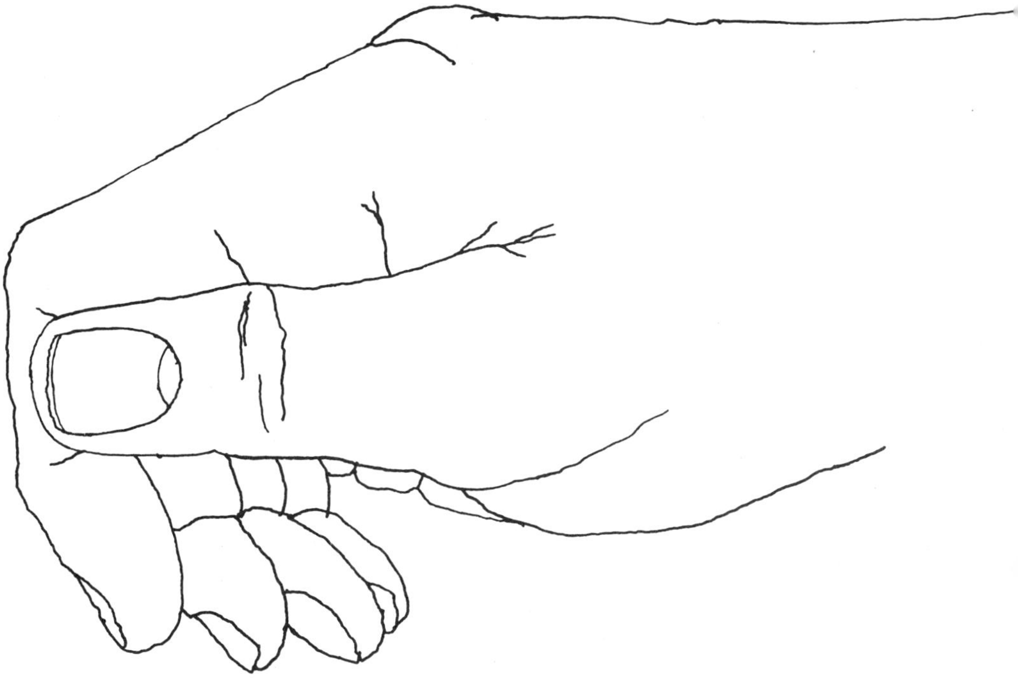

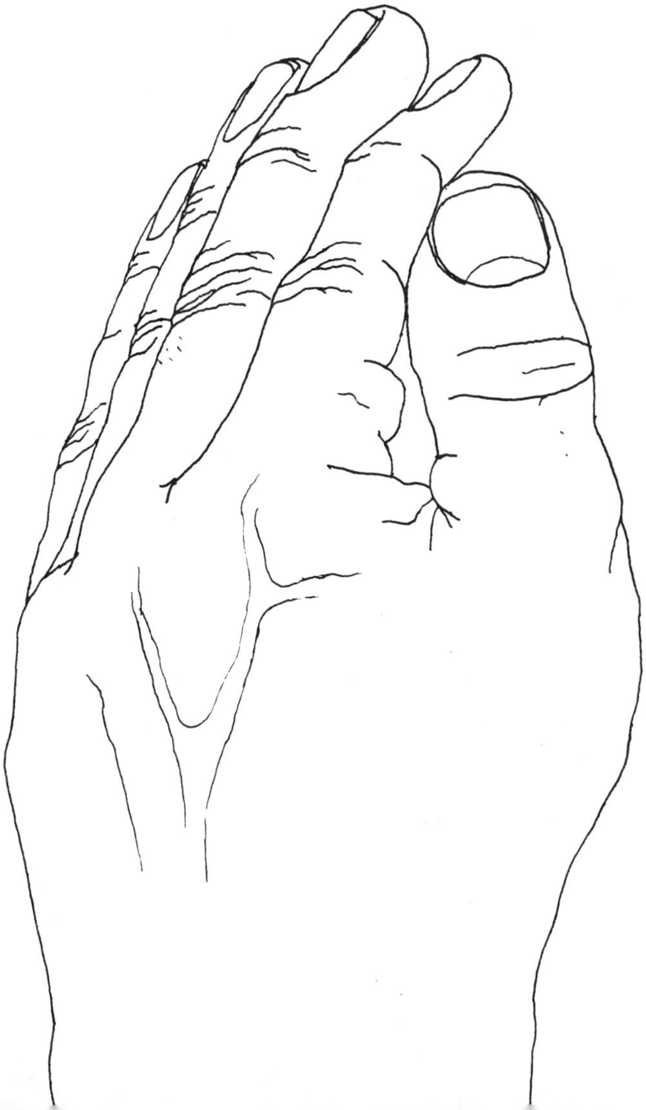

6

HAND TOOLS *three hours*

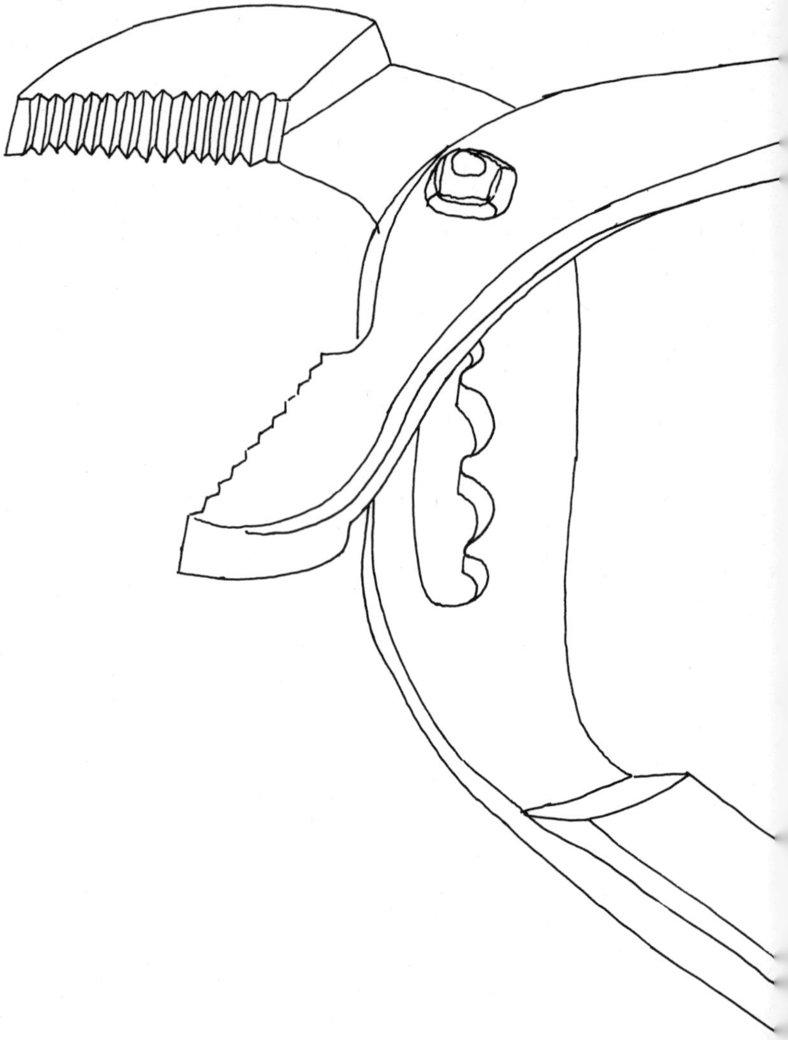

In the previous study we dealt with forms of a very definite character—nongeometrical and, in the variety of types that exist, most expressive. In this problem we consider certain semigeometric forms, man-made to act as extensions of the previous subject. Hand tools that hit, cut, grasp, twist, or turn are, in their own way, as expressive as the various hands that may hold them.

Select for subjects two or three of the following: claw, ball-peen, or tack hammers; jack or block planes; socket, monkey, or Stillson wrenches; "eggbeater" drill; screwdriver, handsaw, backsaw, or keyhole saw; chisel, mallet, C clamp, and so on. Arrange to draw these, singly or in groups, at least life-size. You will note that in most of these objects there is a good deal of geometric quality, quite different from the form quality of the previous studies. Be sure that your drawings represent this character: the lines should be straight, uniform, parallel where required, and unwavering, reflecting the precise geometry of the subject.

In drawing these tools you will encounter certain problems in representing the transitions of one form to another. Here is where an experimental attitude is required. Try it one way; evaluate the results critically and then try it again, a different way. You will probably be surprised to see how little it takes to communicate the exact form satisfactorily, and your critical efforts to find the best way underlie the essence of art.

7

CROCKERY *optional, three hours*

This study involves some of the form-representation problems introduced in the preceding exercise—the transitions between related simple geometric forms.

In a collection of simple, smooth-surfaced, and undecorated plates, cups, saucers, mugs, and teapots (the very thick, white restaurant ware is excellent), you will find a rich variety of precise cylindrical and semispherical forms exhibiting subtle transformations in shape in their connections with handles, lips, and spouts.

Arrange two or three pieces before you on the table and make a careful, slow drawing of them, life-size or larger. Try to preserve the symmetry of the forms as you see them and, more important, maintain an even line, of uniform weight, with no rough joints. As before, you will have to experiment to discover just how much line in just what places will best turn the trick: as a suggestion, it may help to leave out more than you think might be necessary to use.

Do not put in any shades or shadows. Of course the shades, shadows, or reflections you see help you to "read" the form, but you should represent the form by the use of contour line only. Draw only what you can feel with your finger, imagining that your pencil is touching the contour lightly as you draw: you cannot feel a shade or a shadow or a reflection.

As a variation after two or three large studies of several objects, try drawing the same objects arranged upside down, or with some as they were and some inverted or lying on their sides.

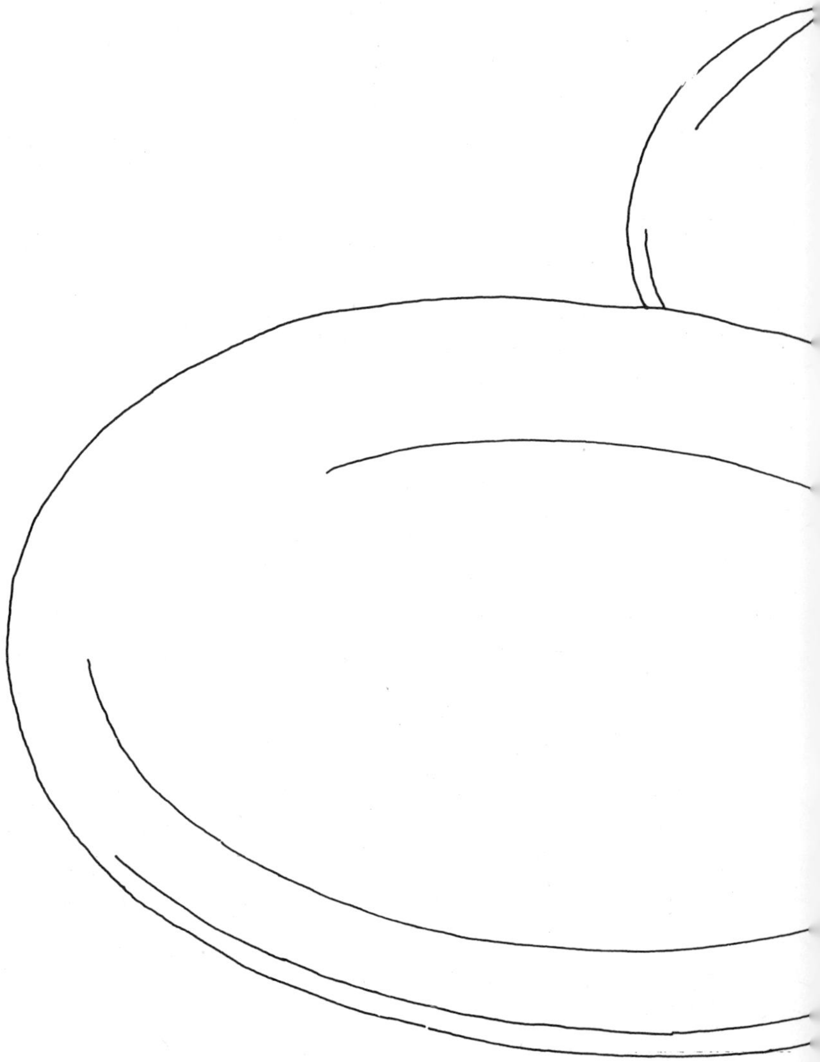

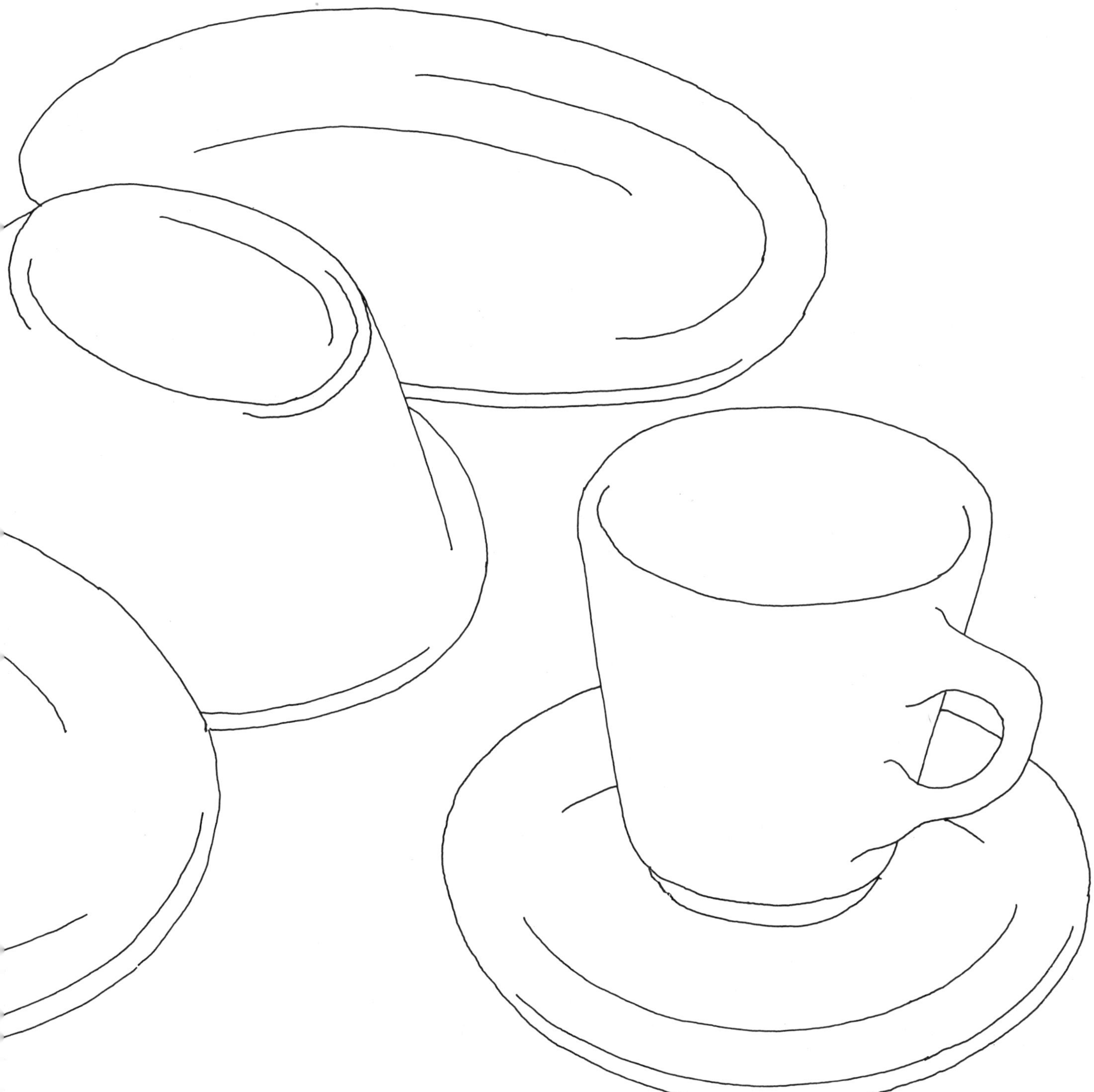

8

SHOES *three hours*

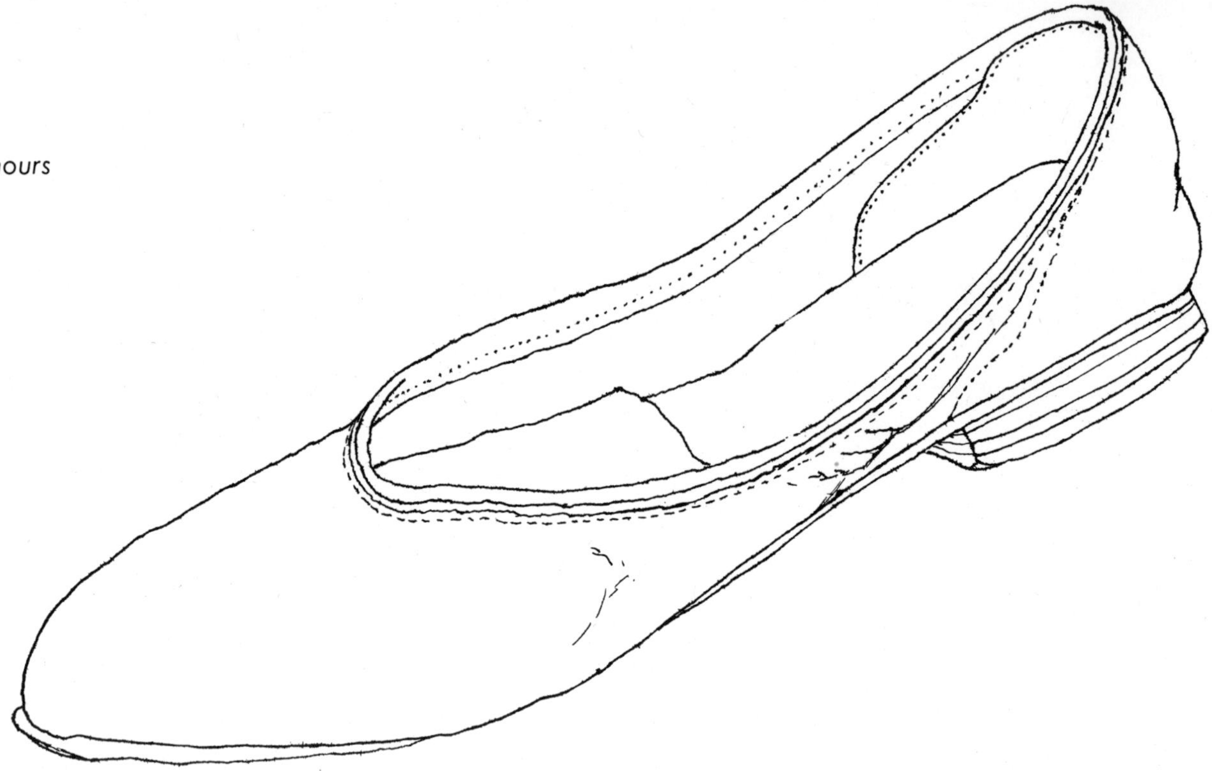

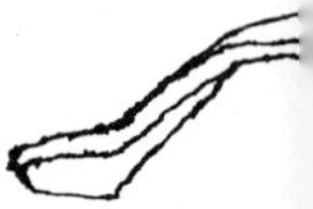

Like hands, shoes are expressive of our contact with external circumstances. They can speak to us not only of the size, sex, and weight of their wearer, but also of his occupation, affluence, and attitude. Imagine a small ballet slipper next to a massive, mud-caked work boot.

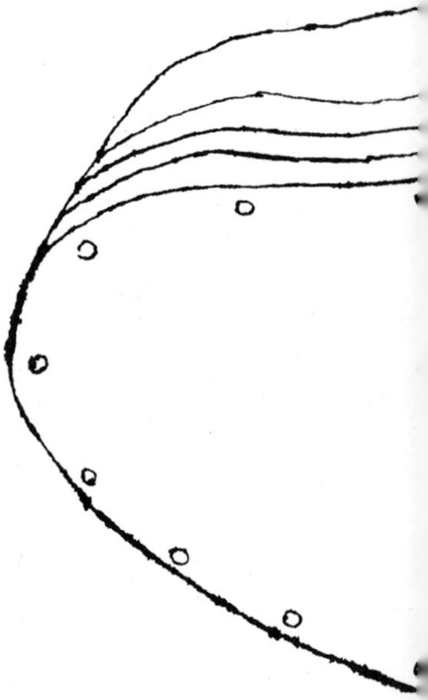

Just as shoes share some of the expressive qualities of hands, they offer somewhat similar problems in representation. There are several points to watch out for, however. A shoe usually consists of several pieces of leather (which has definite thickness, no matter how thin it is) assembled by a variety of seams and joints. Remember that leather, unlike paper, has thickness; representing this is one of your problems. Another problem is to indicate clearly the way the pieces are put together. Probably you will have to stop occasionally and pick up the shoe to examine its construction. To draw it you must understand it.

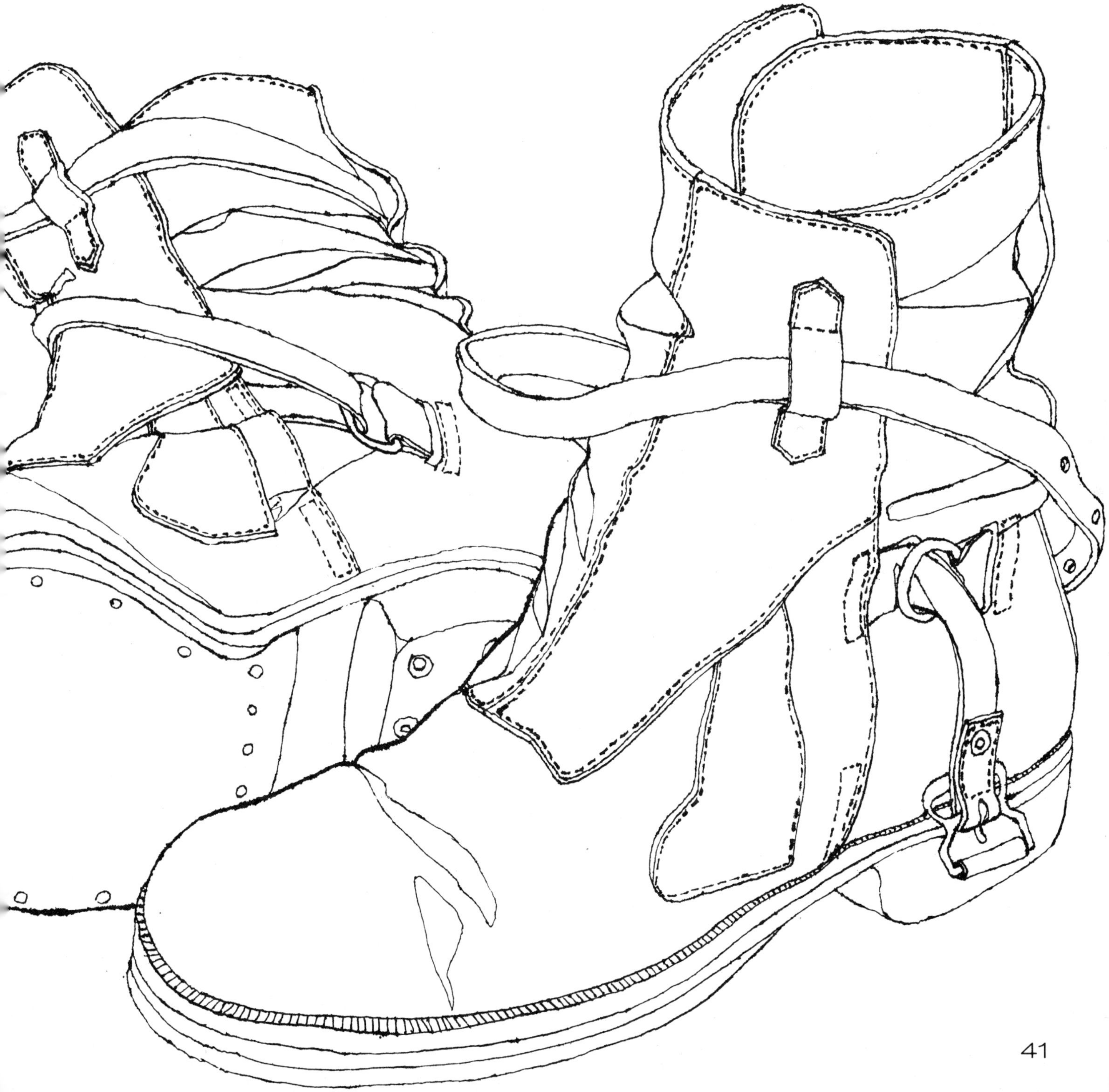

Here again you may worry about proportion, but remember that this is not significant at this time. Rather be concerned with a very clear indication of the seaming and edges.

The shoe should be drawn at least life-size or larger, so that you will have adequate scope for the explanation of the small details. Do not necessarily try to draw the entire object; concentrate, perhaps, on the laces, eyelets, and adjacent parts, or on the area around the heel. If you have time, continue on with the rest of the shoe.

An old shoe may show many wrinkles. Here, as in the case of the hand, you will have to decide on the degree of significance of these details.

A note about laces: if you are drawing braided or similar laces, do not fall into the error of drawing the outer edges and then cross-hatching the space between them to represent the material there. This is a fatuous mistake. A braid, for example, has a very specific form, and you cannot even suggest it by scratches on paper. You will have to draw it very well or else omit it altogether.

Remember to keep your line fine and of an even quality. Any start you become dissatisfied with should be completely abandoned: **start over again on a new sheet.** Do not try to "correct" or salvage something that you realize is not what it should be. The act of starting over is an indication of your growing standards of discernment and quality and (perhaps only in retrospect!) should give you meaningful satisfaction. Remember Hokusai! And any time you start over, use a different viewpoint—even slightly different—or a different shoe. Above all, concentrate on clearly explaining the method of assembly and the nature of the materials.

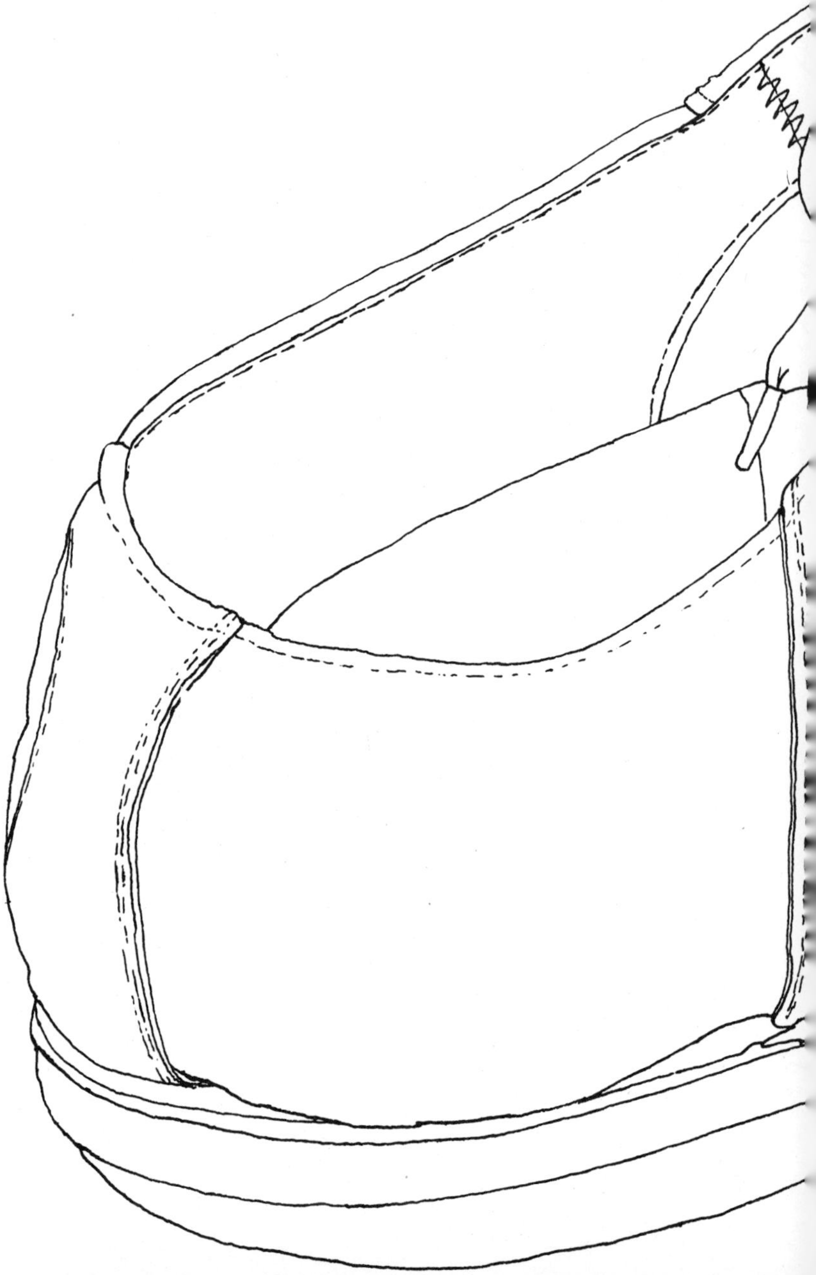

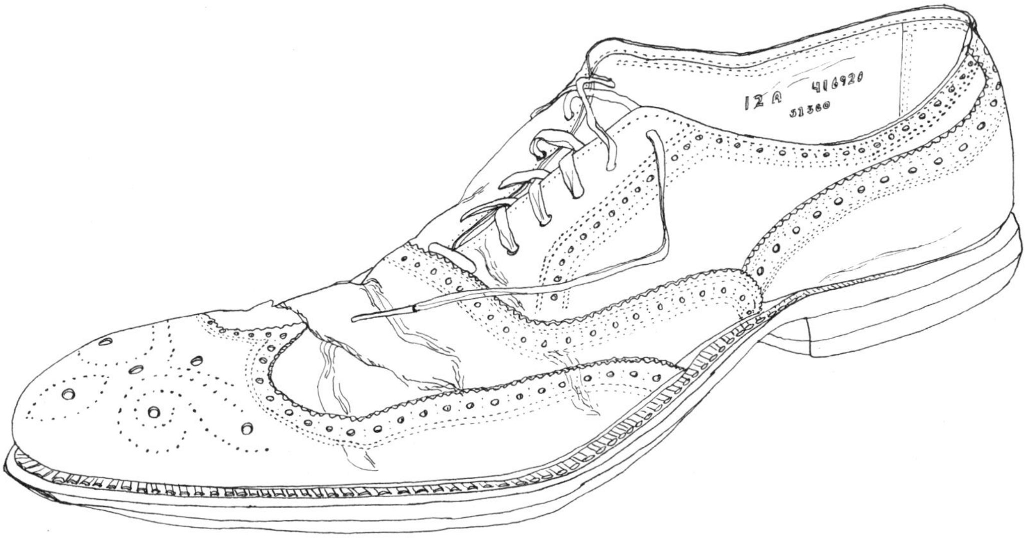
12A
416920
51360

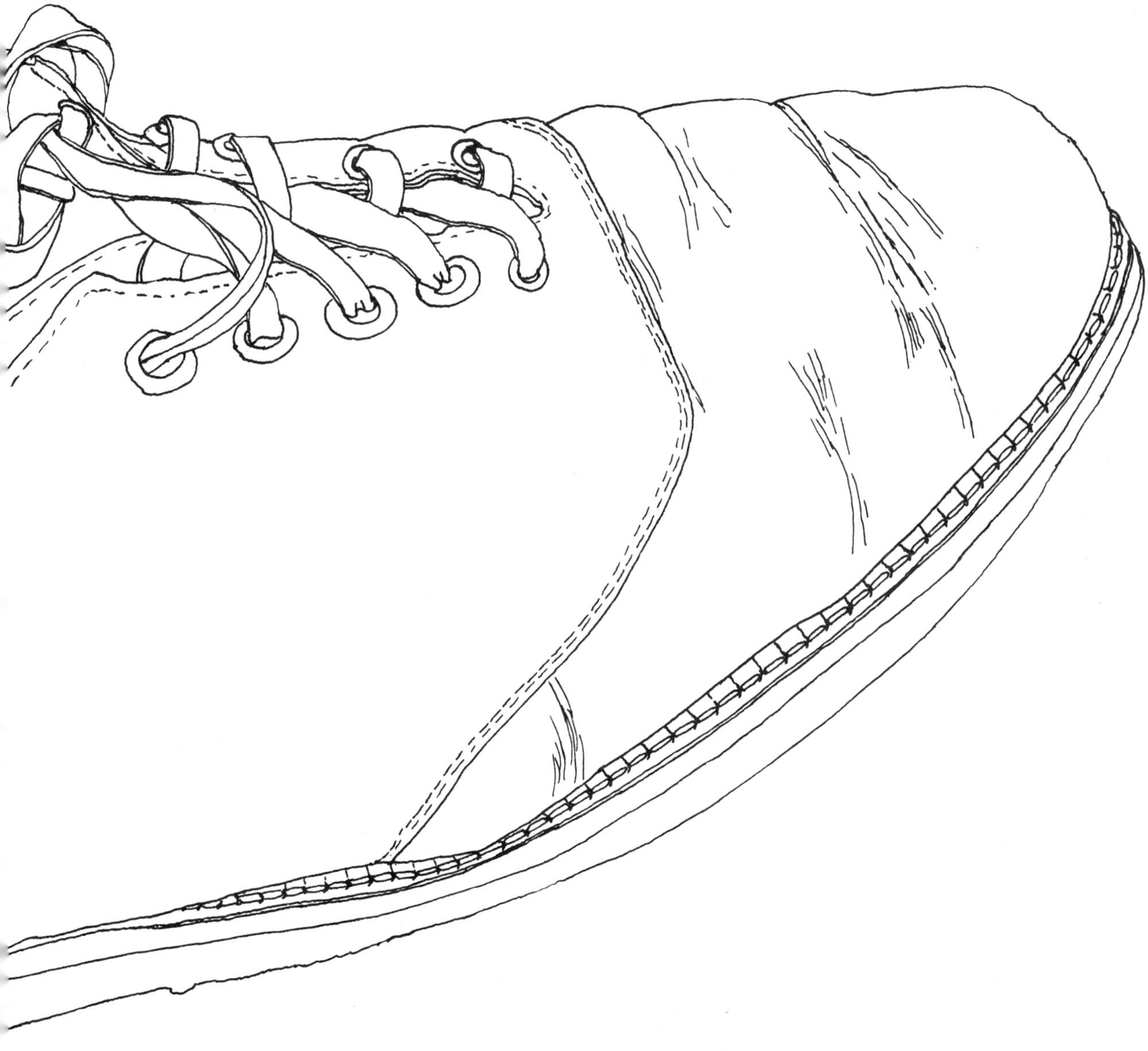

9

TYPE FACES *three hours*

For this study your subject will be some specimens of bold-face display type. Examples can be found in magazines and in newspaper headlines and advertisements, particularly supermarket ads. Collect a variety of large, thick, fat faces, at least ¾ inch or 1 inch high, including some with serifs (the flourishes at the end of the vertical strokes) and some sans-serif faces. In assembling such a collection you will begin to notice the specific character of each face.

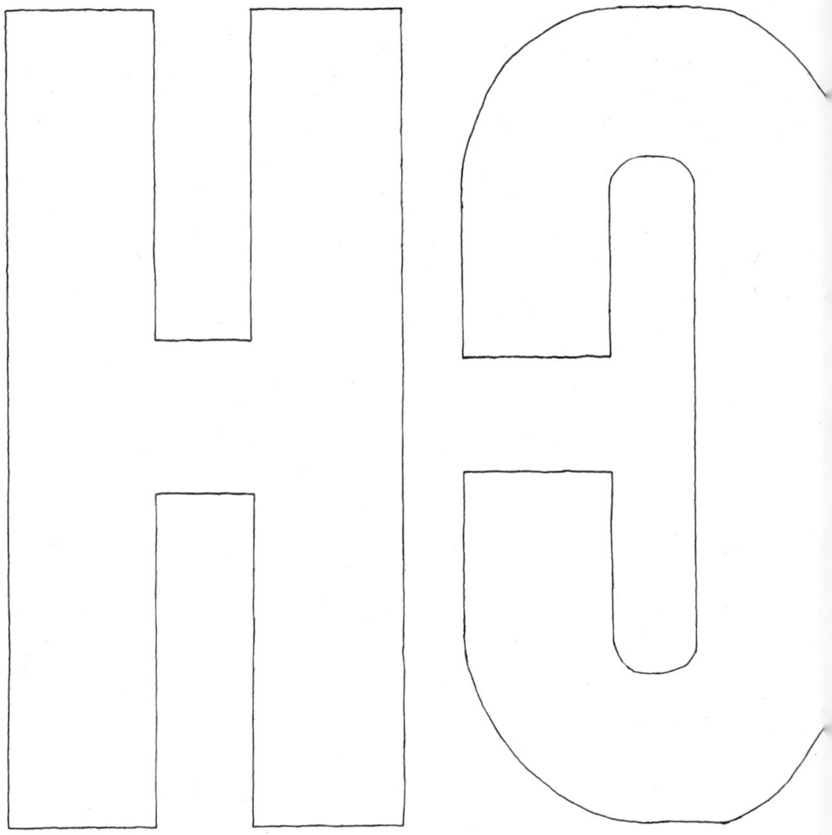

Take a short word of four or five letters (or four or five letters from a longer word) and turn it upside down so that you can more freshly appreciate the form quality without the distraction of the literal meaning. Then begin to draw the outline of each letter, enormously enlarged so that the four or five letters will just fit on your entire sheet of paper. Do not change the proportion or spacing of the letters, and of course do not make any preliminary block-out of the proportions. As you see, this is a study in both the discernment of proportion and the control of line quality. Take care to keep your lines straight and parallel and of even weight. Note the form of the "negative" spaces between the letters; their shapes are often as interesting as those of the letters themselves.

Check yourself to see that the letters you are making are of a uniform height. And **watch the proportions**—the relation of width to height, of the parts of the letter to each other and to the letter as a whole. Some of the curves, you will find, are very subtle; hardly any of them are really circular arcs.

LUN

LUNCH

OATMEAL

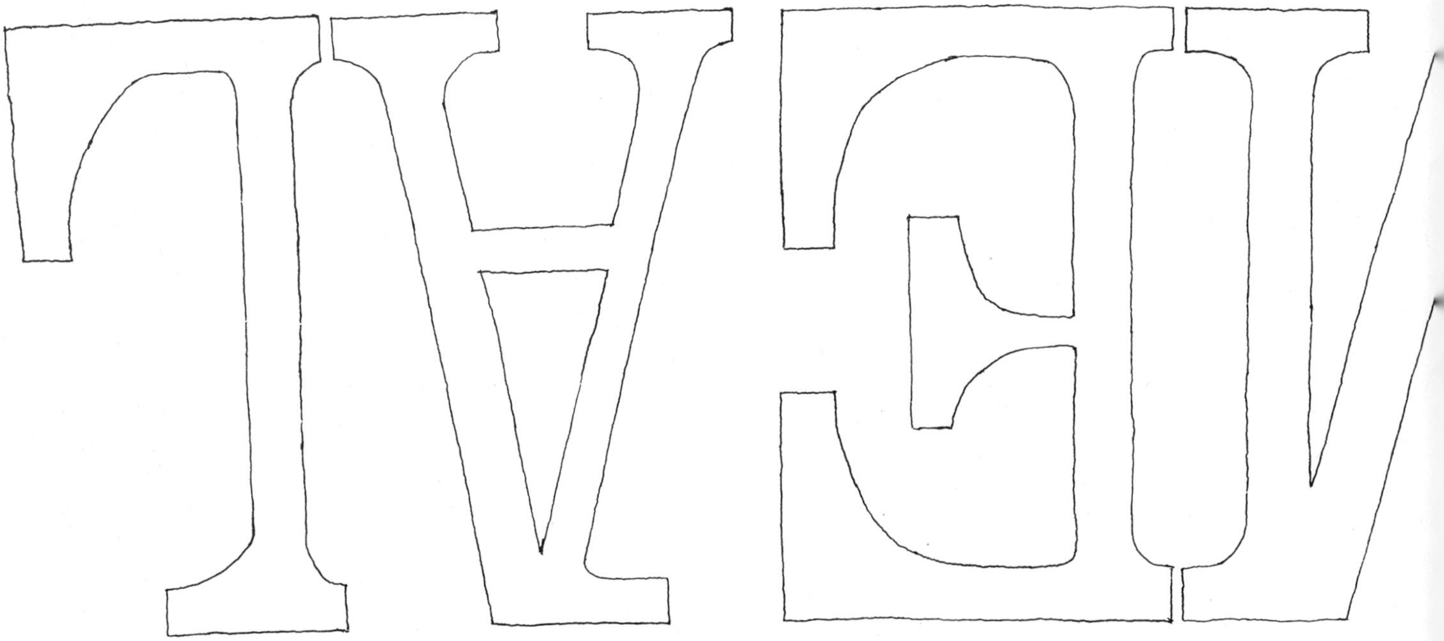

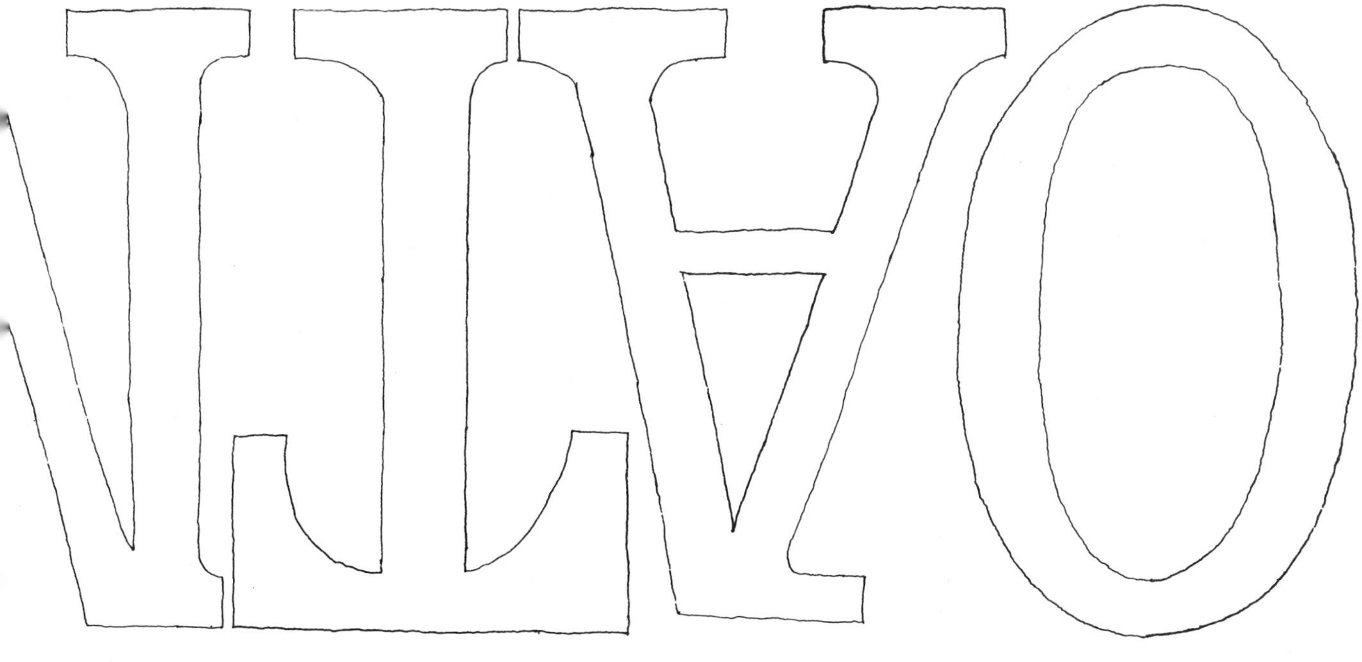

10

PAPER, CLOTH, ROCK *three hours*

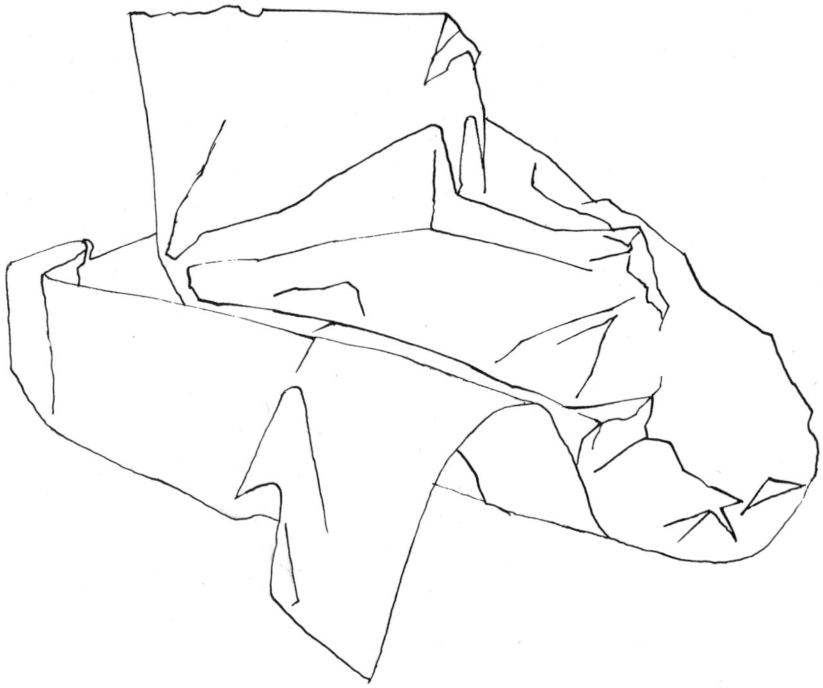

An 8½-by-11-inch piece of white typewriting paper, if crumpled up a bit in the hand and released, will offer a wonderful "landscape" of ridges, mountains, plains, and valleys. A piece of white cloth, such as a freshly ironed handkerchief, will also show a rich variety of forms when it is picked up and dropped on the drawing board. These forms are similar to those of the paper, you will notice, but with significant differences: the cloth forms are softer and more rounded, with fewer points.

You may also be able to find some chunks of rock that exhibit similar faceted surfaces with ridges and planes. But in this case there will be neither the thin edges of the paper nor the softer folds of the cloth. Thus, all three of these objects are basically similar in form, yet each has its particular distinguishing nuances.

Drawing a group of two or three of these objects, in contour line only, is a good challenge. To test your success, ask someone who has not seen the original subjects to identify what you have drawn; or look at the drawing yourself, a few days after you made it, and ask yourself the same question.

It may be that the matter of "significant detail" will trouble you in this problem, too. (Refer to the problem on hands.) It is always a revelation to see how little it takes, if that little is done perceptively, to tell the story. What you are really seeking here is the visual essence of the paper, cloth, and rock.

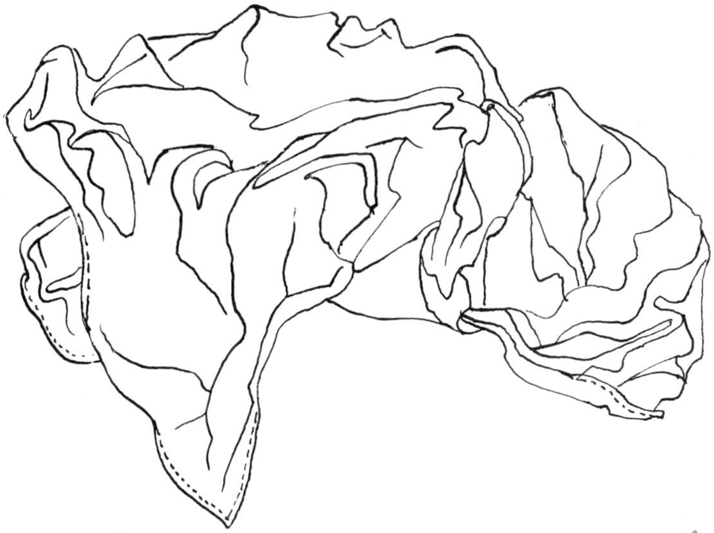

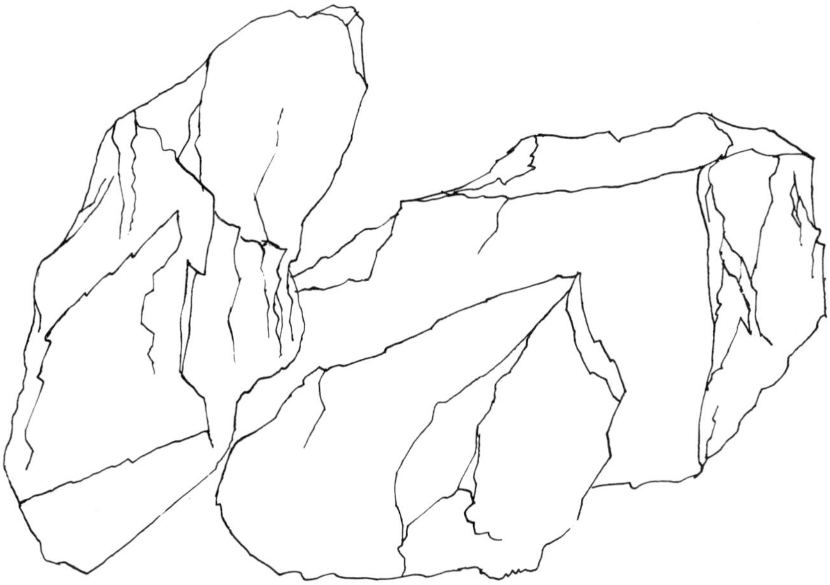

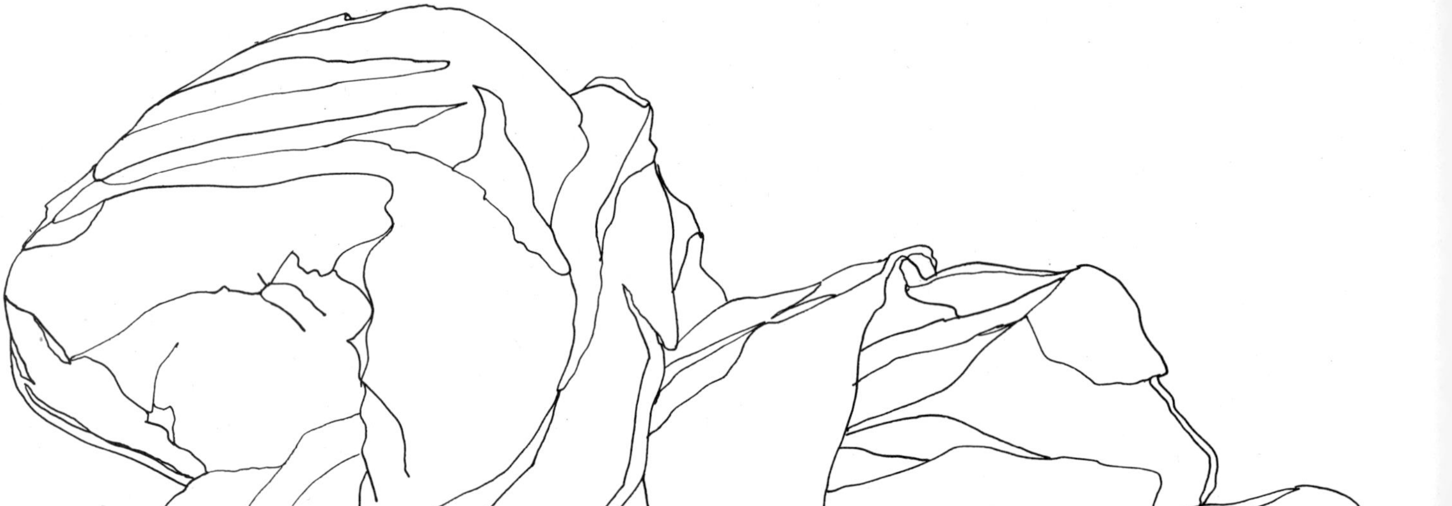

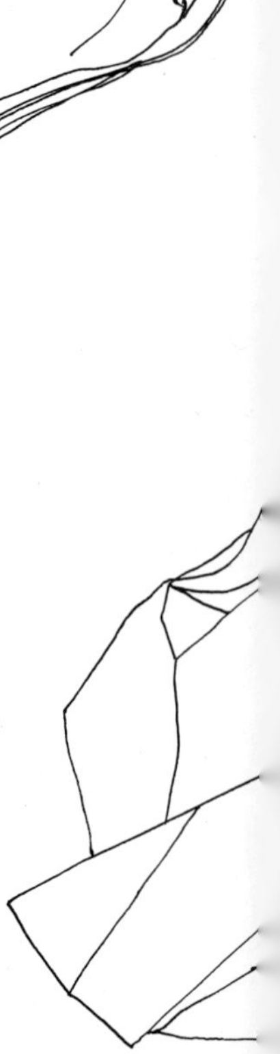

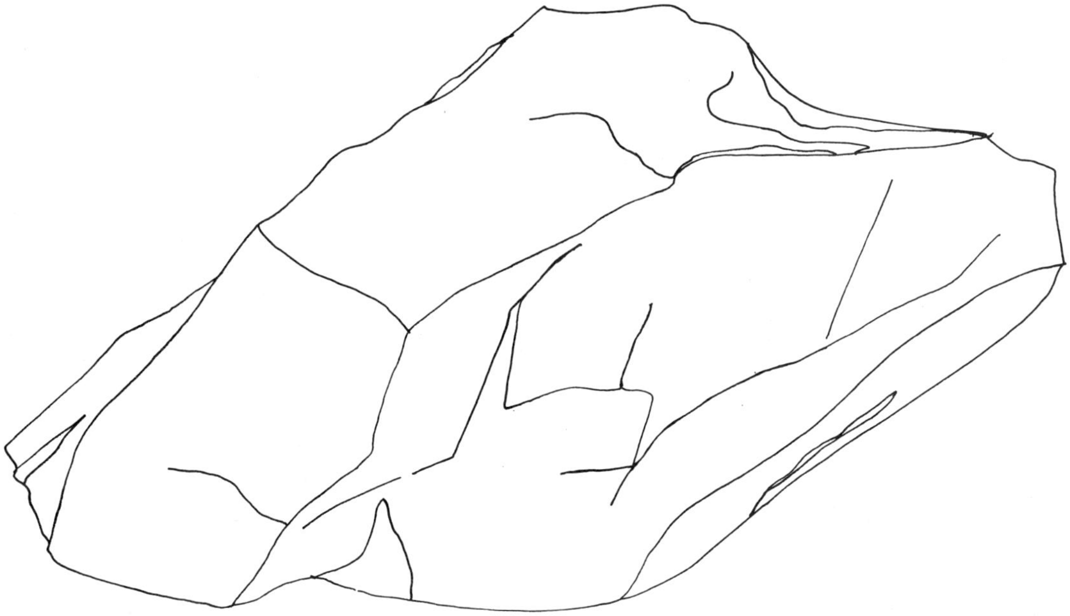

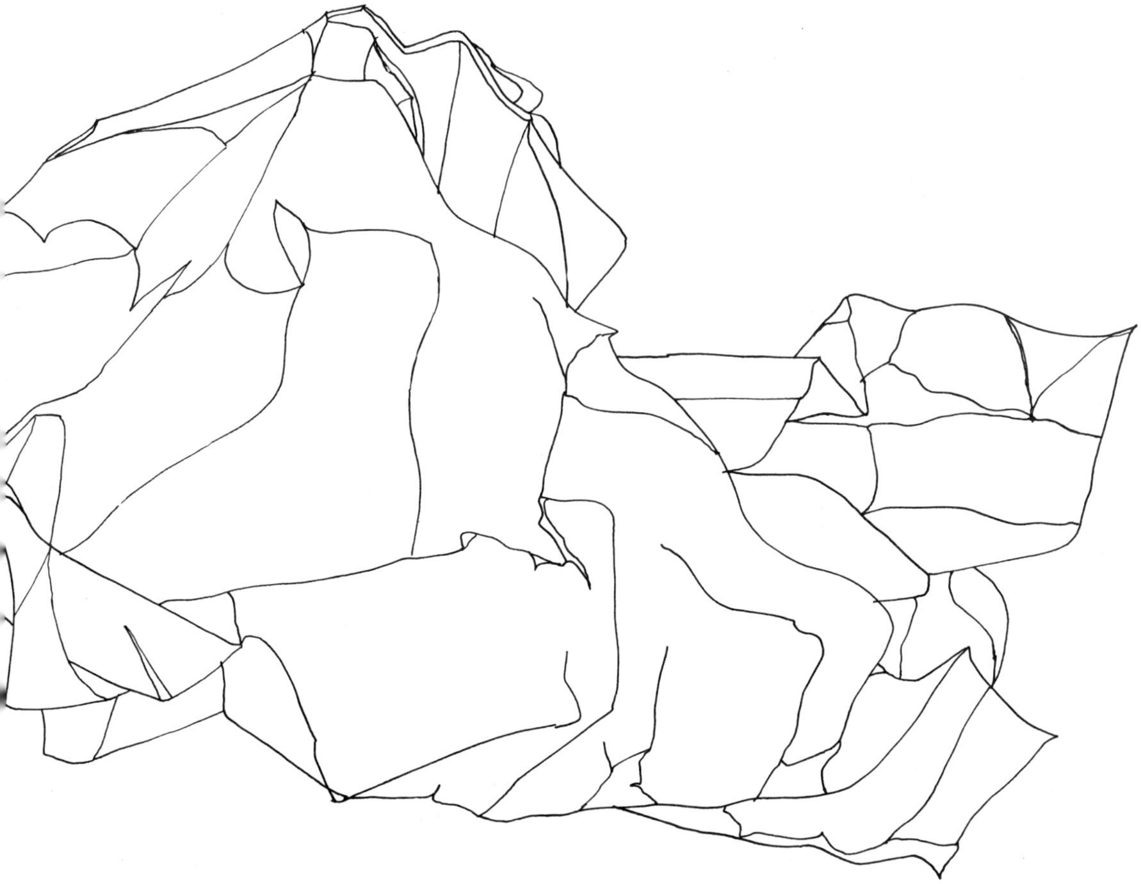

11

MACHINERY *three hours*

A mass of complex machine parts, piping, and pipe fittings is the next subject. Perhaps you can use for a subject a commercial refrigeration or electrical plant, a mechanical engineering laboratory in a university, the engine of your automobile, or even a junk yard.

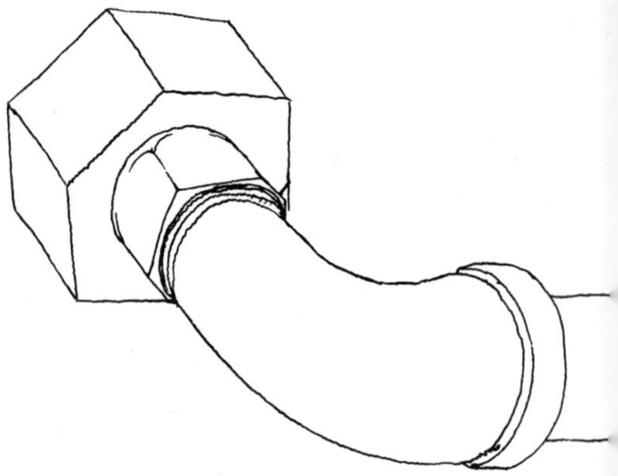

To draw all this may strike you as being impossible, if not ridiculous. But the problem is not to draw **all** of it. Take a look at a bit of it. You will notice that the forms are chiefly geometrical, again with the challenging transitions between one simple part and another. It is suggested that you spend a little while reconnoitering the situation until you find some shape or group that interests you, and then sit down to draw, full-size, just a small part of it; perhaps just one nut, or pipe flange, or bolt head.

When you have discarded two or three starts, and finally have this item drawn as you would like to have it, go on to the adjoining object. And do this again. Keep going until you run out of machinery, time, or paper.

You may not have some of the proportions just right, but if you have at least noticed this fact, and if your line quality is good, your parallel lines are parallel, and your straight lines really straight, you have made considerable progress. And if you got up and examined the subject more closely or even made some careful, enlarged studies on another sheet, you are indeed to be congratulated.

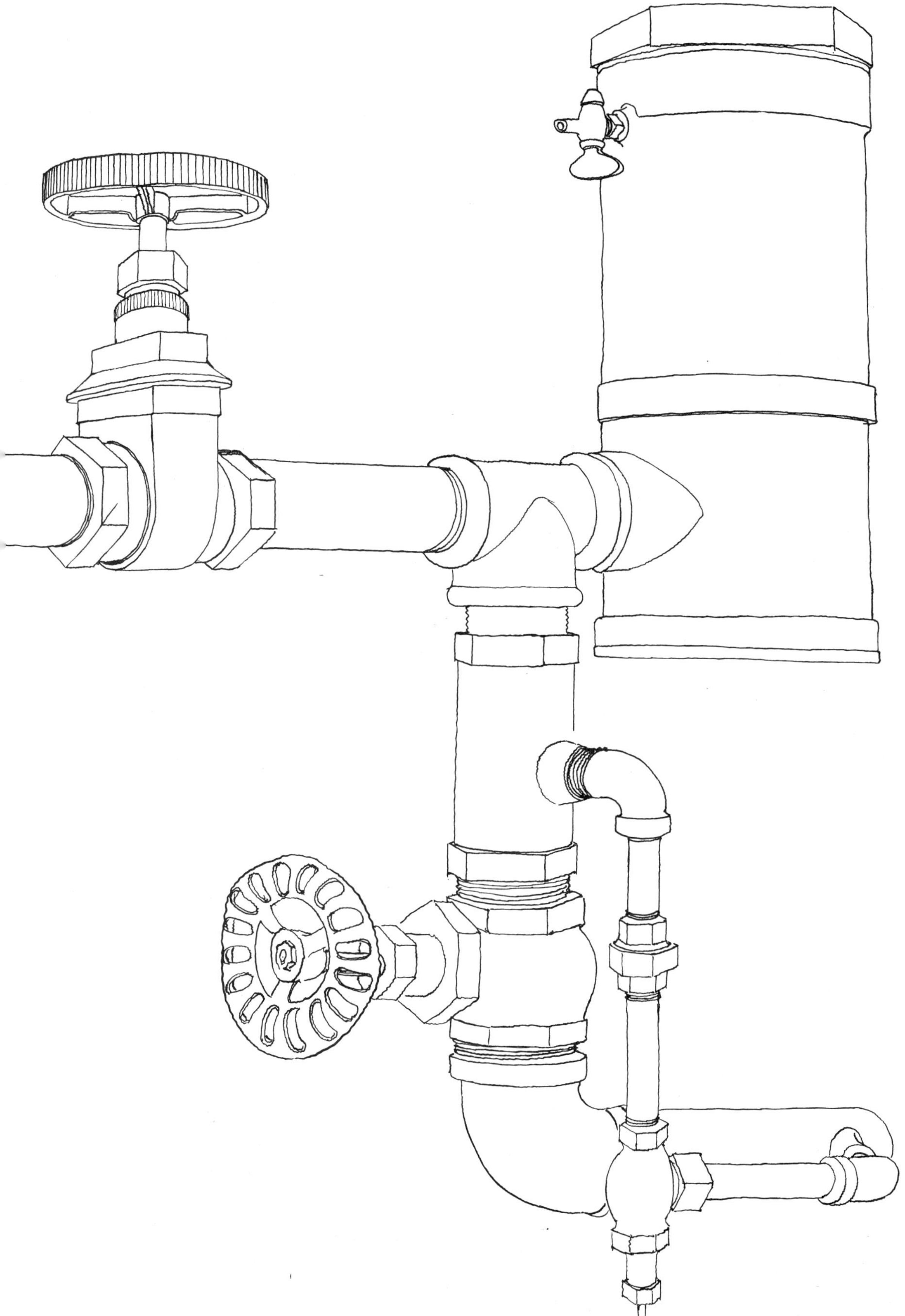

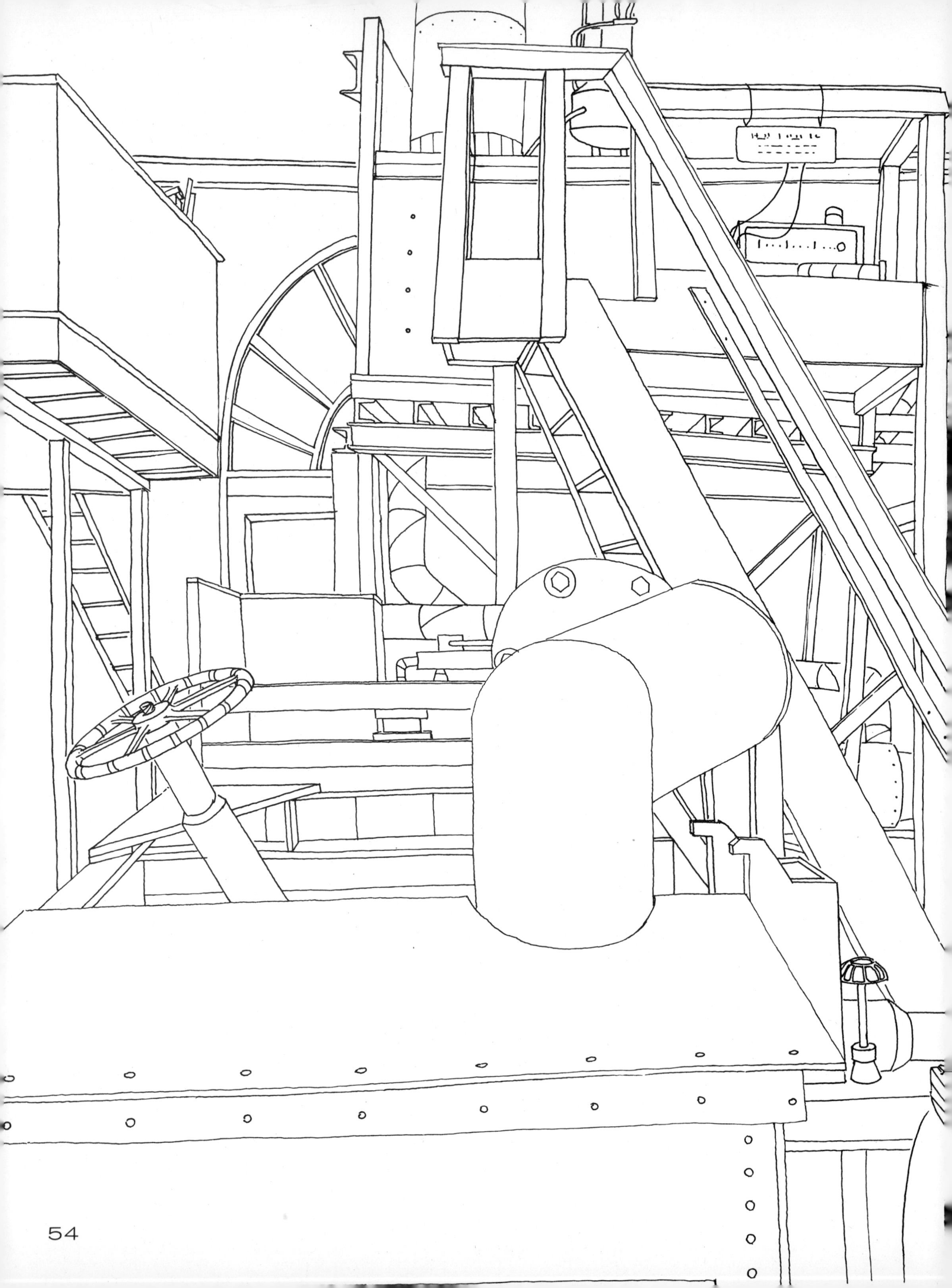

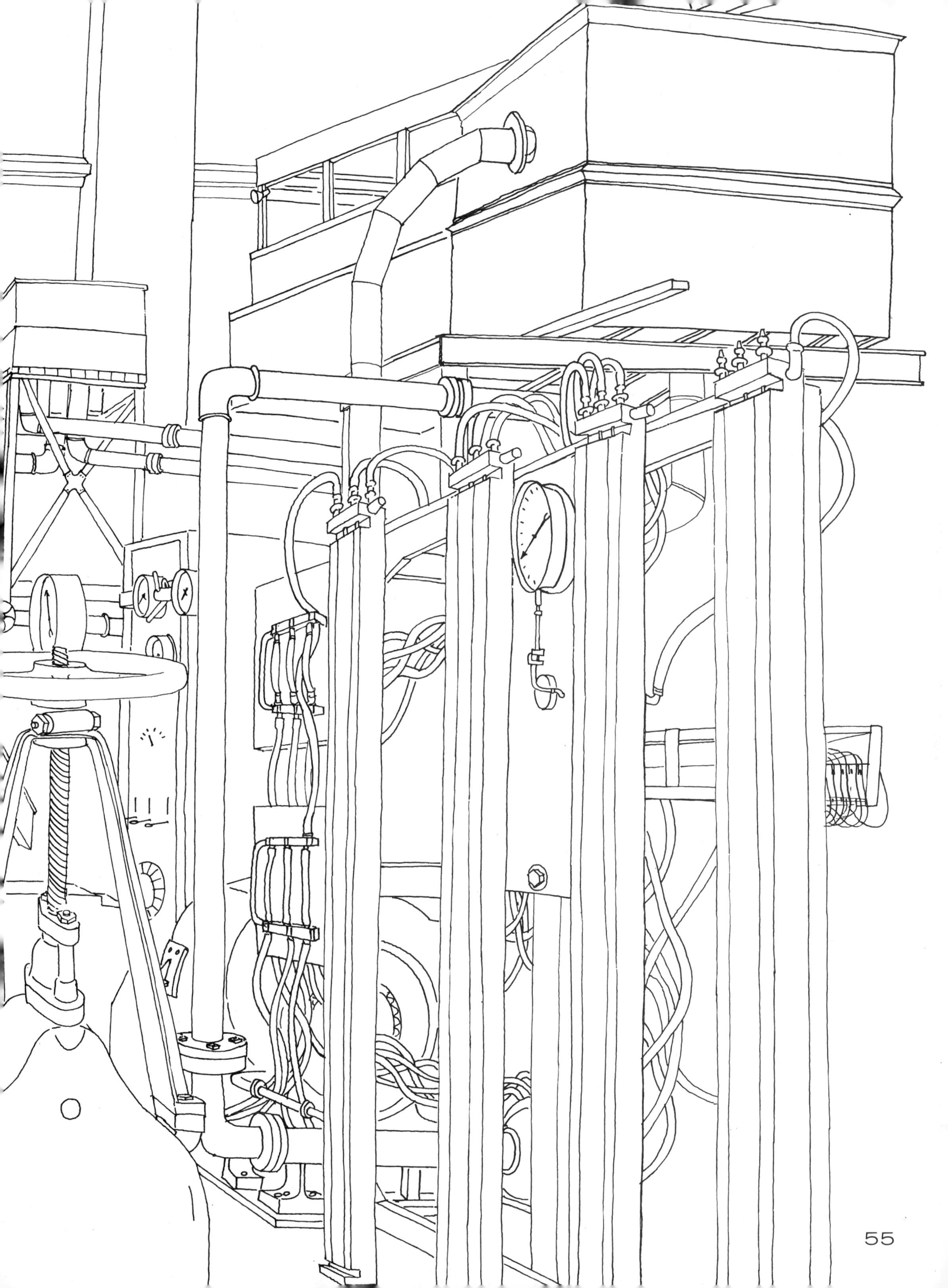

12

JACKETS *three hours*

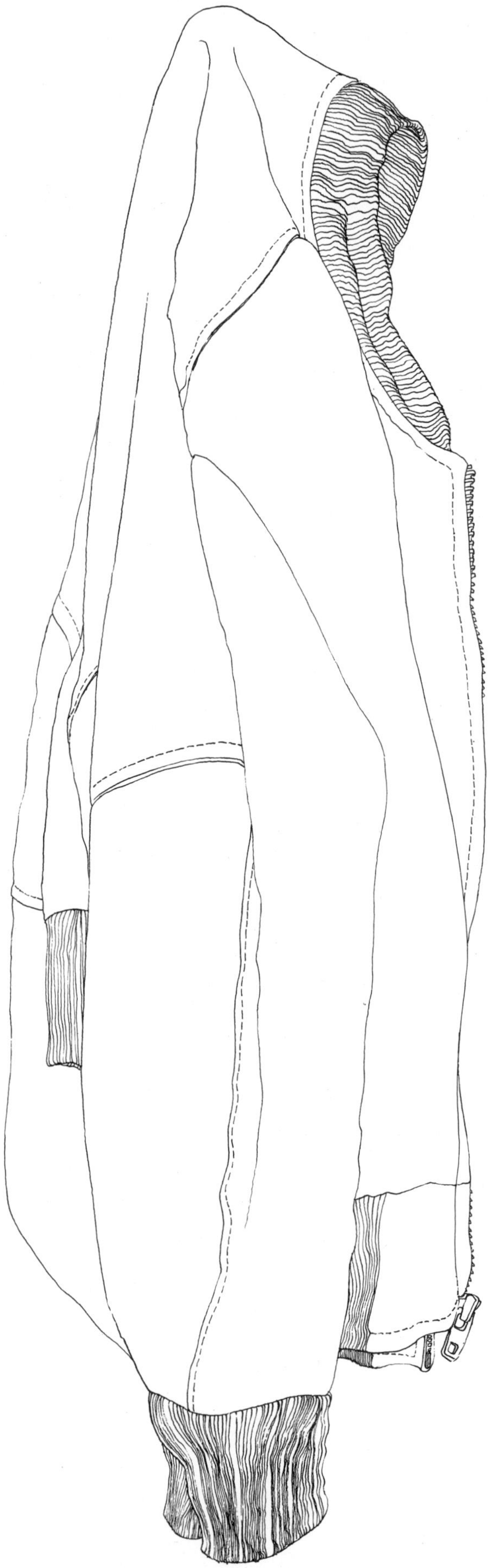

In drawing shoes and handkerchiefs, you have dealt with the problem of the representation of leather and cloth in contour line. In this study we take the matter a bit further and get into the problems of representing the form and connections between draped pieces of cloth or leather and such fittings as zippers, buttons, and accessory materials.

A man's windbreaker or mackinaw makes a good subject. Hang it from a hook or drape it over the back of a chair. This problem is really very similar to the shoe problem in that it requires you to see and understand the way the pieces are connected, and to invent for them an adequate representation. Here you will also encounter problems similar to that of the shoelace: textured fabrics (corduroy, for instance) are not adequately represented by the scratches of cross-hatching. Start drawing at any part of the jacket that interests or challenges you and stop when the problem no longer excites you. There is no value in drawing beyond that point. A small fragment, drawn with absorption and care, is better than the world drawn with superficial indifference.

Remember that the drawings as such are really not the issue here. They have primary meaning only as the tangible evidence of a process of observation and invention you have performed. In a sense, they are graphs of **you!**

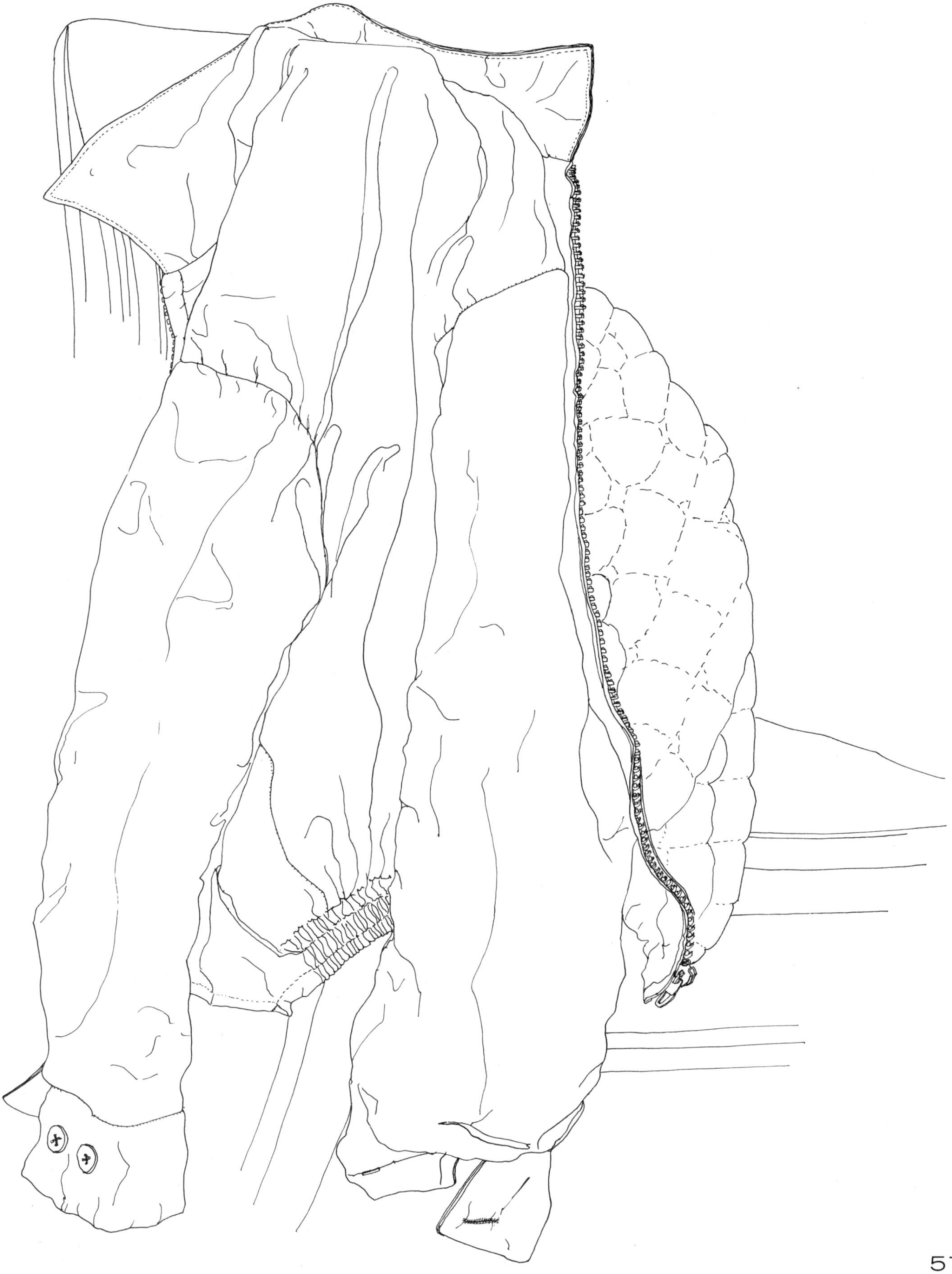

13

GLASSWARE *optional, three hours*

A collection of glass tumblers, empty wine bottles, pickle jars, cut-glass decanters, and so forth will provide you with some new form experiences and new challenges in the representation of materials.

The various degrees of transparency of this material, glass, will permit you to struggle with the problem, again, of the significant, simple evocative line. When you arrange a varied group of the objects so that some are partly seen through others, you will find that you have a good puzzle to decipher: which of the refractions, reflections, or forms is significant and essential? Can you preserve the transparent quality of the material?

It will be worthwhile and interesting to spend some time in assembling a good group of glass objects. Some commercial glassware is of very handsome form, and you may find its subtleties and transitions in shape very rewarding to study.

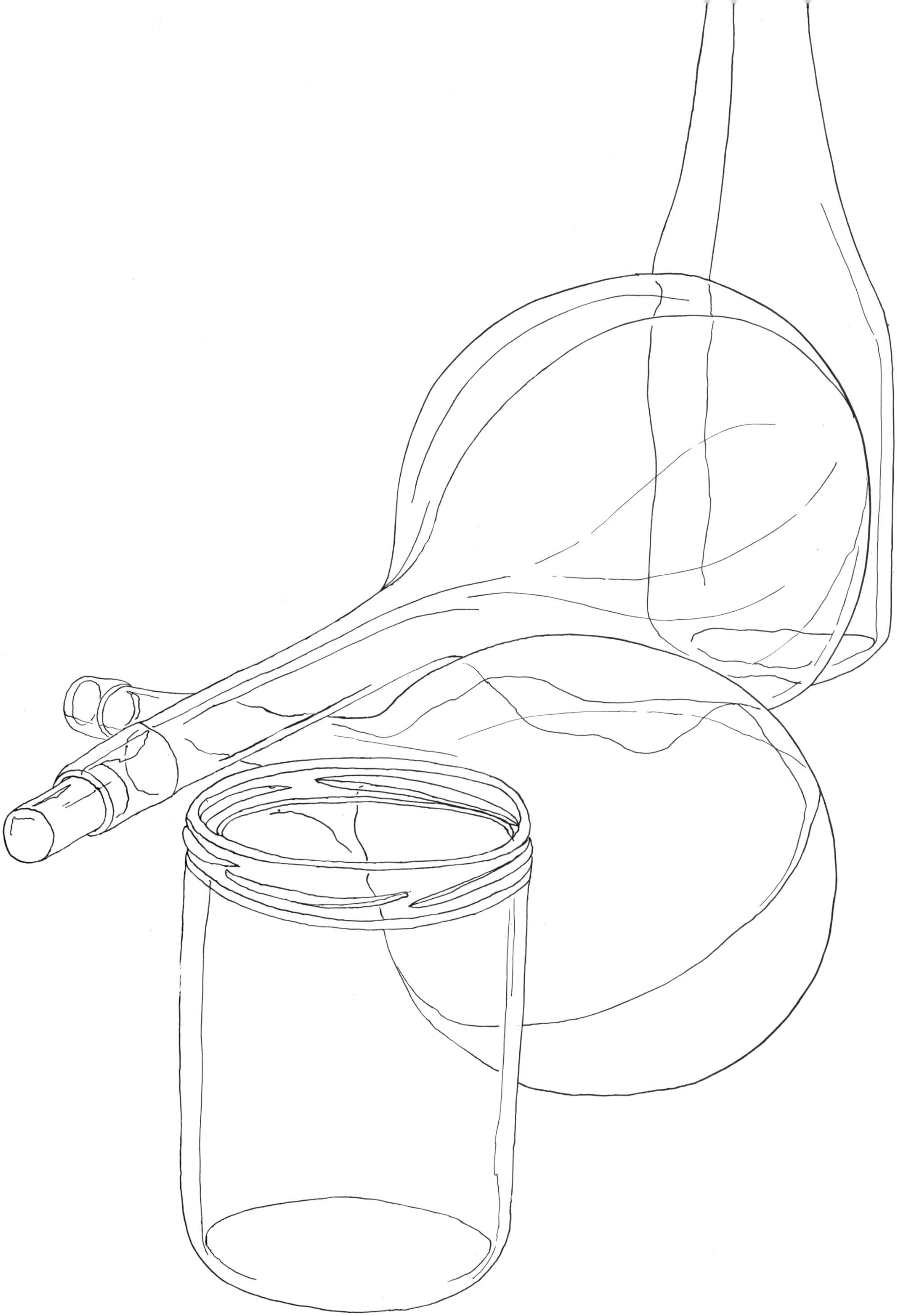

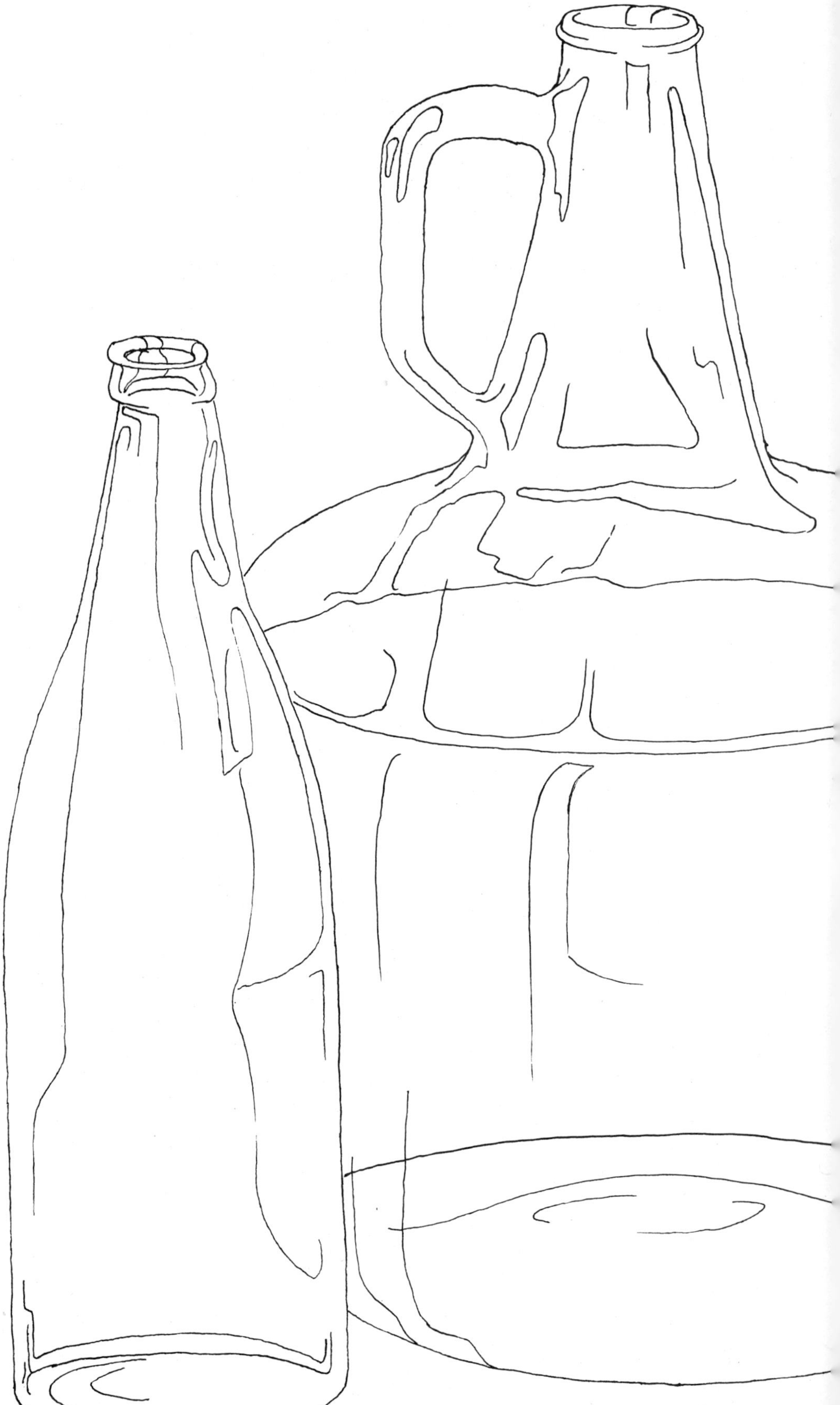

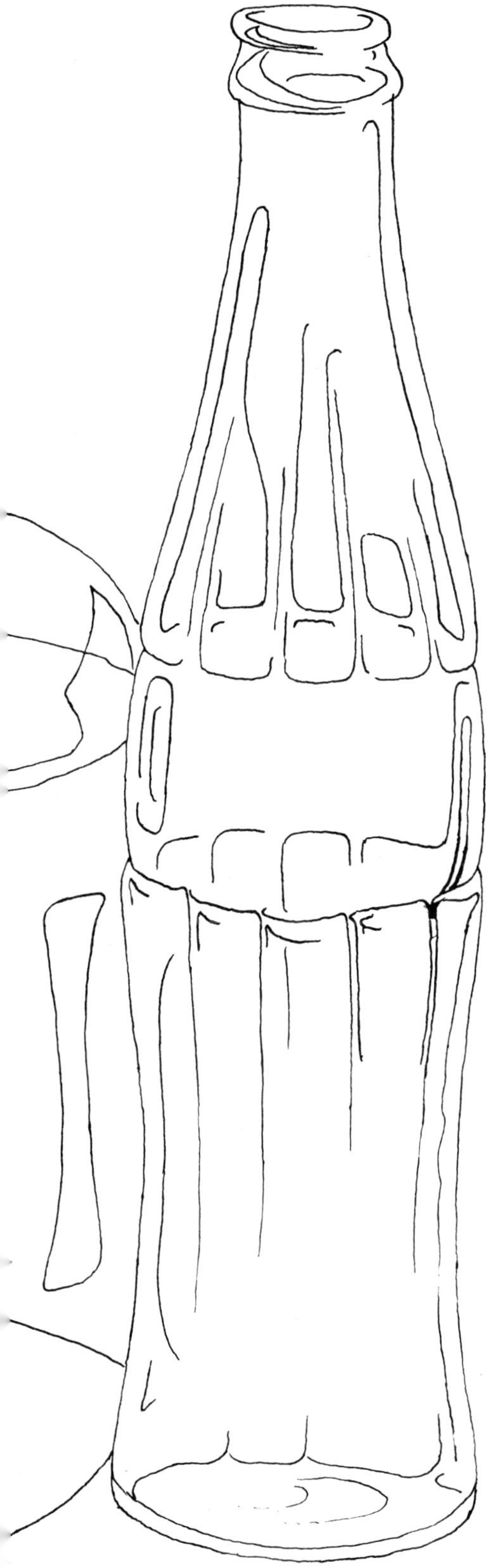

14

FLOWERS *three hours*

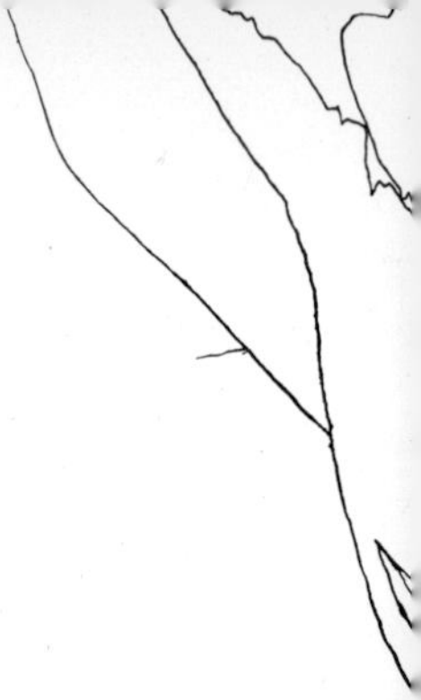

A close-up study of the architecture of a rose, or any other flower (including a portion of the stem and some leaves), will be of interest. The forms and the materials are unlike any you have drawn so far, and this problem will broaden the frontiers of your form experience.

The trick is to draw this subject about twice life-size, so that you have a fair chance to explain what you have seen. Changing the scale this way is a wonderful means of experiencing the subject anew: can you imagine what a rose would look like if you were the size of an ant? Perhaps it will help you to draw larger and see better if you do imagine that the relative sizes of you and the flower were changed.

In any event let the amount of time you have available determine how much you draw; an excellent fragment is better than an indifferent whole.

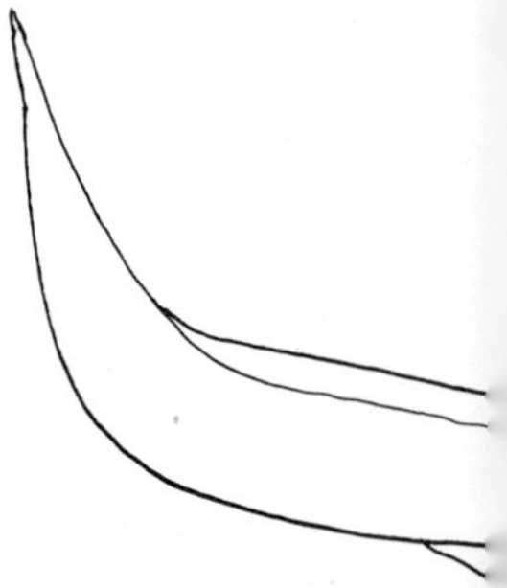

Keep this drawing on your wall for a few days. This is a good idea to use with all your work, for it gives you an extended opportunity to review and evaluate your work. Self-criticism (before or after, but not during the process) is most important to your development. It all comes down to the point that ultimate responsibility is always in your own hands. You can build the confidence and courage for this by the experience of continual evaluation and criticism.

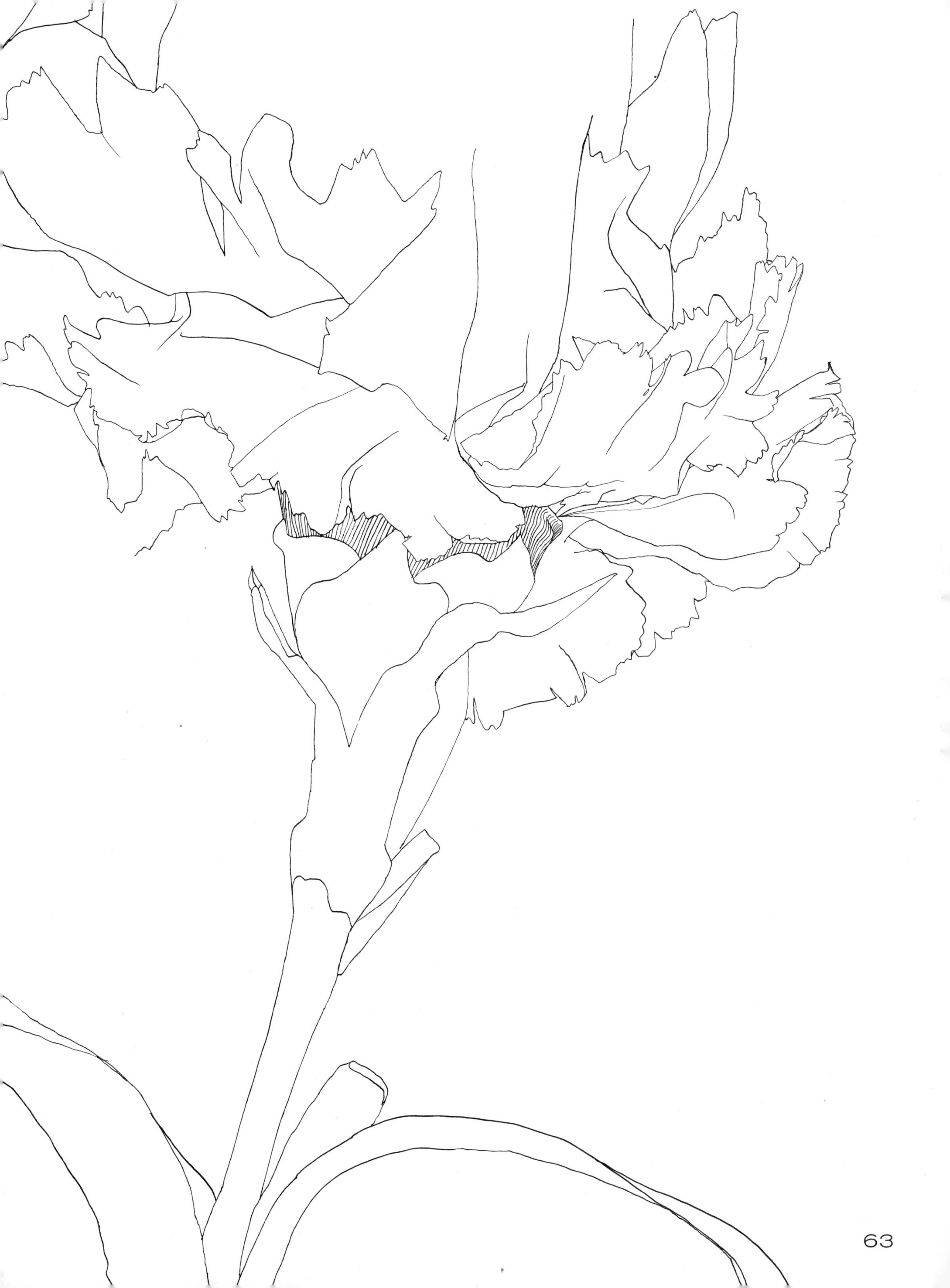

15

LEAVES, BRANCHES, BARK *optional, three hours*

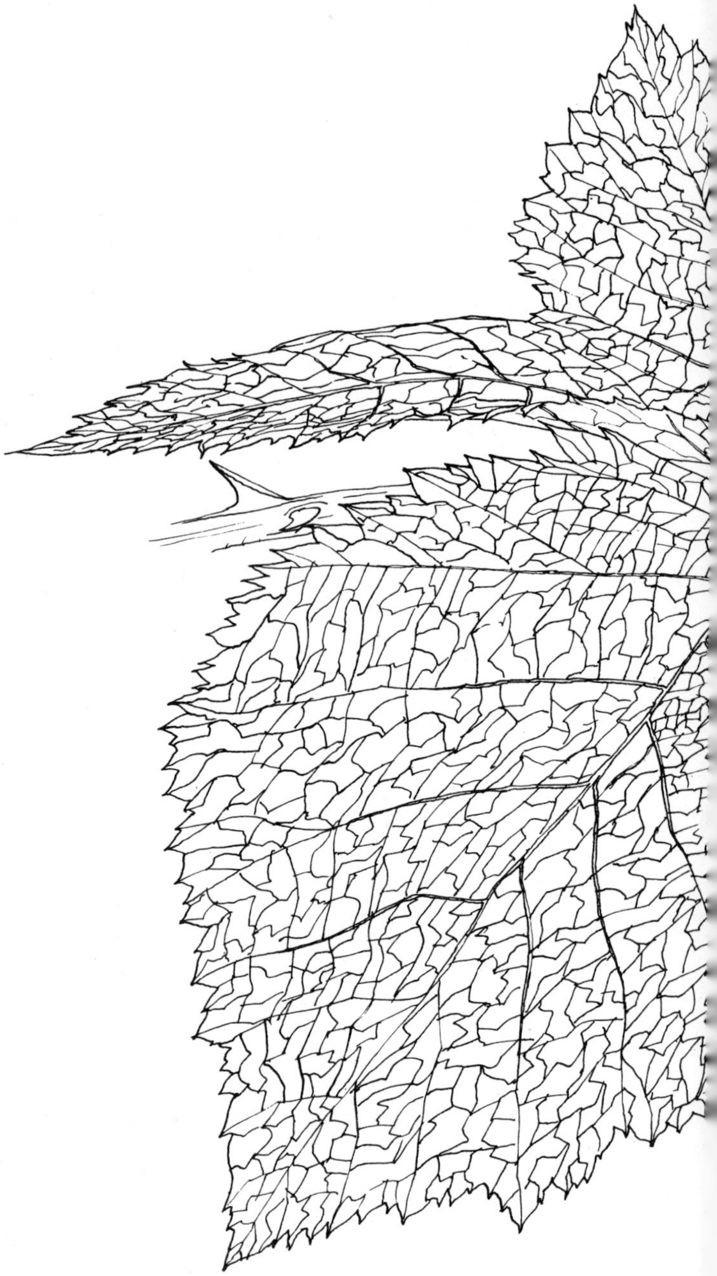

Man's most intimate form experience in the past has been with the natural landscape. Today, increasing numbers of us are city dwellers, and nature becomes a week-end or a harried holiday experience. For this next problem you are invited to examine certain components of the natural world—leaves, branches, and the bark of a variety of trees or shrubs—and, by drawing some of them (at least life-size), to rediscover a little more of the wealth of natural forms.

A good procedure would be to collect a half-dozen or so specimens of different trees or shrubs. In each case obtain a cluster of leaves with their stems and a portion of the branch. A critical examination of each of these will leave you with an interest in one or two specific examples, and it is suggested that you draw only these.

You might follow the same procedure with the bark of a variety of trees. Examine several before you choose one to draw. In all cases you will have a problem, not only in the discrimination of significant detail, but also in the development of ingenious ways to represent new form and surface qualities. (In a sense, you should think of yourself as a researcher, trying experiment after experiment to find the best answer to a problem.)

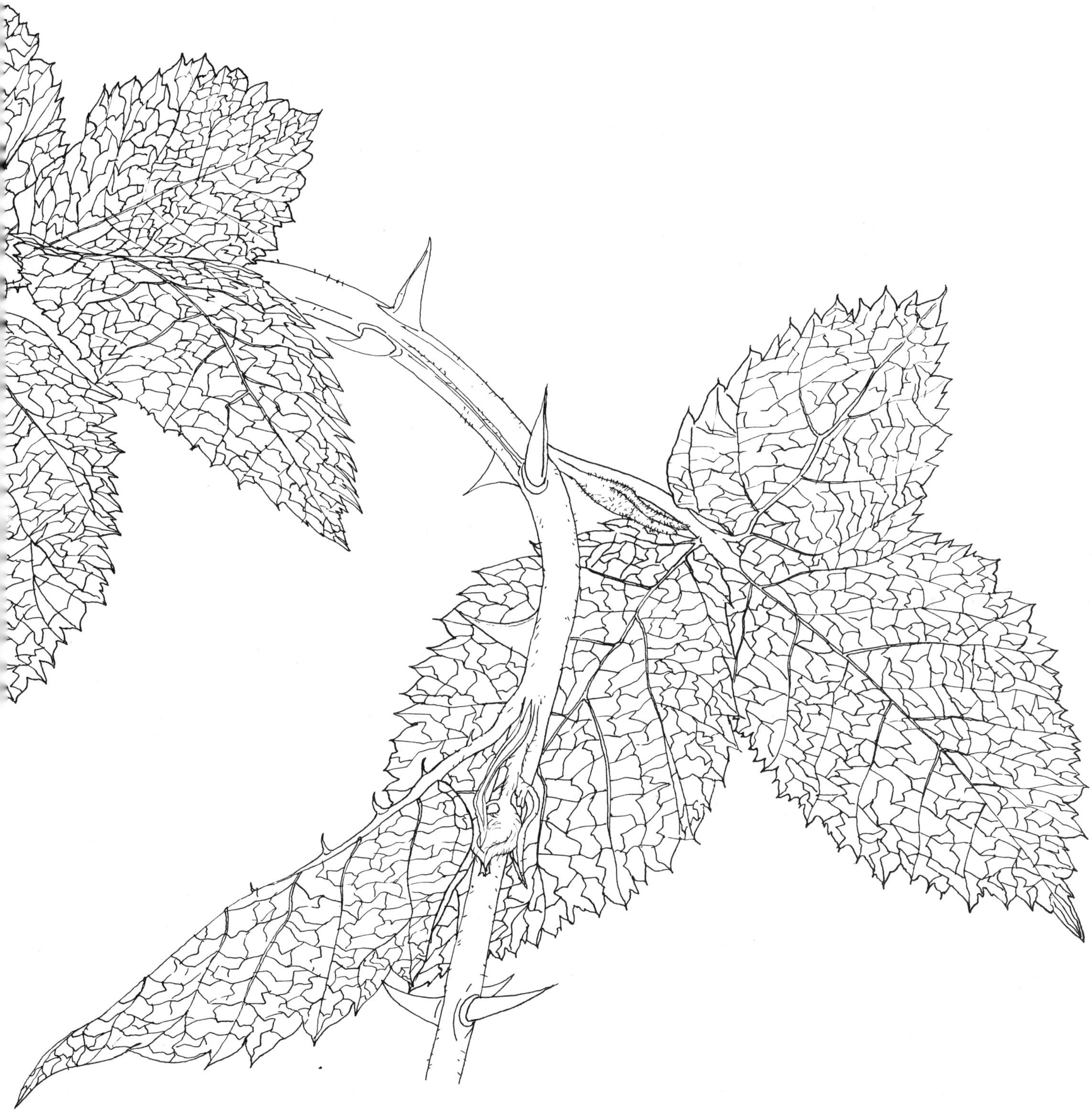

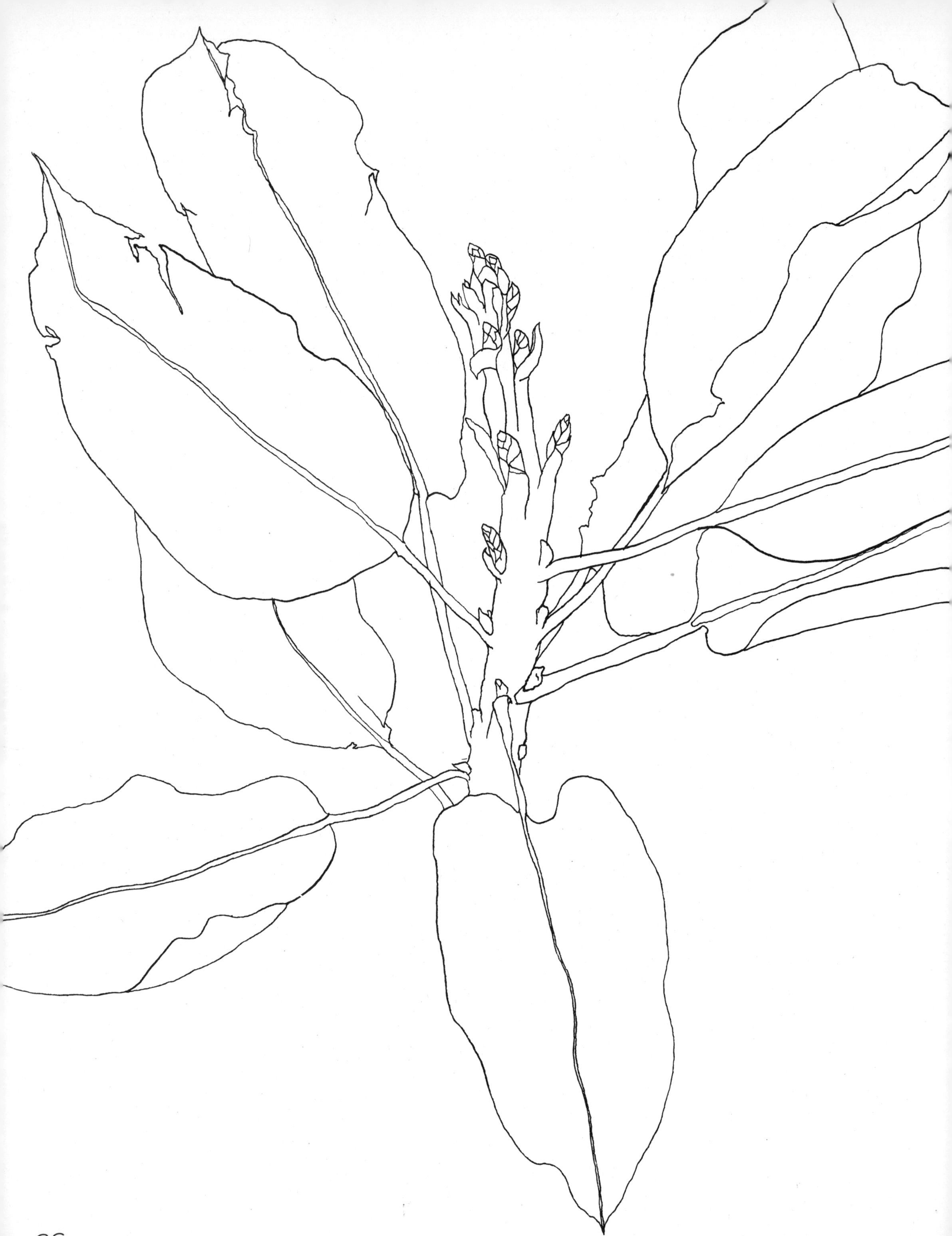

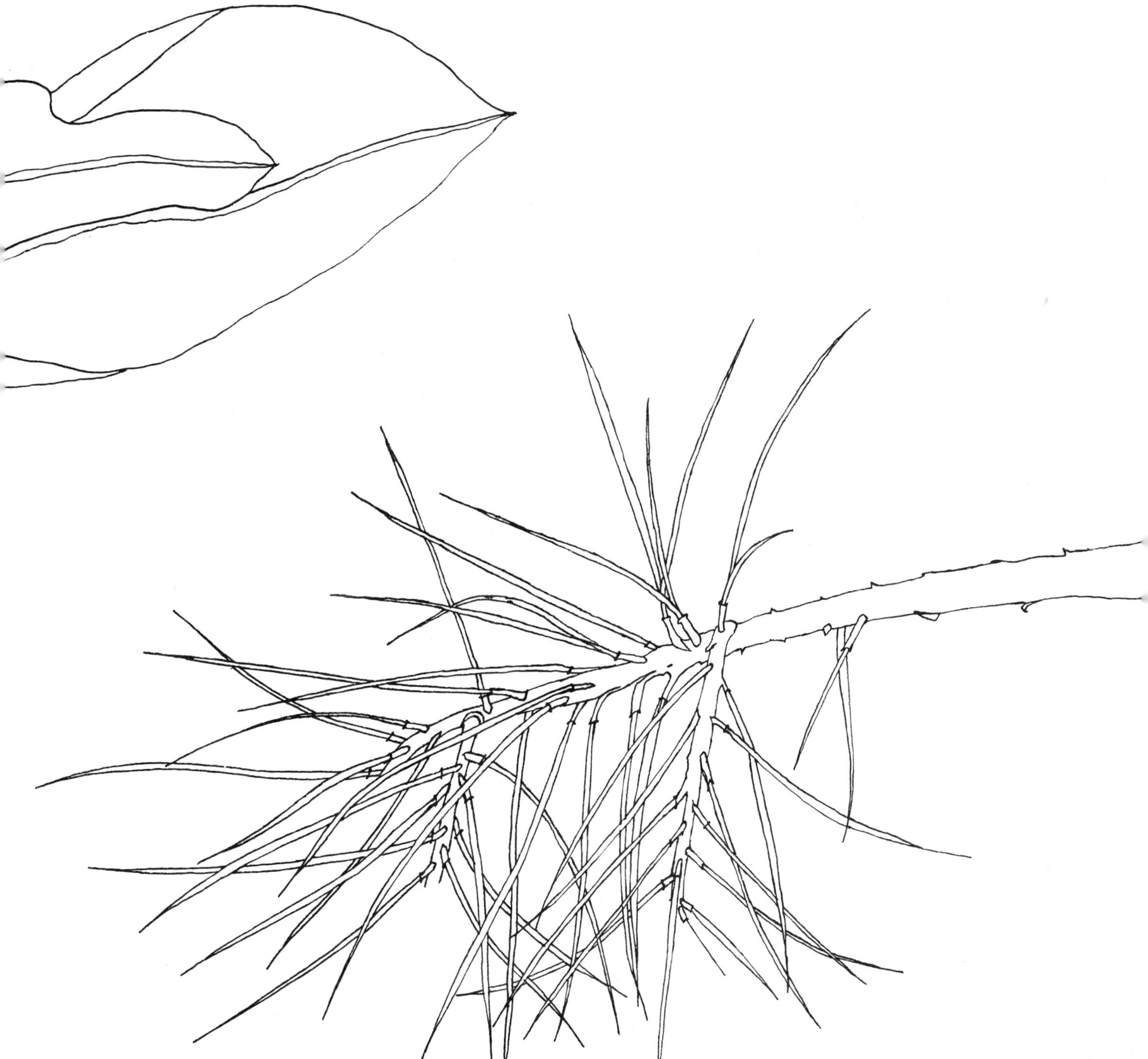

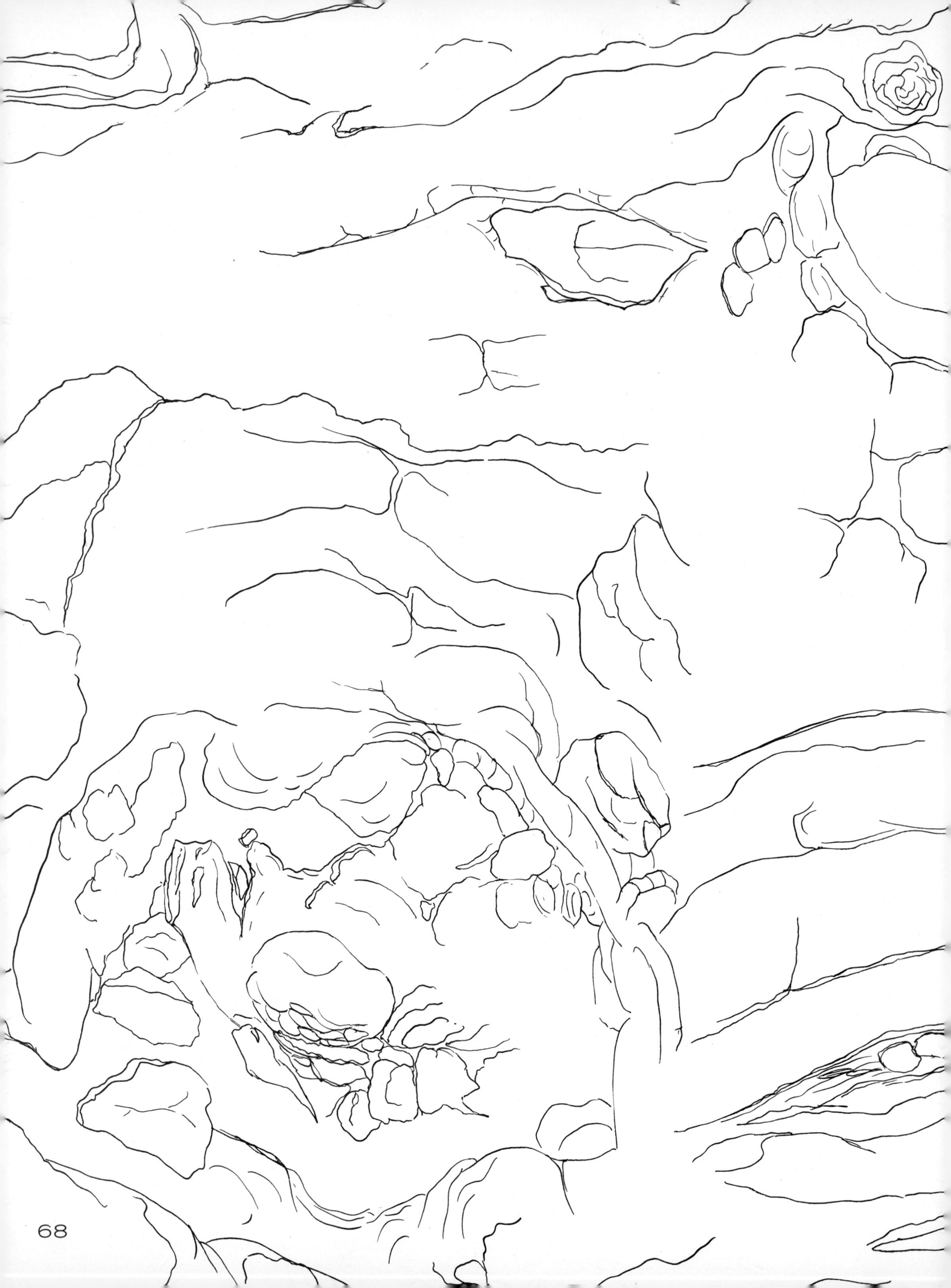

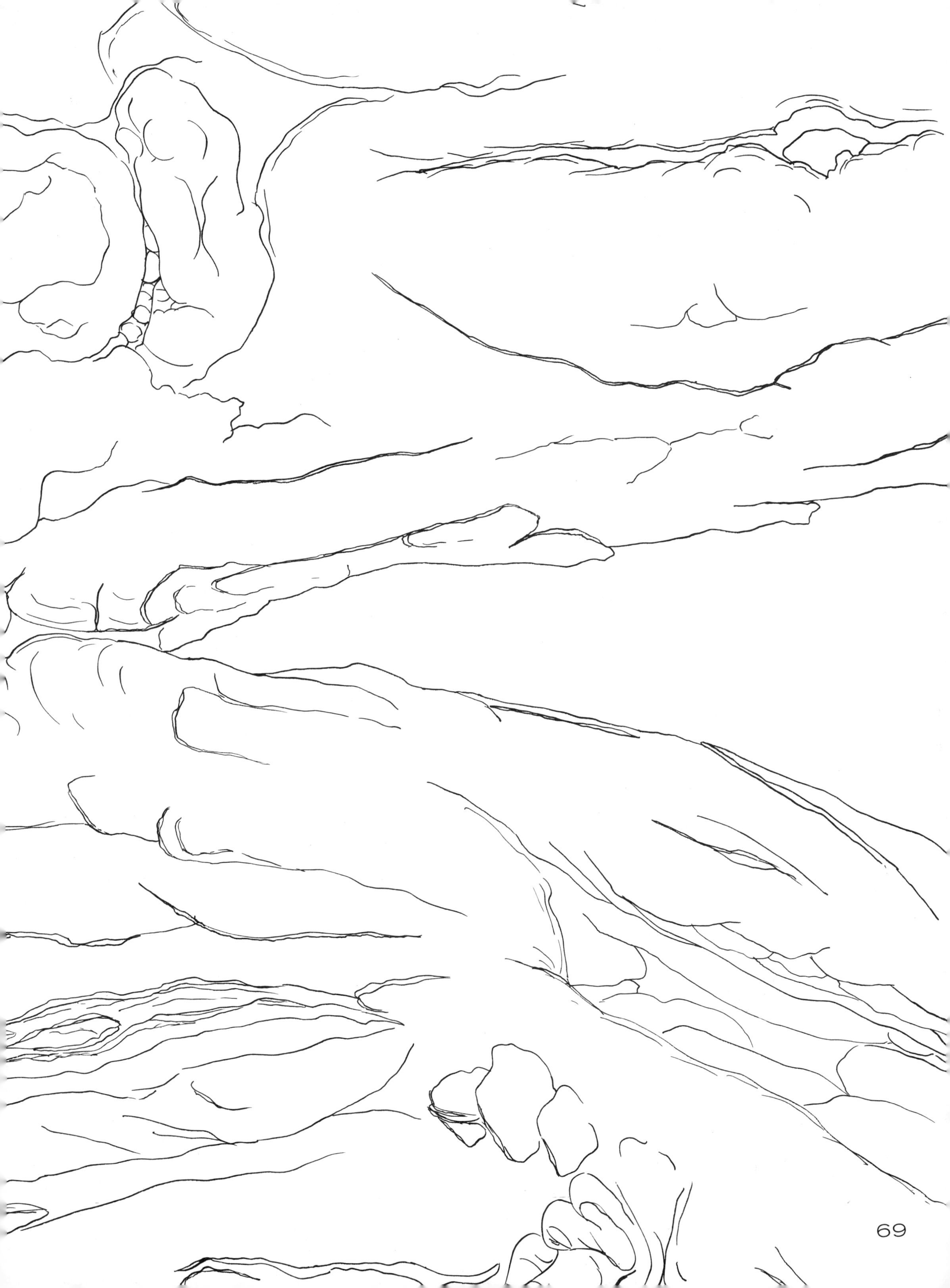

16

HUMAN FEATURES *six hours*

Next in our series are the human features. We will take them up in three groups: first the ears, along with an adjacent area of hair; then the eyes with the eyebrows; and finally the nose and the lips. All these studies, with the exception of the eyes, should be at least life-size. The eyes will have to be studied at a larger scale because of the intricacy of certain details.

It is most advantageous to have a model for this work. You can, of course, use yourself as a subject with the aid of a mirror, but this procedure limits the variety of angles and viewpoints from which you can draw these features. Perhaps you can take turns acting as model with a friend.

At this stage ears will give you no problem. Remember that you should use line only, and avoid the use of shades or shadows to represent the form. The inch or so of hair area about the ear that you should also include with your study will, however, require some words of advice. And the advice is, specifically, to **draw every fifth hair.** Unfortunately, there is no short cut to this problem, and you will find that the best results are obtained when you actually do single out an individual hair and draw it just as you see it. Then count over five hairs and do the same for that hair. Anything other than the exact observation of specific hair elements just cannot have any meaning. But cheer up: after the first five thousand hairs you will not even think about it any more; you might even become fascinated with the nuances of direction and line or form that hairs demonstrate.

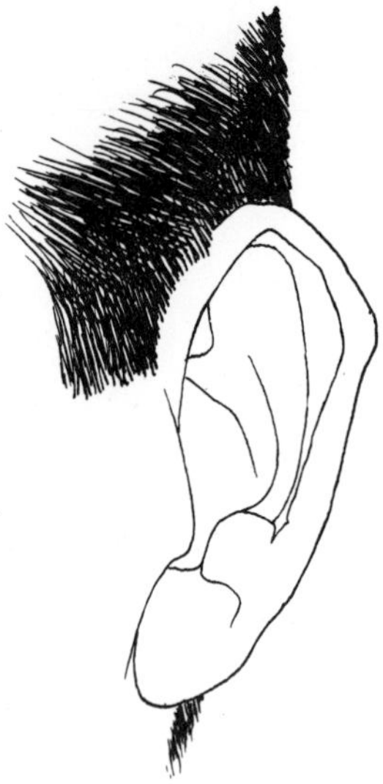

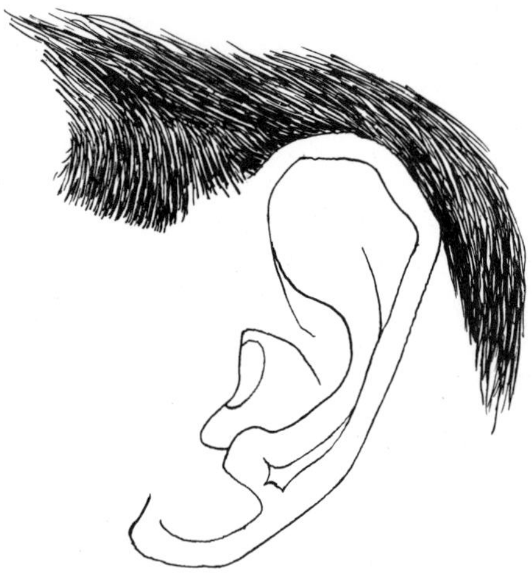

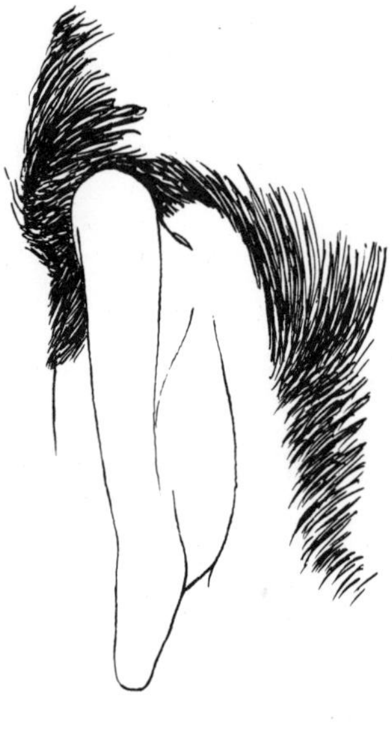

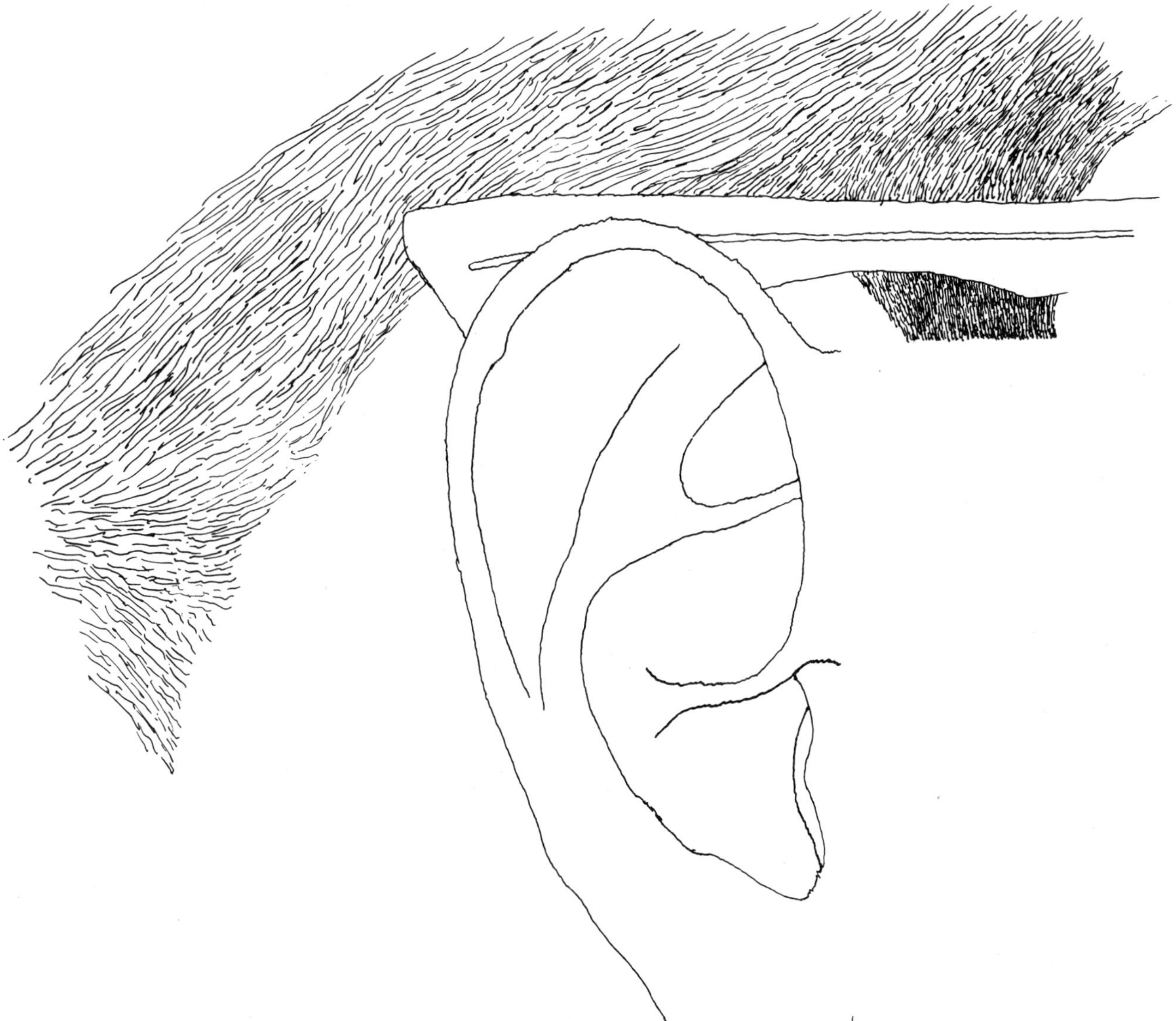

These observations on hair also apply to eyebrows and eyelashes. Two other comments should be made on the eyes. The first is that eyelids have definite thickness, and that the corners of the eyes show very tricky forms. The second is concerned with the matter of significant detail, with particular reference to the iris and pupil of the eye. It will probably require a certain amount of study and critical evaluation before you will evolve a satisfactory idiom for their representation.

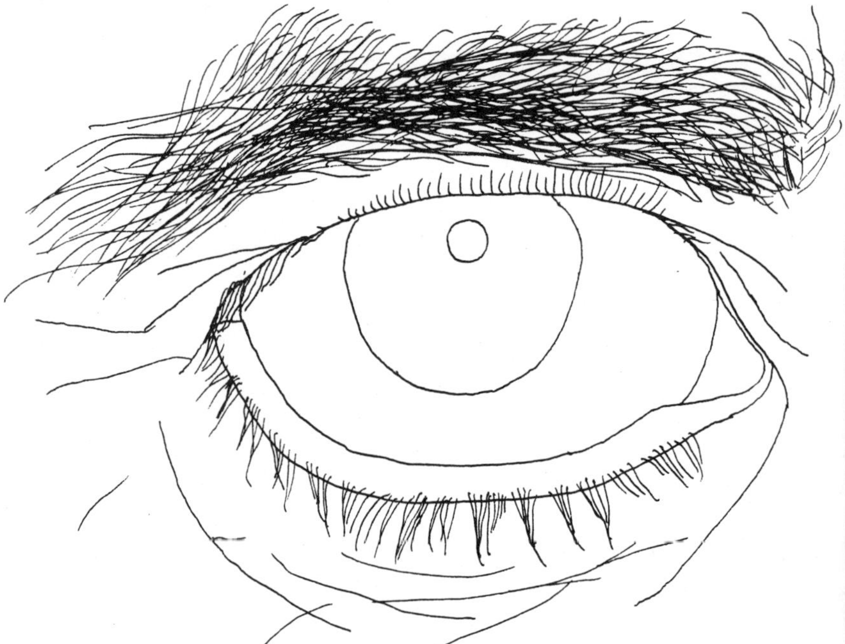

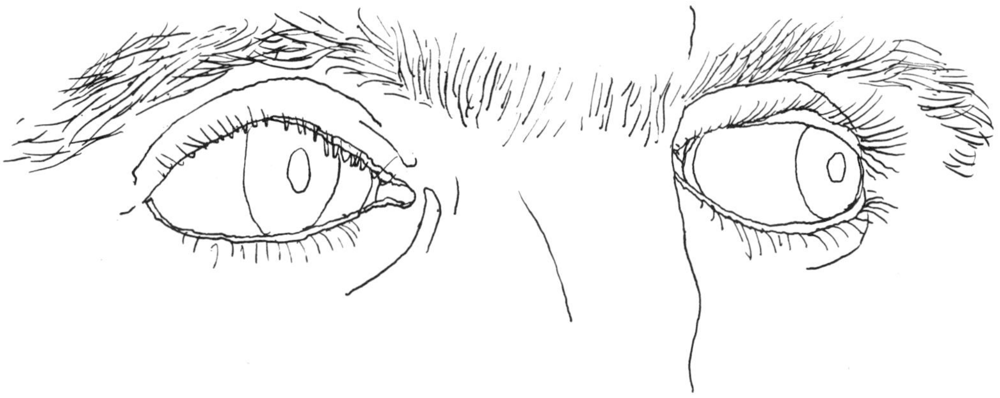

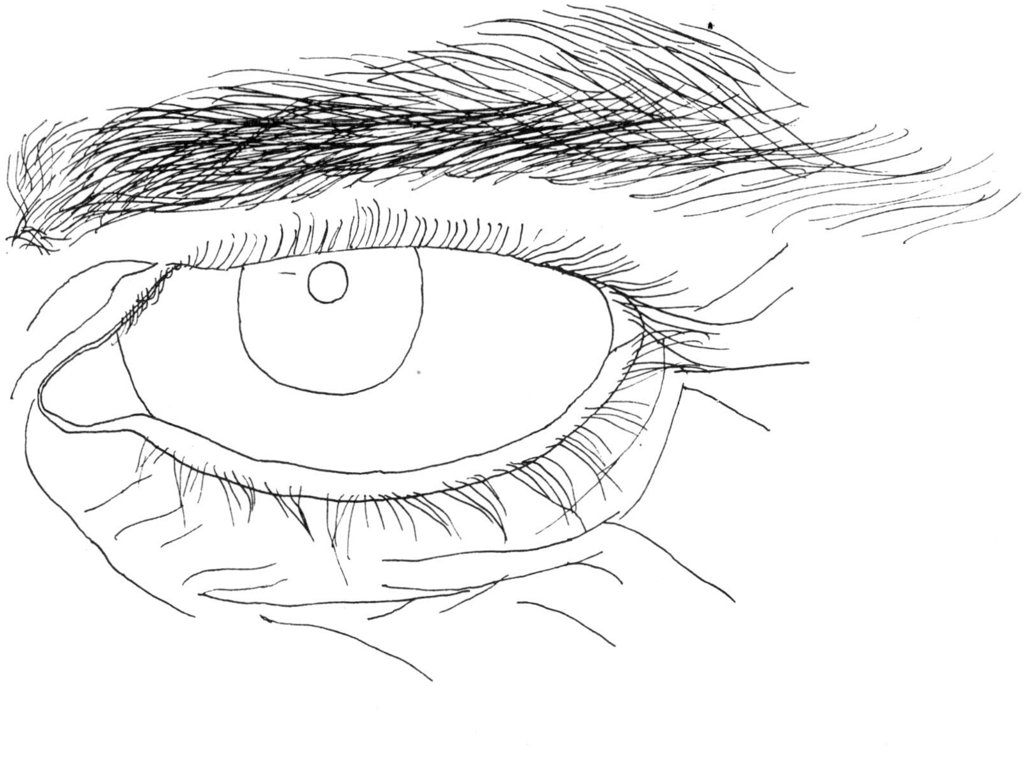

The only comment on drawing the nose and lips again draws attention to the question of significant detail for the surface quality of the lips.

In all three parts of this problem you should draw each group from at least three different viewpoints: from the front, from the side, and from above or below.

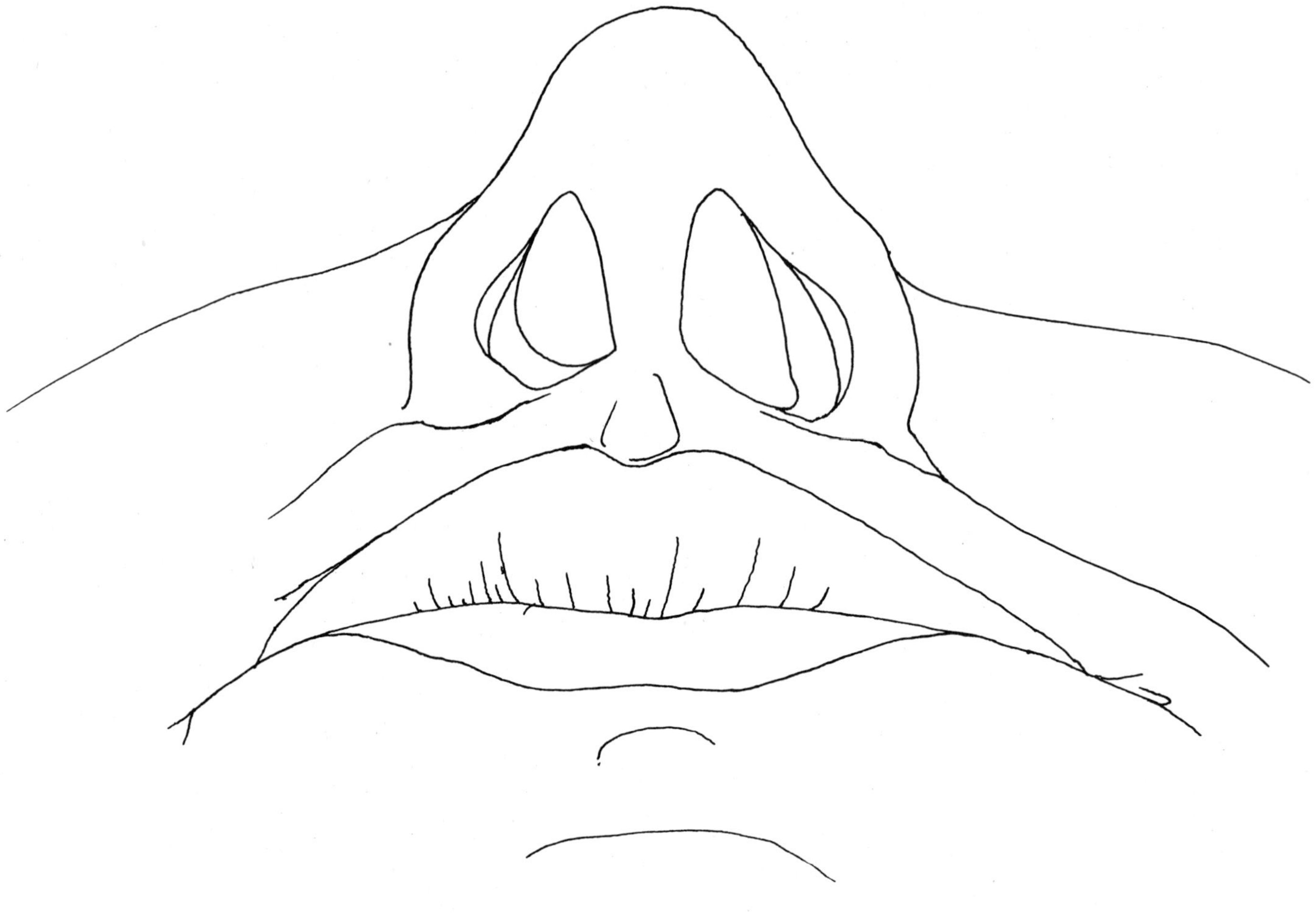

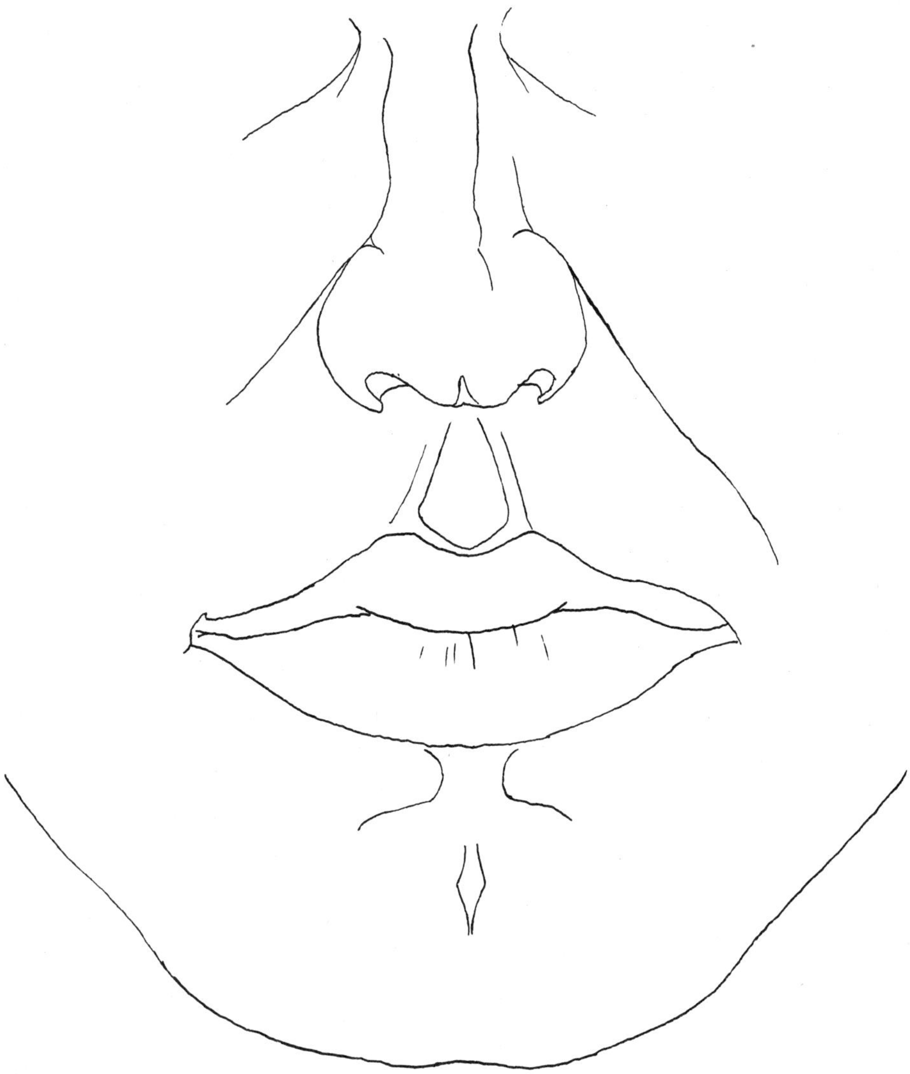

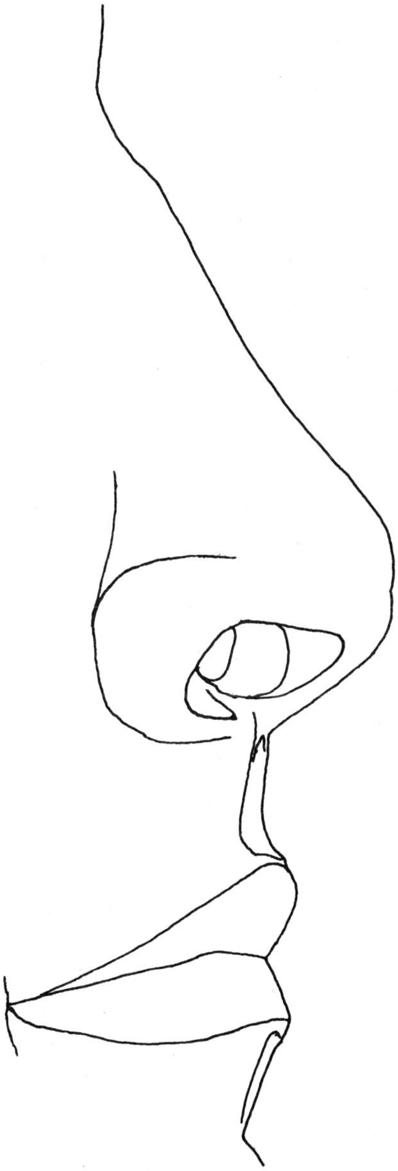

17

TREES *optional, three hours*

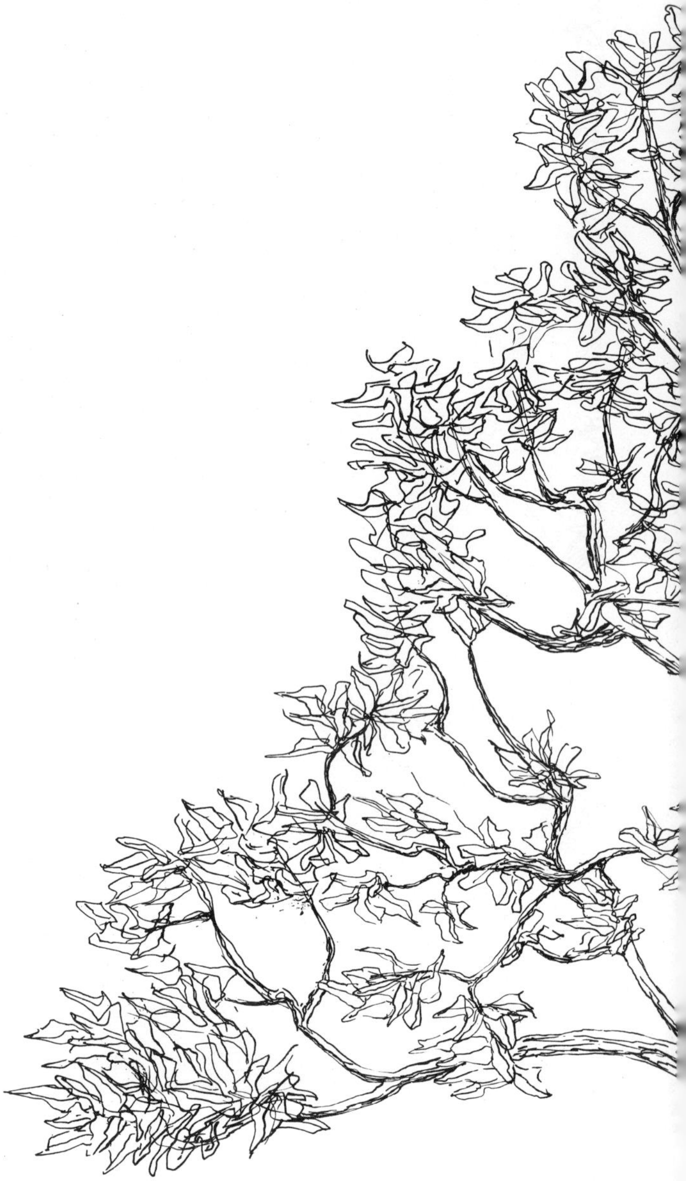

Having already encountered leaves, branches, and bark, you are now ready to step back and take a look at the whole tree or bush. For this study we will draw trees from several different distances, and this will require that you locate a subject that can be readily seen from a medium and from a long distance. You may deal with an individual tree or a group of trees.

From a greater distance you will not be able to show individual leaves. The problem here is to develop, by trial and error, suitable graphic texture indications that represent masses of foliage of different scales. The "masses of foliage" may at certain closer distances be composed of a representation of generalized, individual leaves; here is where your earlier studies of different leaf forms will be of use.

Be sure to use a consistent line quality and avoid all tendencies toward shading or cross-hatching.

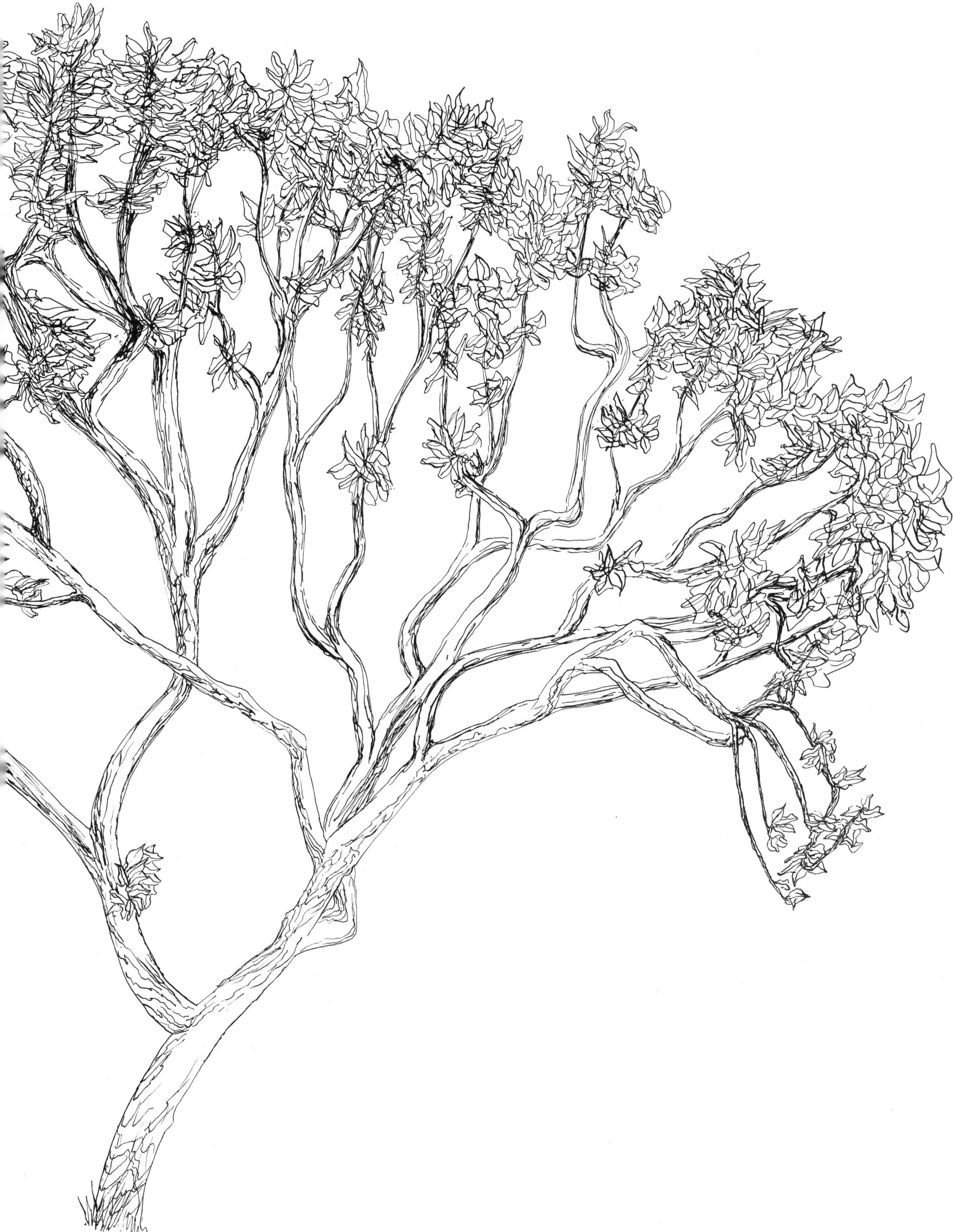

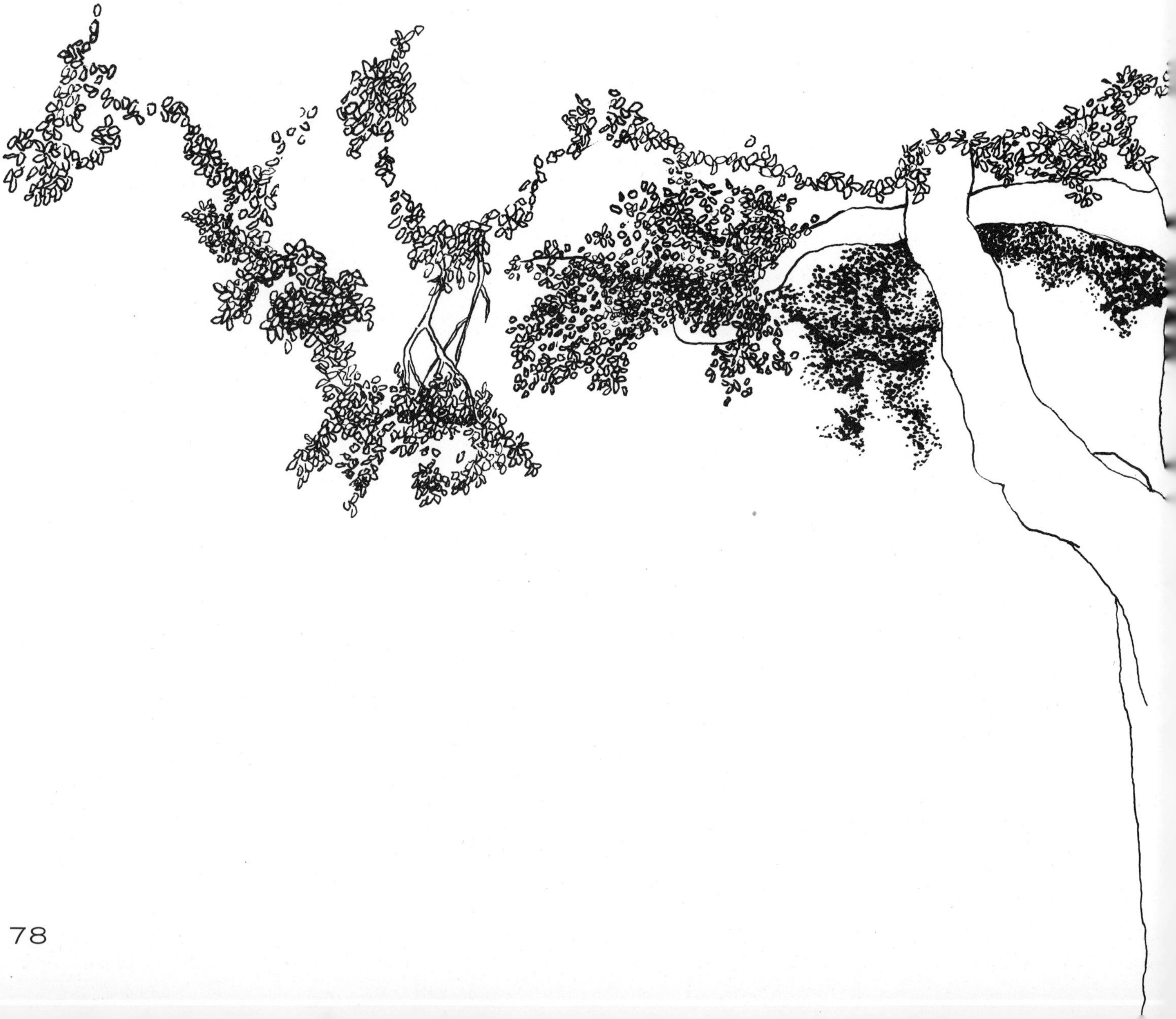

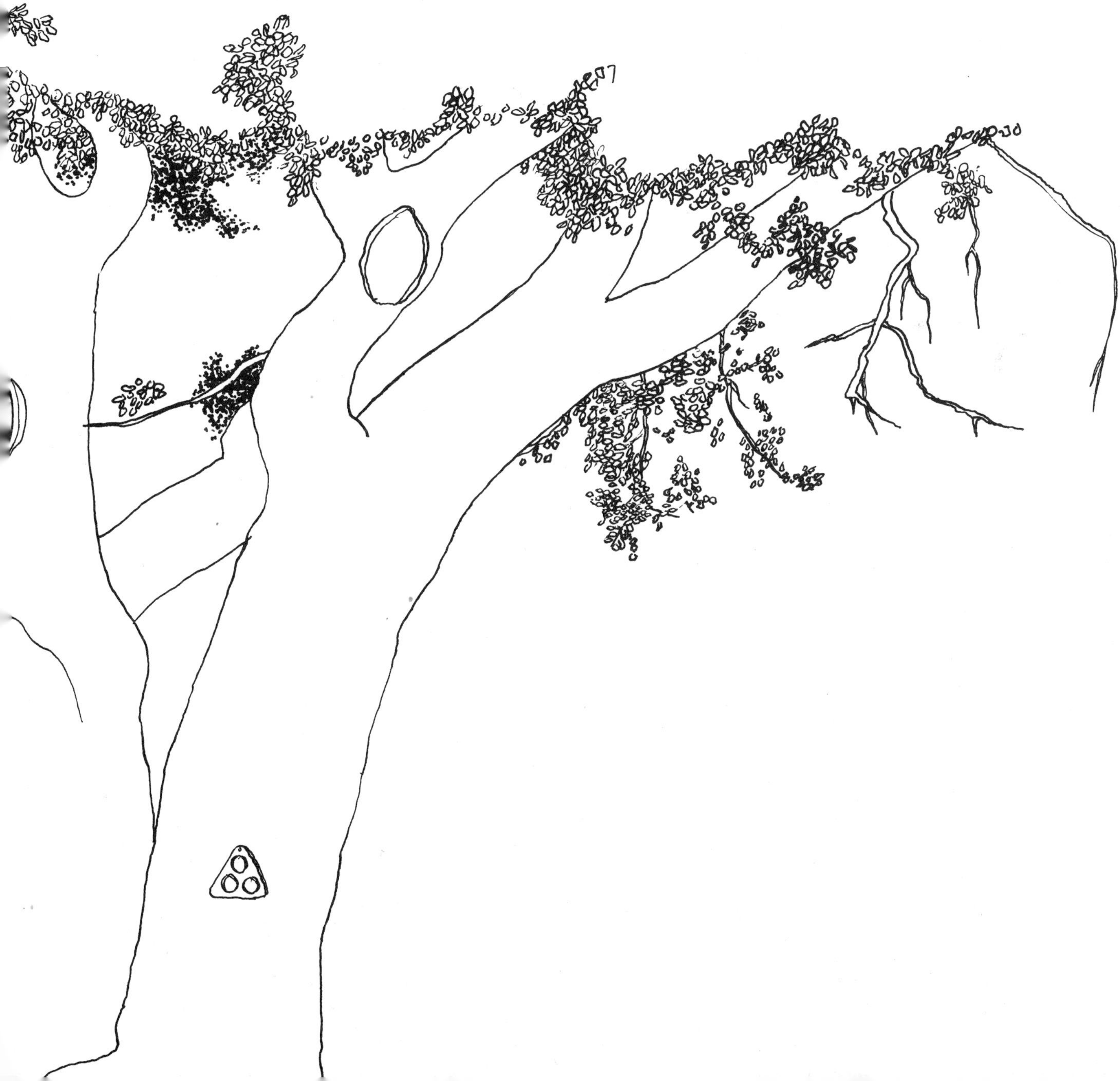

18

HUMAN FACES *three hours*

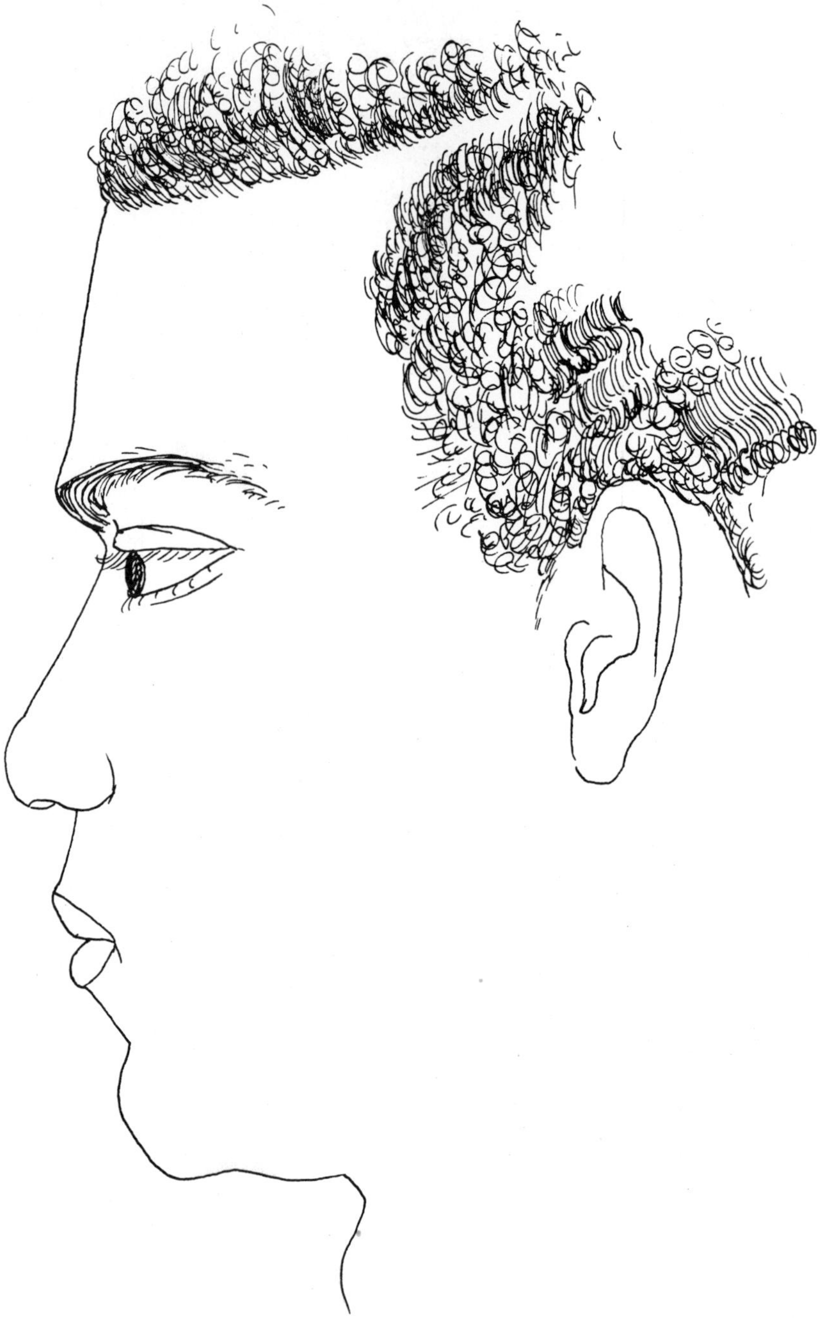

Here also it will be advantageous to borrow someone else's head for a while rather than using your own. An excellent procedure is to have your model recline in a horizontal position and to draw his face from above or below his eye level. From this unusual viewpoint you will experience the assemblage of features as a fresh, new landscape, and thus tend to avoid stereotypes.

You have, of course, previously drawn each of the features separately, from a variety of viewpoints. So you see that there is nothing new about this problem. Select any part of any feature, and draw it; then go on to the next; and so on. When you are all done you might take a look at the proportions—obviously while you were working you were much too involved to bother about this consciously. But keep in mind that this is a drawing and represents a record of your response to a stimulus. As such the "distortions" that you may notice are a wonderfully candid expression of your perhaps unconscious interests and preoccupations. The human interest of such a drawing lies in just these unconscious stresses.

A note again about the hair. You will recall the suggestion given earlier, in connection with drawing the ears and hair. The same comments apply here. Draw the hair or omit it if you will; but if you draw some or all of it, respect it, give it all the time it deserves, and let your responsibility show in each line.

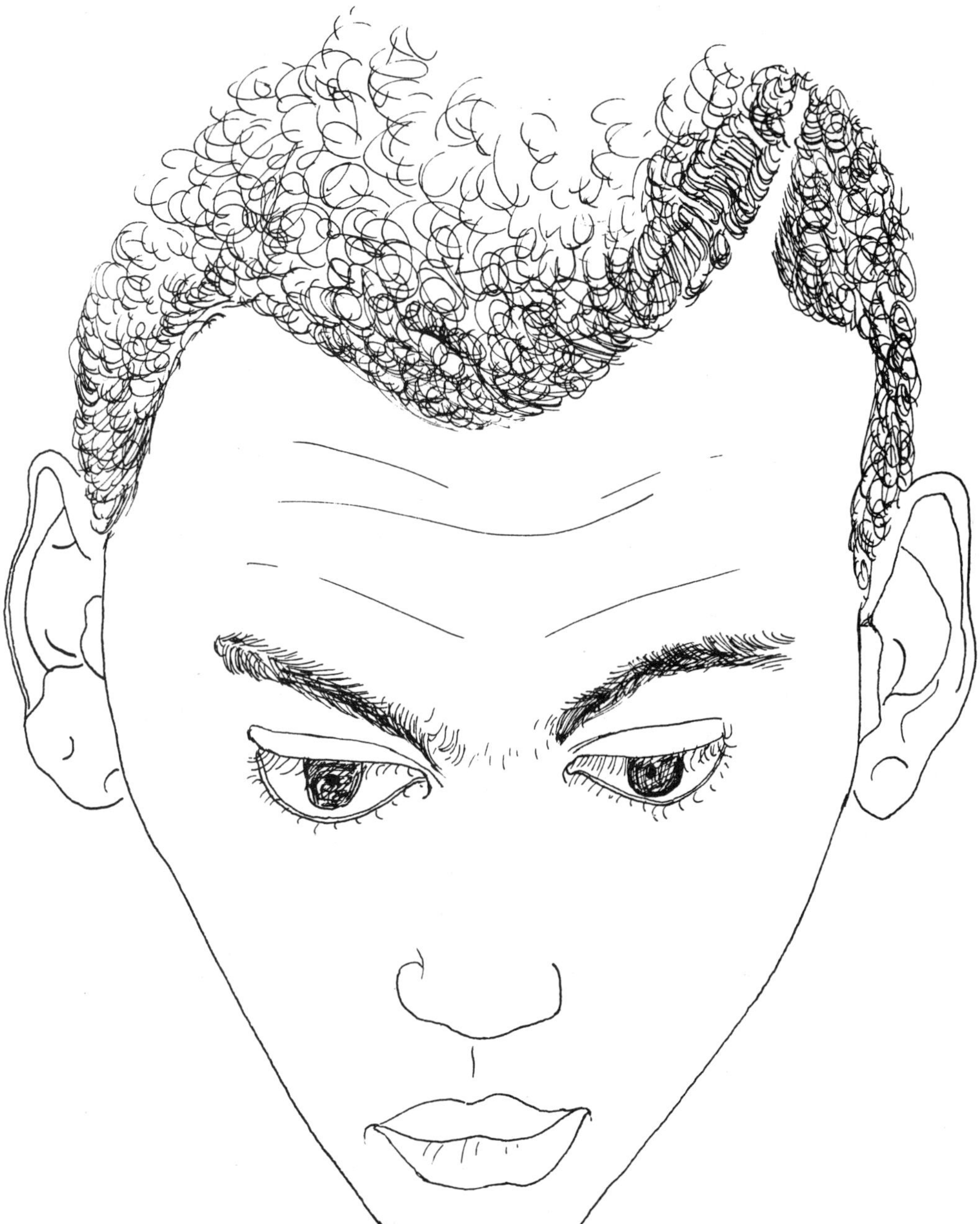

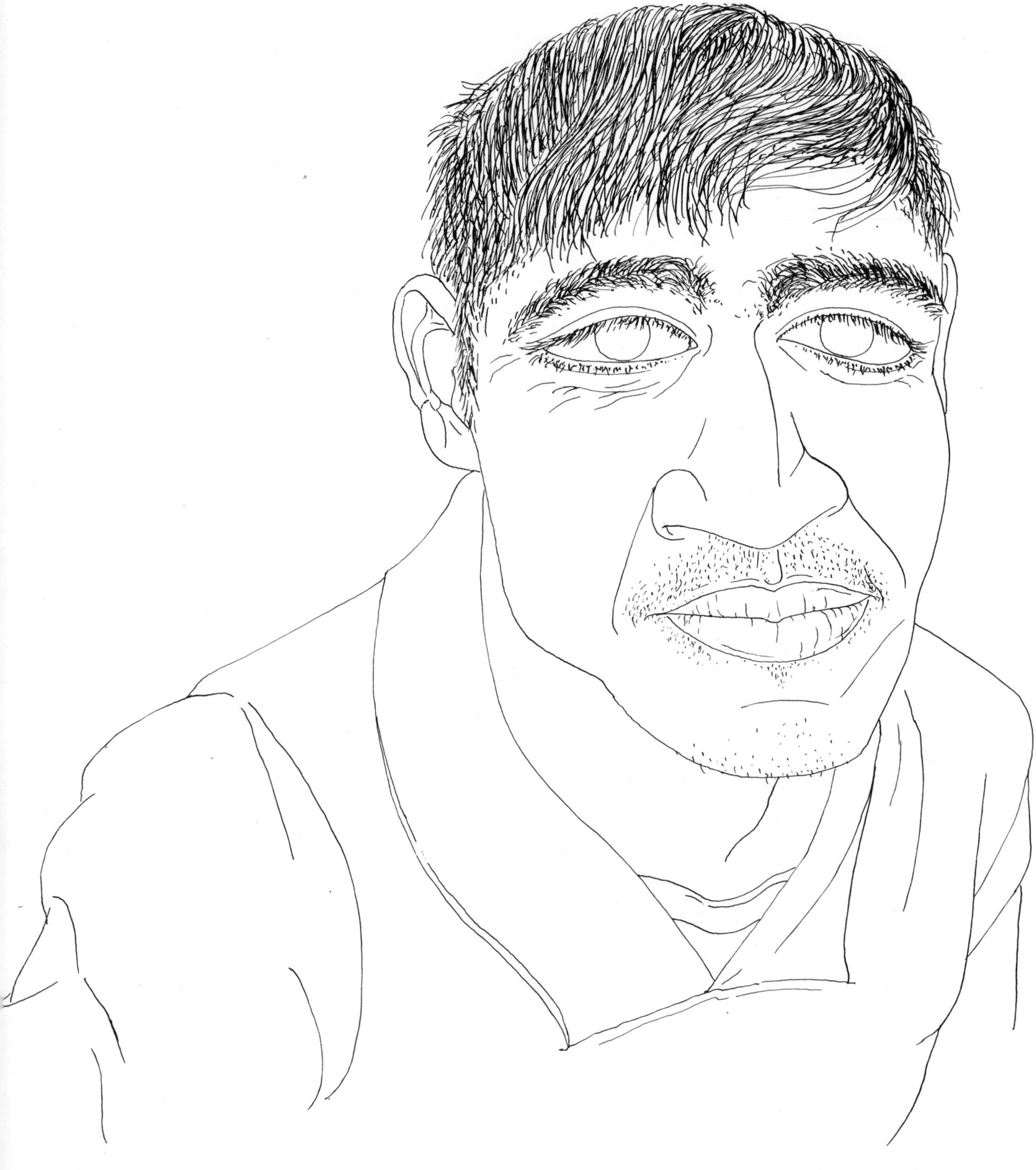

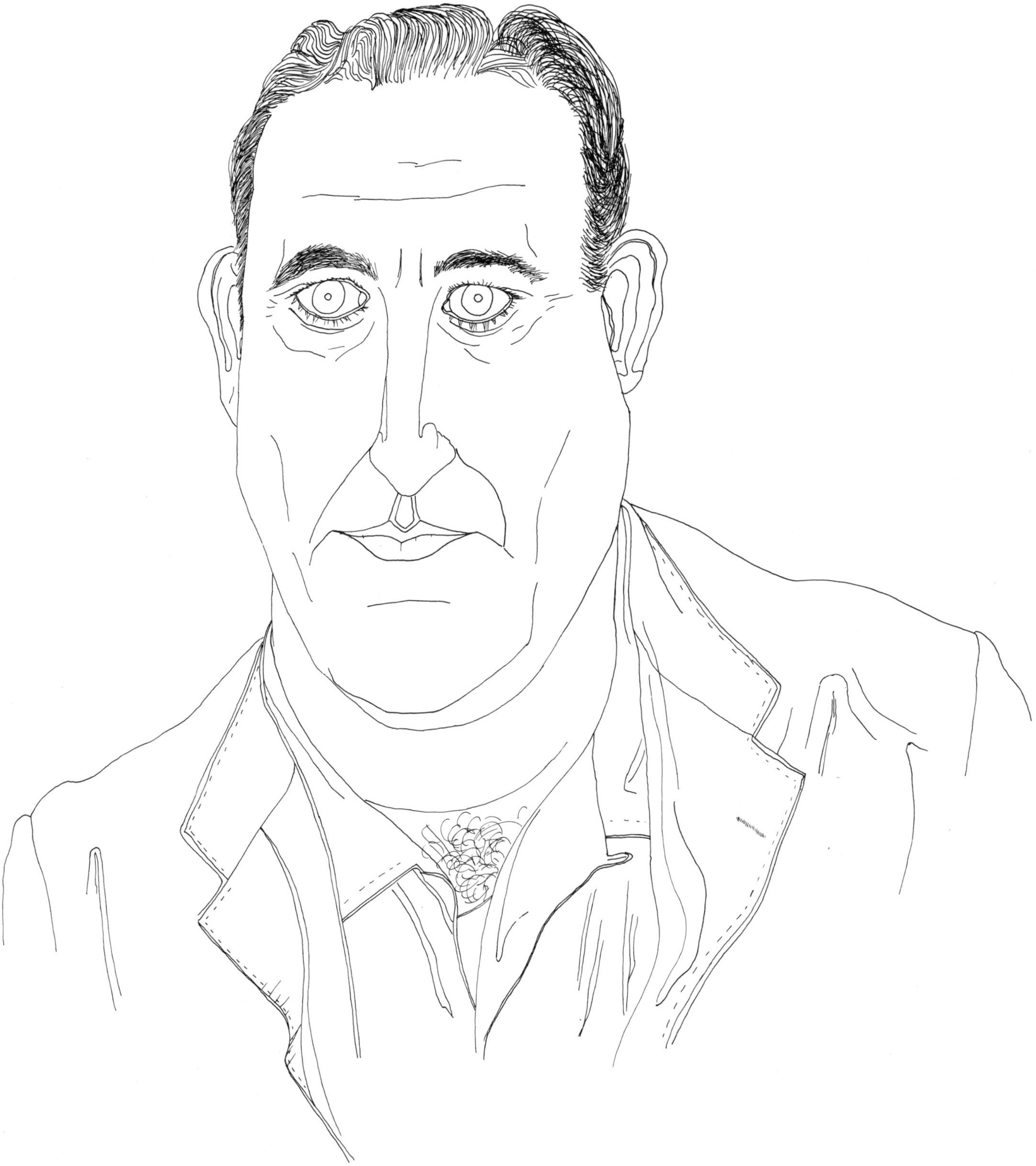

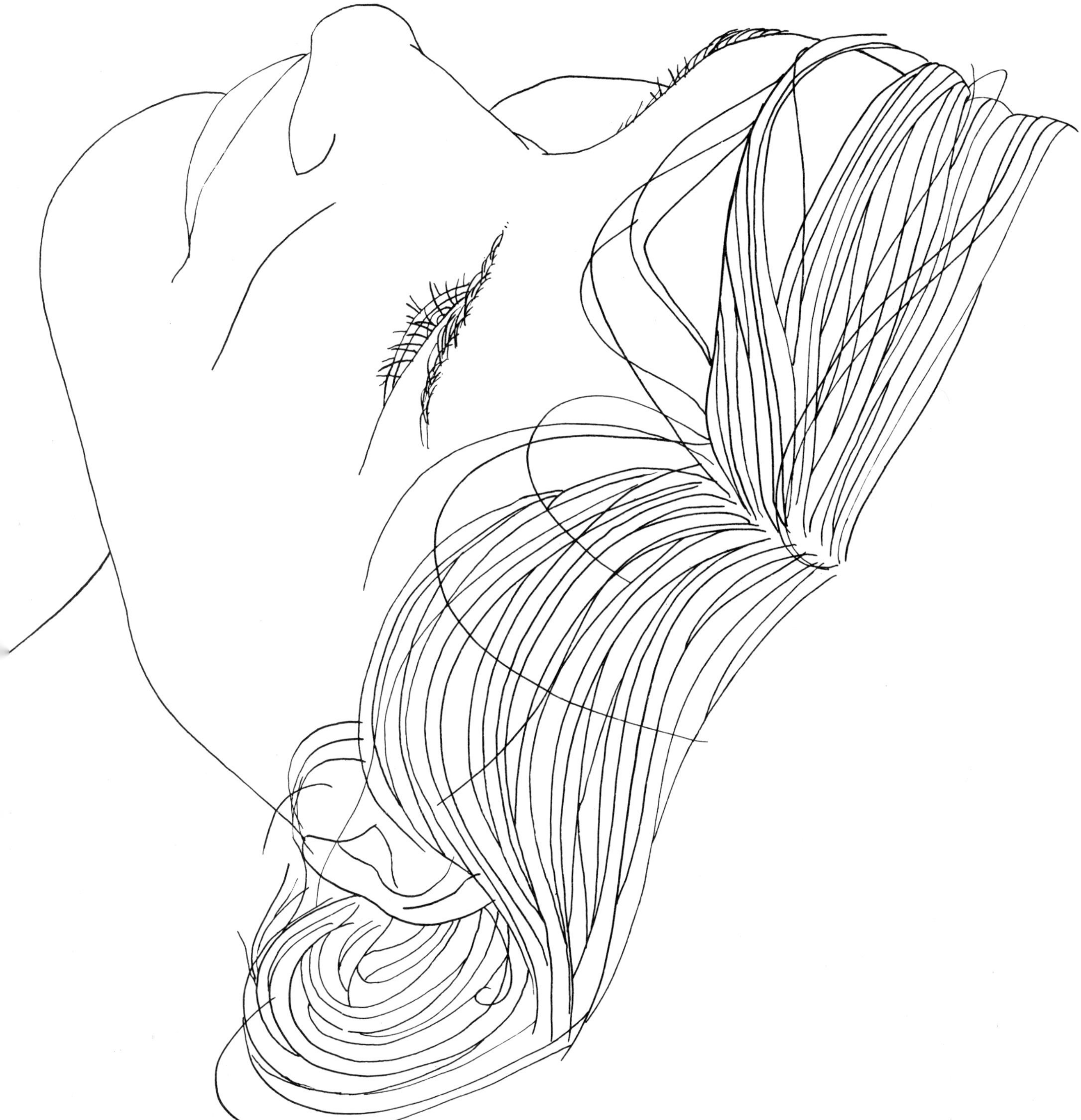

19

STILL LIFE *three hours*

An assembly of three or four objects very different in form and surface quality is a good challenge. For example, try such combinations as an empty wine bottle, a large splintered block of wood, and an eggbeater; or a large wire-mesh kitchen strainer, a lamp bulb, and a pineapple; or a three-foot length of bare, crumpled-up iron or copper wire, a large withered leaf, and a tennis ball. These three examples combining natural and man-made, geometric and organic forms exhibit strong basic form and surface contrasts and analogies, and you may find them a real delight to look at and draw. As you draw them you will grow increasingly to appreciate their qualities in combination.

All these things should be drawn in line only, and life-size or larger. Take time to locate and select and arrange your subjects until they really excite you. This matter of selection and arrangement is as important as making the drawing.

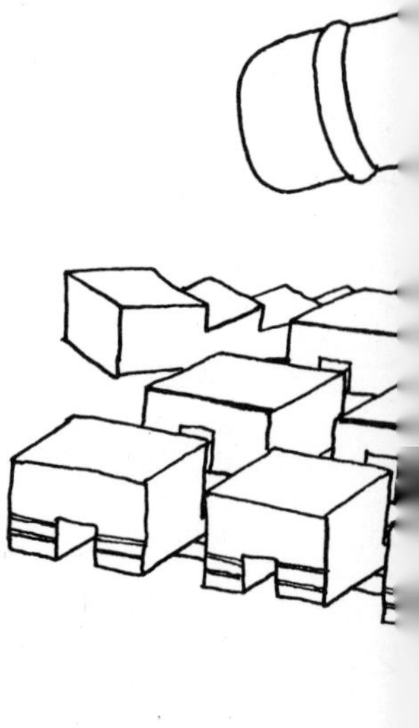

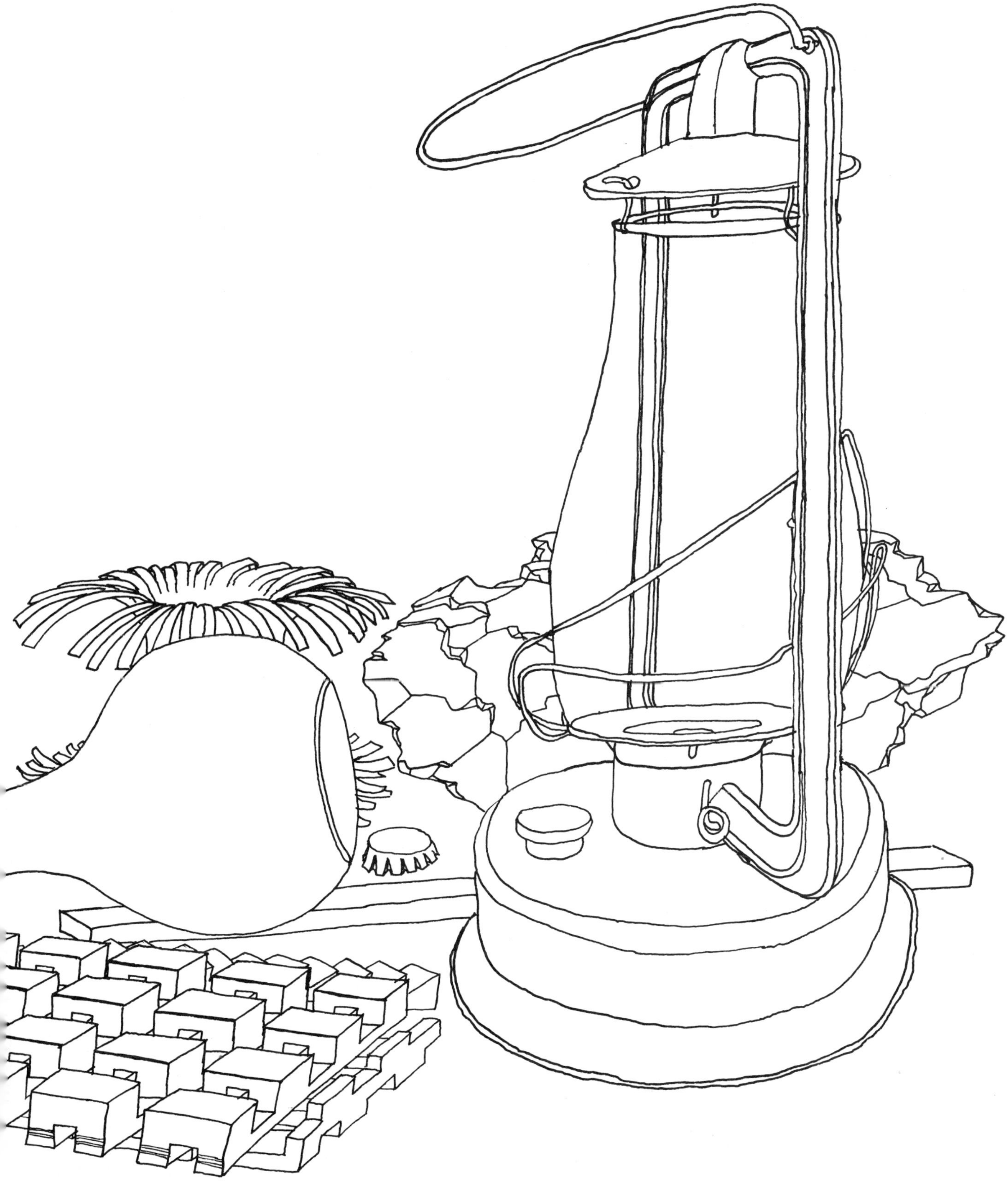

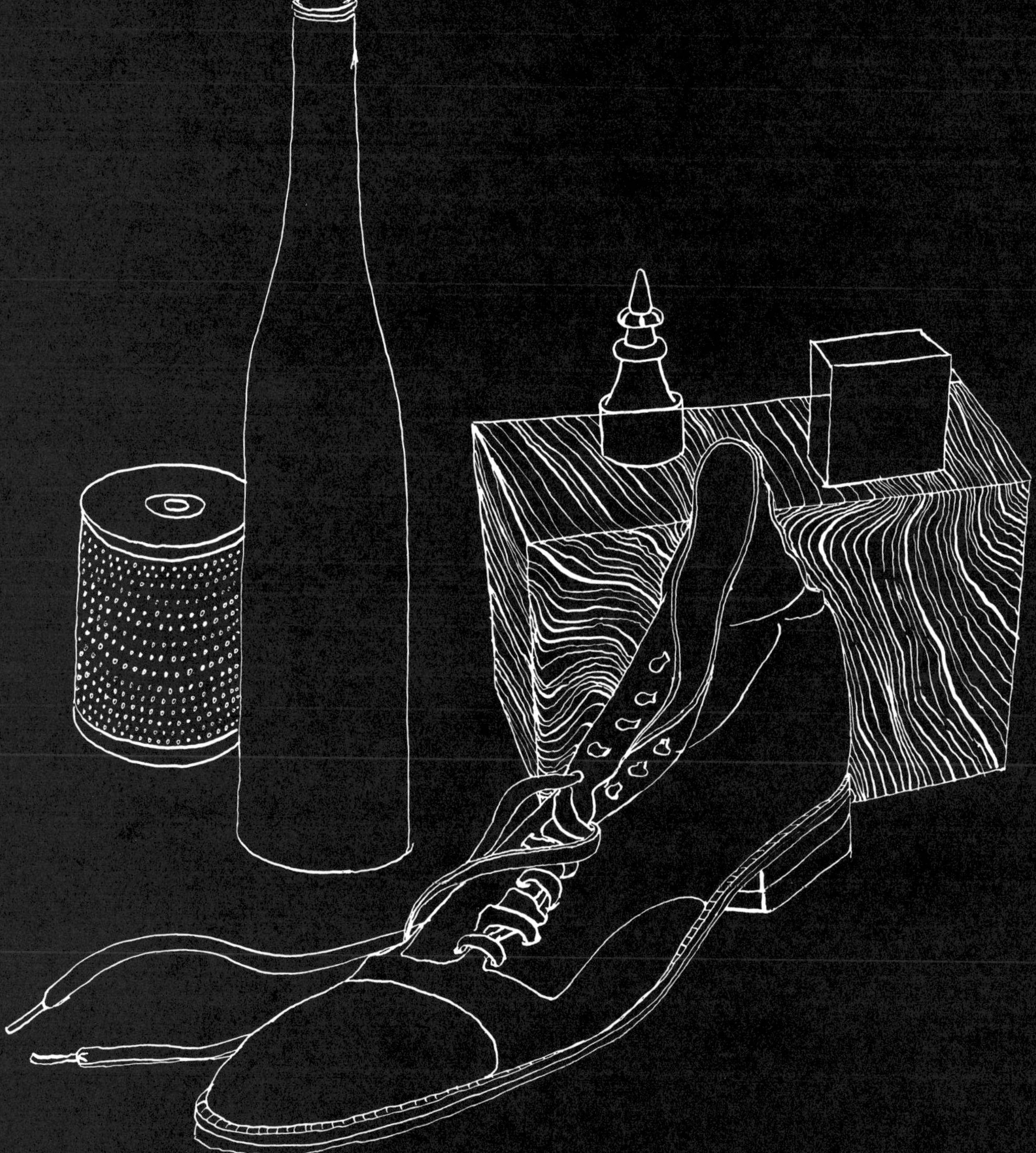

20

CLOTHED FIGURES *three hours*

This study combines several previous problems. You have already worked with chairs, fabrics, shoes, jackets, features, faces, and hands. Here they all are together again before you, in a model or a cooperative friend —reading a book, perhaps.

Just as in the case of the machinery drawing, this may seem like a big order at first, but you will find that if you start at some familiar spot (the ear, for instance) and just keep working slowly and carefully, adding detail to detail until time, paper, or interest gives out, you will conquer all.

Again, do not look for a "likeness" in the first fifty studies. And draw only the part that interests you enough so that you will do it well. A good fragment is fine.

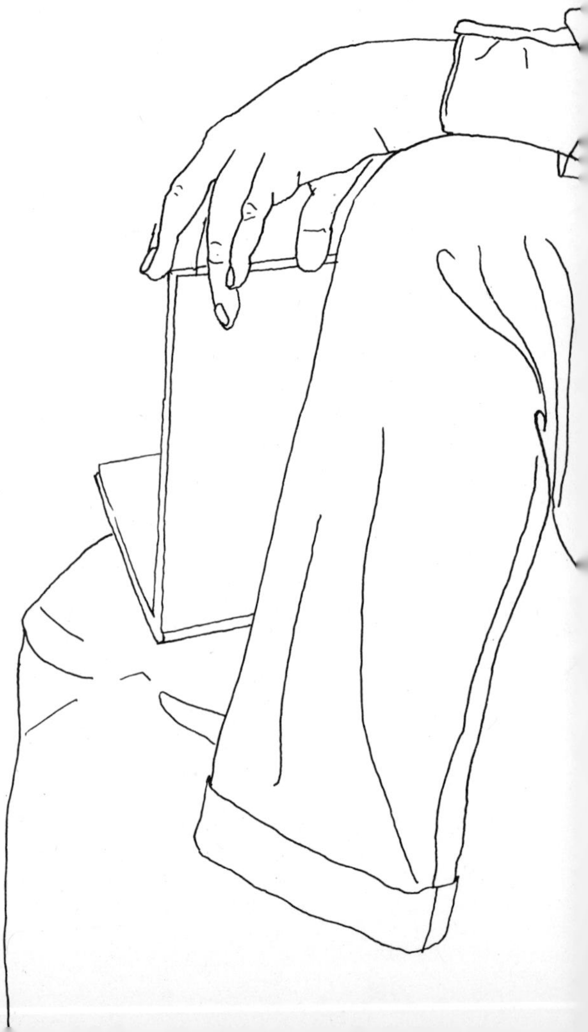

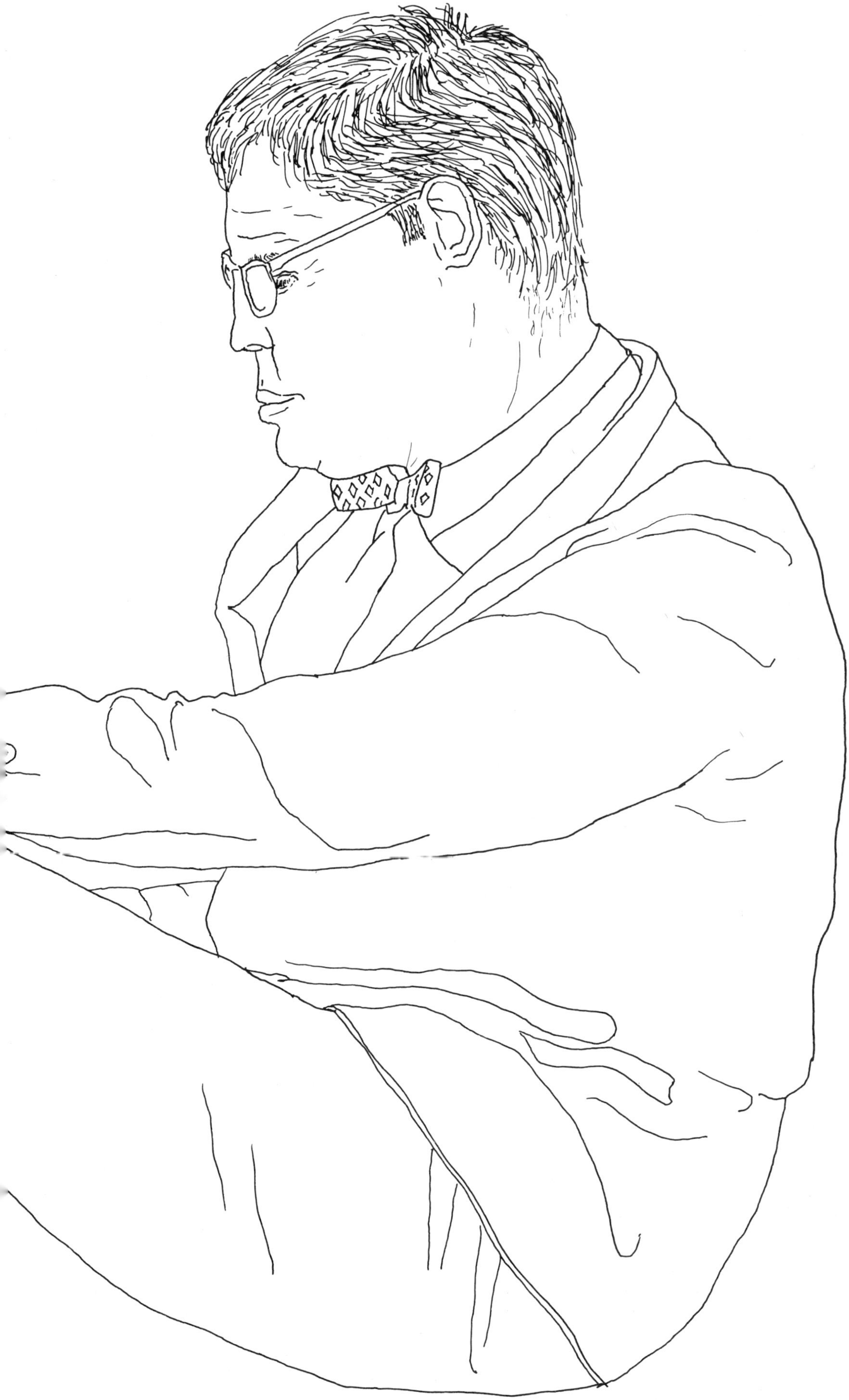

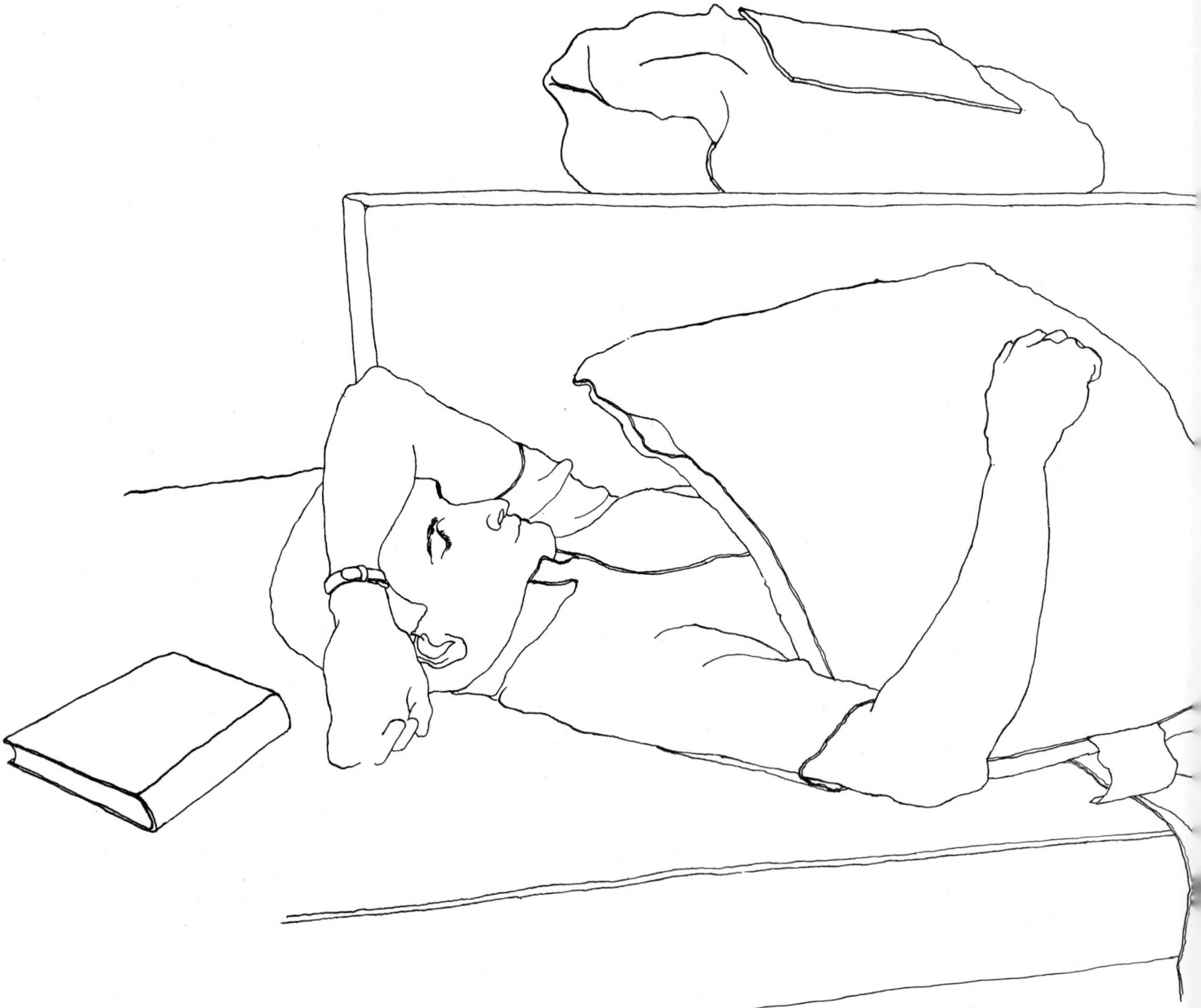

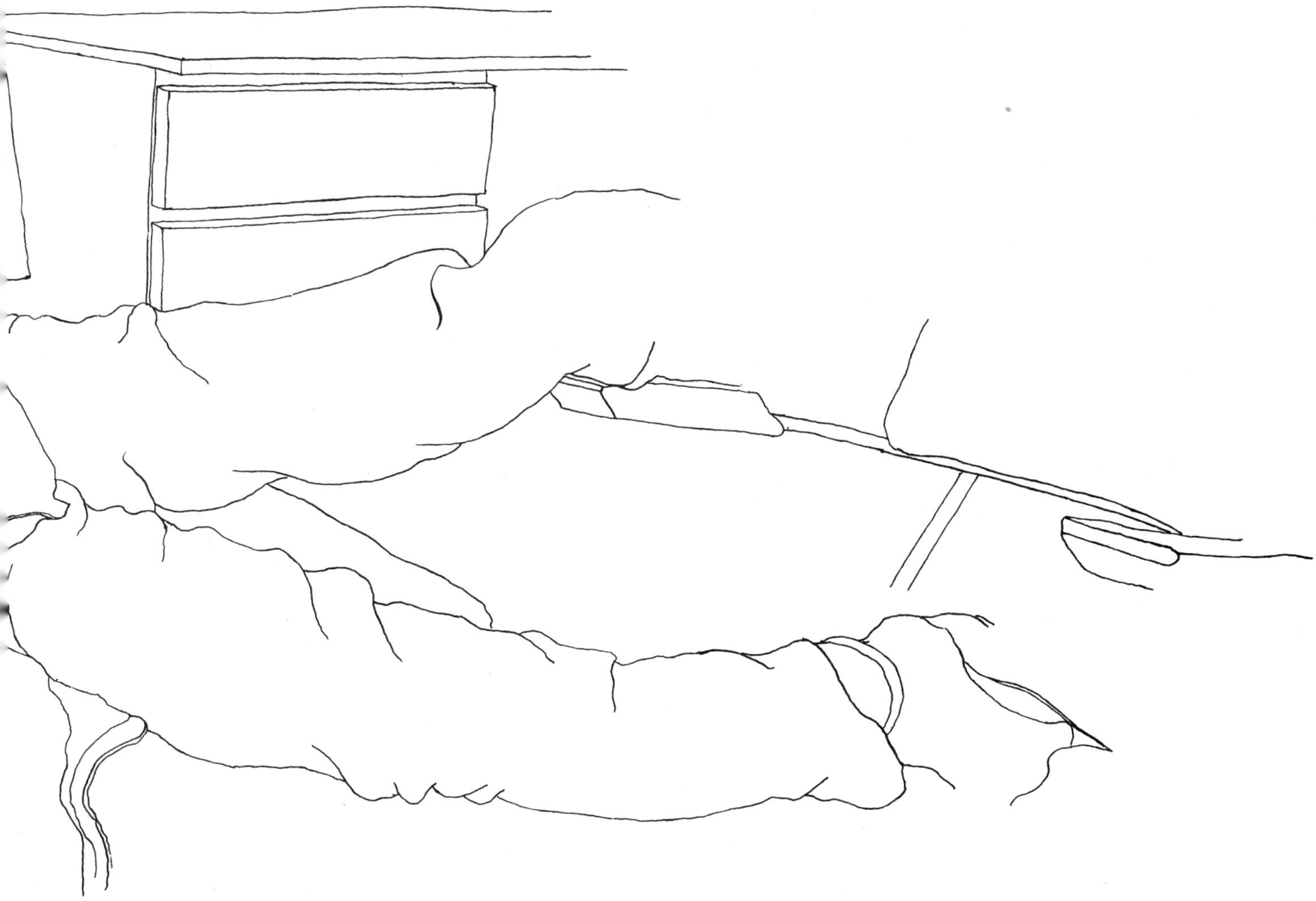

21

STAIRS *six hours*

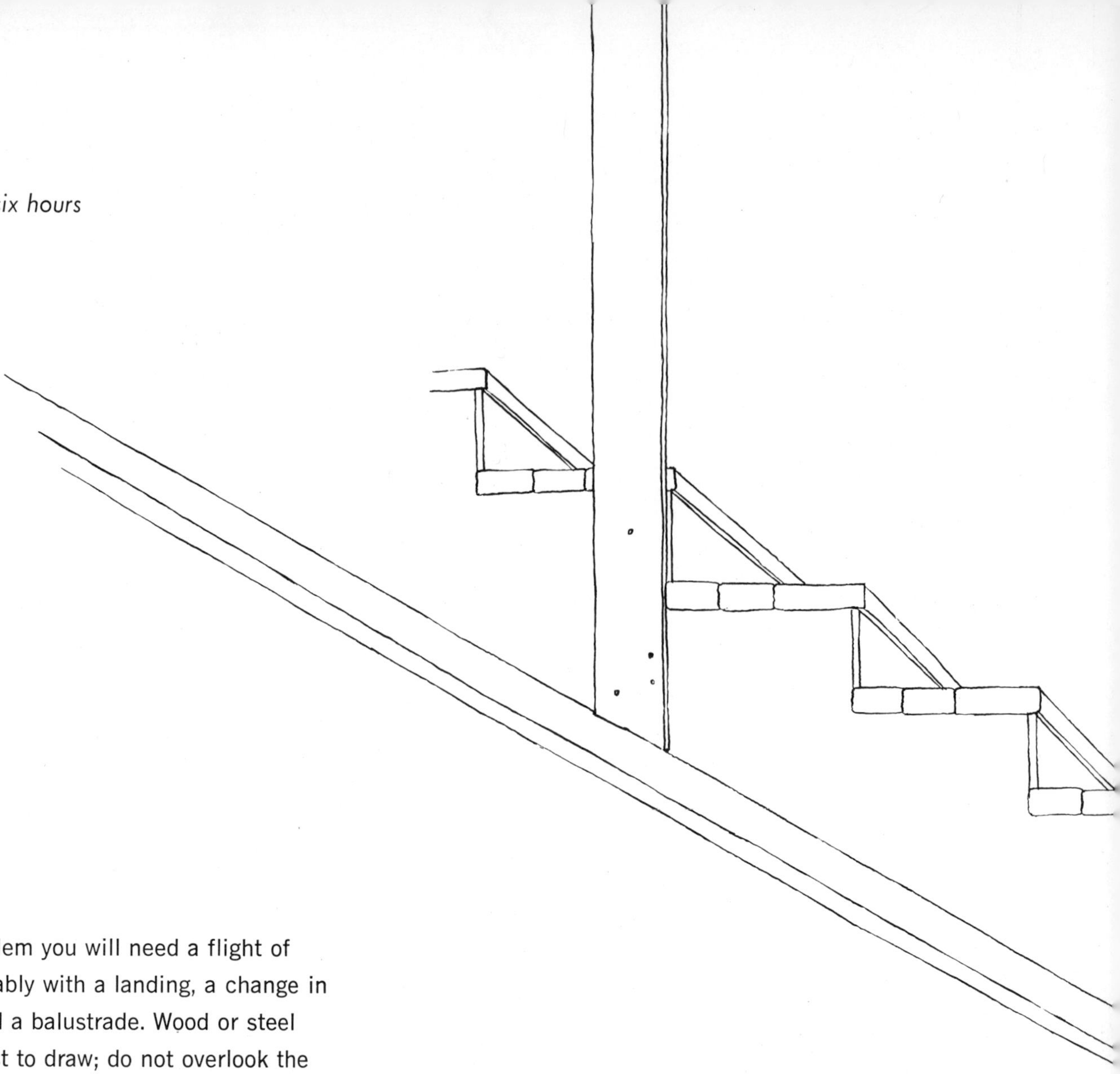

For this problem you will need a flight of stairs, preferably with a landing, a change in direction, and a balustrade. Wood or steel stairs are best to draw; do not overlook the possibilities of a fire escape.

Select a viewpoint off to one side, or one which, if possible, permits a view up and down the stairs. You will see that this problem is nothing more than a special application of the earlier box problem, along with some references to the problem on chairs. The elements—mostly straight lines arrayed in space—are pretty much the same, with only the addition of more variety and some new detail.

Here you will be challenged in proportion and perspective. Here again, if you discover an "error," do not try to "correct" your work. Shift to a different viewpoint, and go at it again, trying to do better.

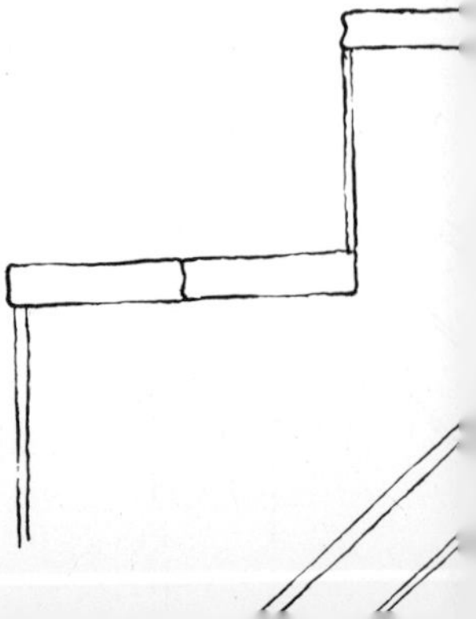

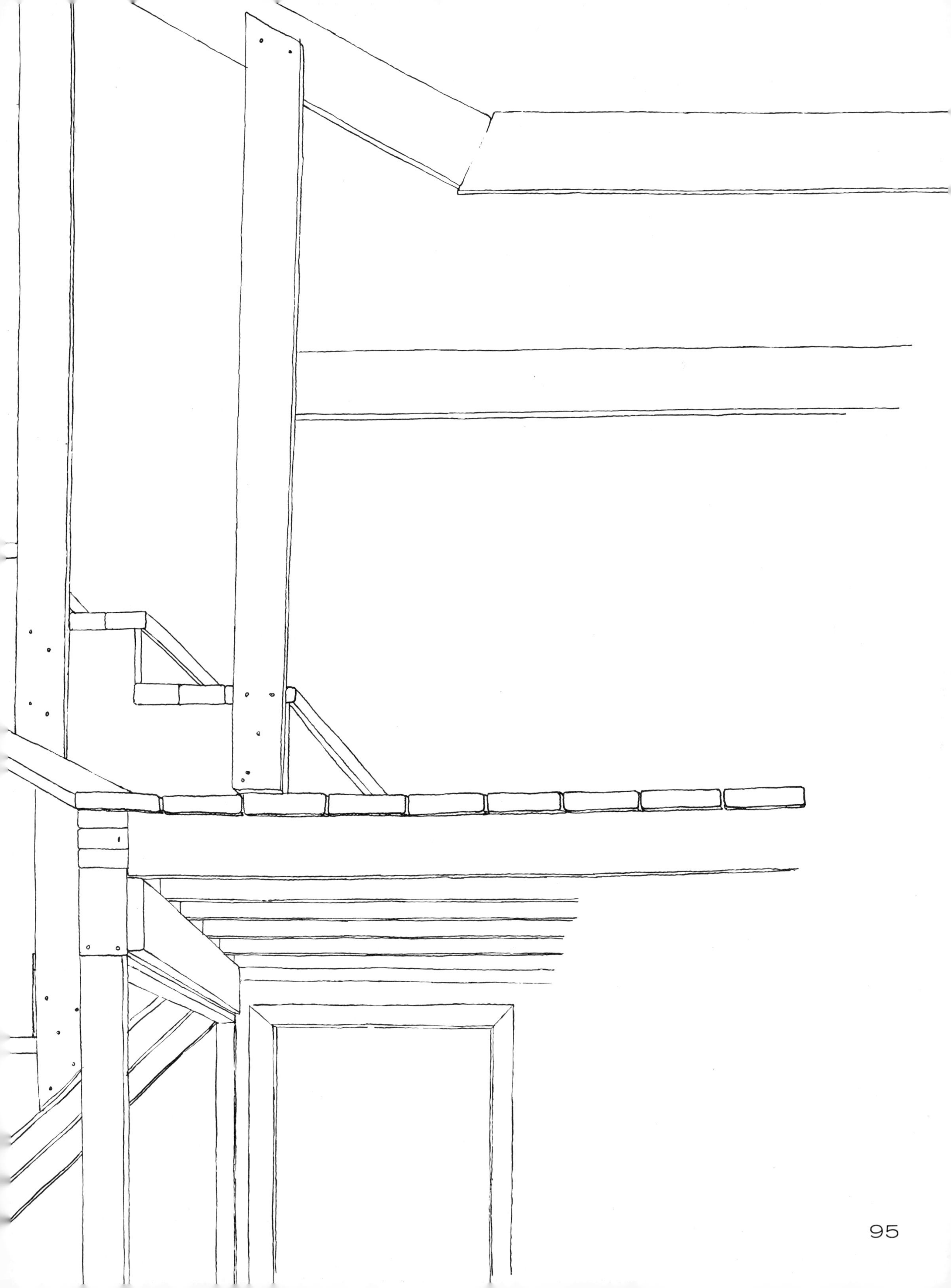

22

ARCHITECTURAL DETAIL *six hours*

This is a study in the relationships of a variety of materials seen in conjunction. Wood, glass, brick, stone, concrete, metal appear in combination in such places as window frames, eaves, exterior corners at grade, porches, doors, and so on. The interest of these elements may be compounded if they are seen in an old building, which provides in addition the effect of wear and weathering.

Select some limited portion of your subject that has two or three different materials in association, and make a good-sized drawing of just this detail.

When you have made several good studies of a variety of details, back off a bit and do a large drawing of more of the building: a corner of a wall with several windows, an open door with some stairs, a hallway with doors and windows. Do not try to do too much: just start at some point near you, and keep adding to it.

The problem here, of course, is in your control, so that straight parallel lines that converge in perspective will really be straight, and the proper distance apart throughout their length. Refer back to the first exercises in control, and remember your success in producing really straight lines.

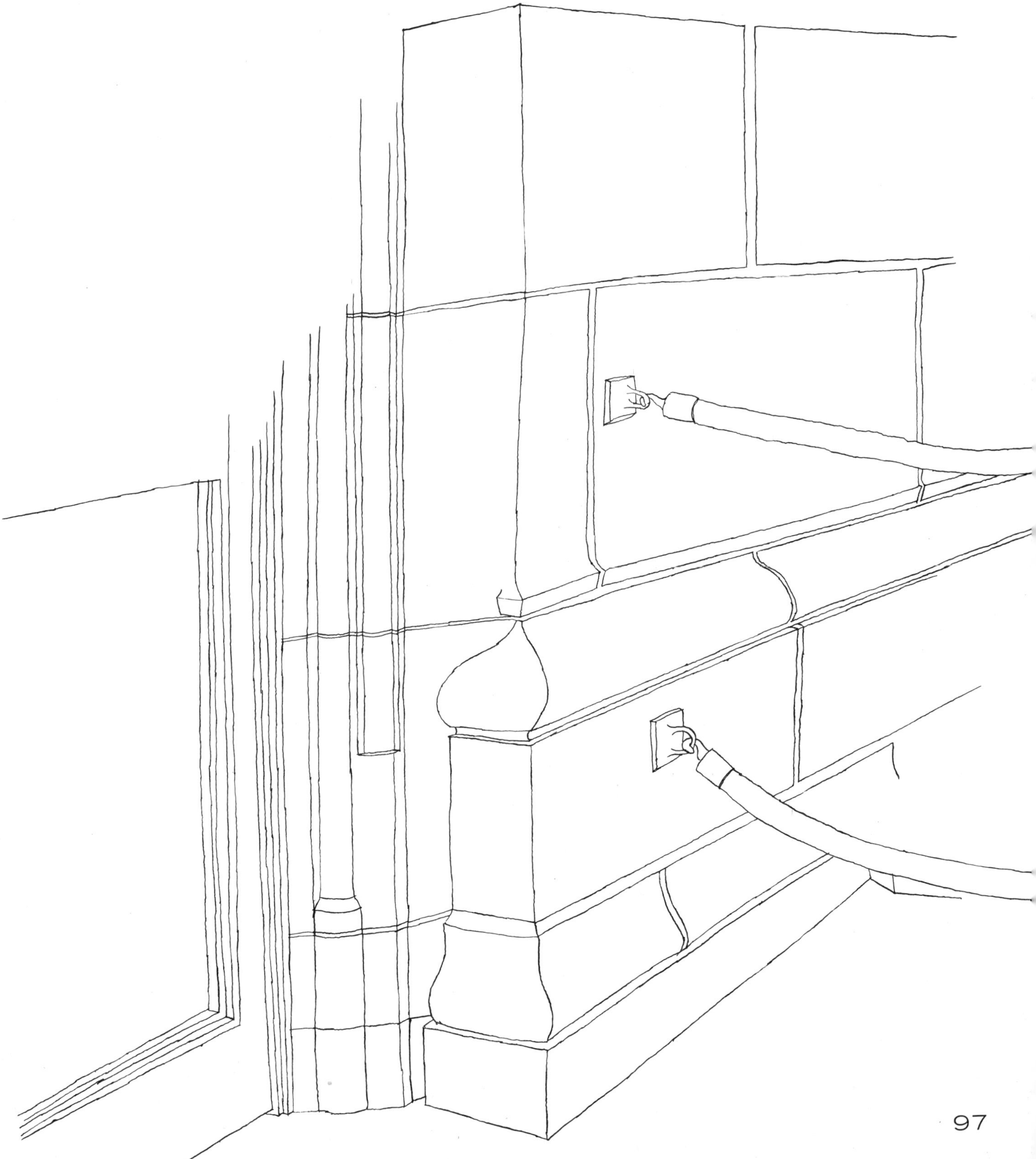

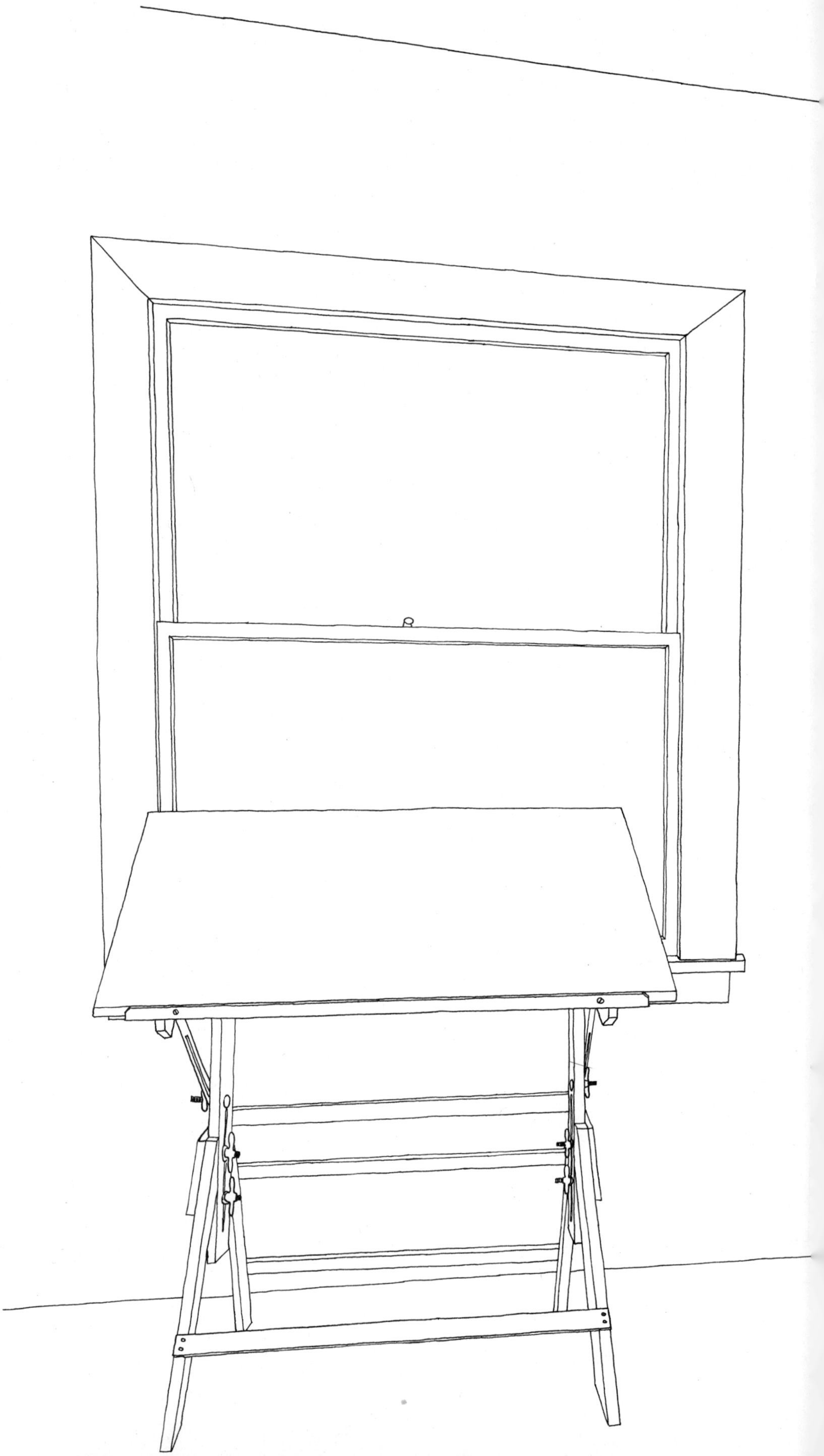

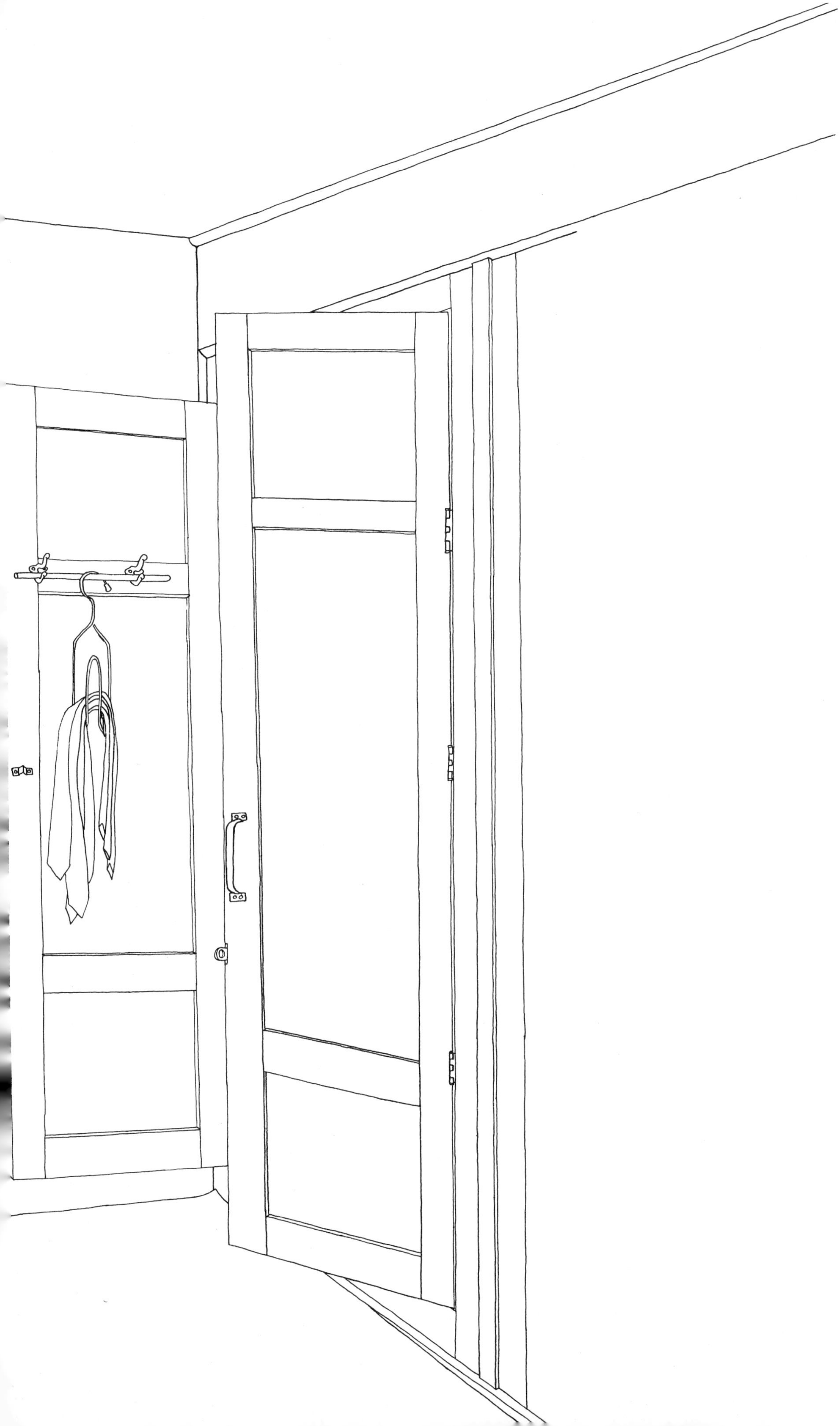

23

THE NUDE *six hours*

Figure drawing presents some new problems in subtle forms. The human figure is all convexities and concavities, and the contour lines change radically with each fresh viewpoint.

Since the time limit for the average pose is about twenty minutes, and since you have already had some work on the face, features, and hair, it might be well not to spend the limited time of each pose on these matters, but to concentrate on the form of the torso and the extremities.

Arrange your paper so that it will permit the **largest drawing** of the entire figure, and start in at any point. The neck (or the ear) is suggested for a start. Remember to imagine

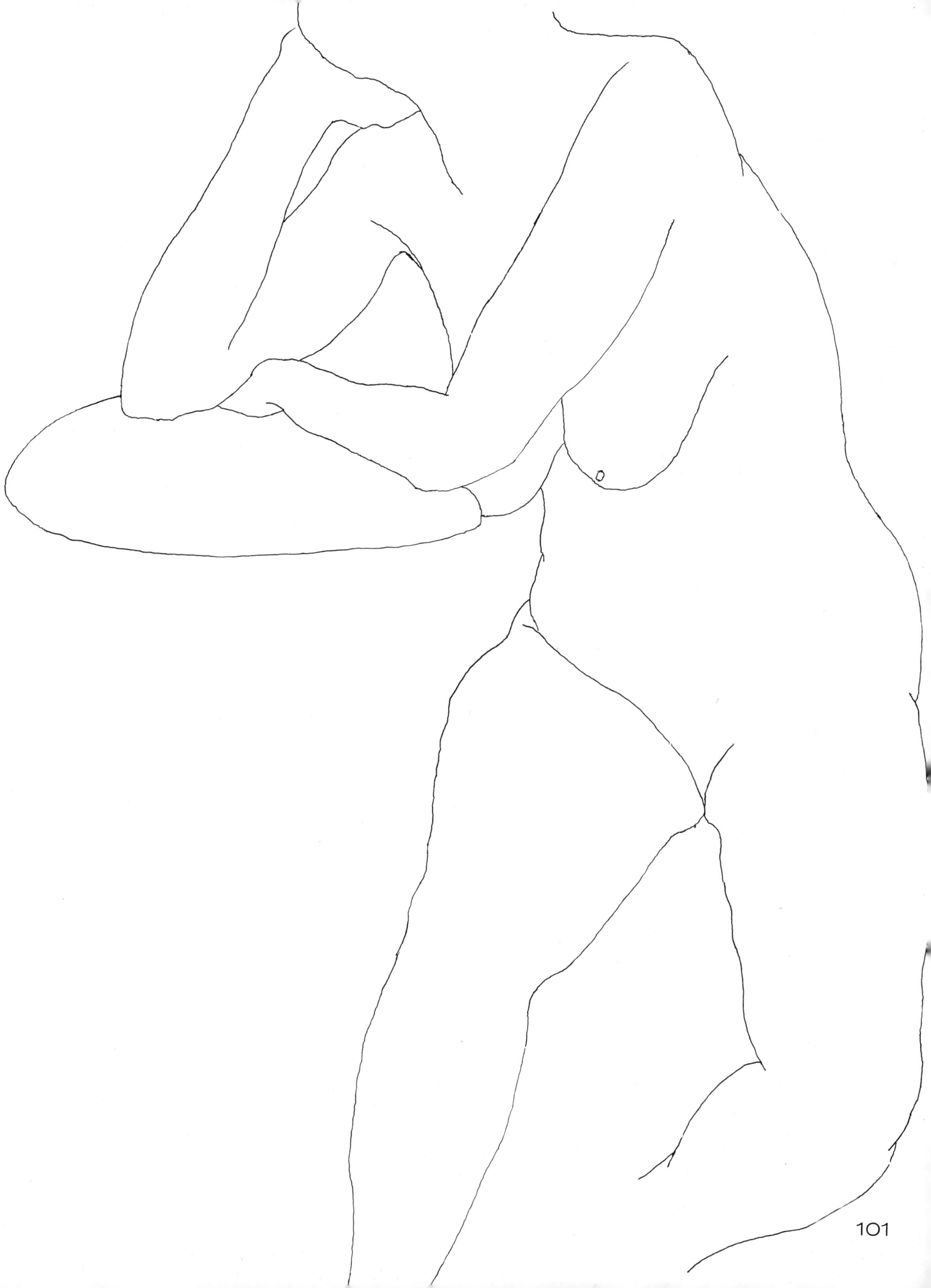

that you are touching the contour lightly with your pen: keep "contact" as you slowly draw, and do not press too hard. Do not worry about proportion while you are drawing. Forget it, and have a wonderful time tracing the contours. Check the proportions when you are finished, but then forget this when you start to draw again. You will probably be concentrating so hard that you will be surprised when the twenty minutes are up. It goes without saying that you should do no preliminary "blocking out" or sketching before you start. Expect to make lots of what you will call "bad" starts. This only confirms that you are a student, and that is nothing to be ashamed of. When you feel that a drawing is not what it should be, just turn the sheet over and move to a new viewpoint; then, after a bit of study with the eye alone, start in anew.

The model should take a variety of relaxed, natural poses. These may include a standing position, hand on one hip; sitting on a high stool, one leg on the floor; sitting sideways in a chair; kneeling with one leg up; lying prone with one knee raised and the torso twisted. The value of drawing the model is in just the rich variety of configurations that are available to you—the same elements each time, but so different each time.

Never have the model repeat a pose. Use a new one each time. Probably you will be getting only fragments of the figure; that is fine. Go slowly, **draw large,** and with time, much time, you will find that you are getting in more and more. Try to draw each part of the body, however. Do not specialize in knees. If, after awhile, you become aware that certain parts (feet, ankles, necks) give you trouble, do not shirk them, but bring the matter out into the open and make some extra large studies of them separately. In this way you will get to know and conquer them.

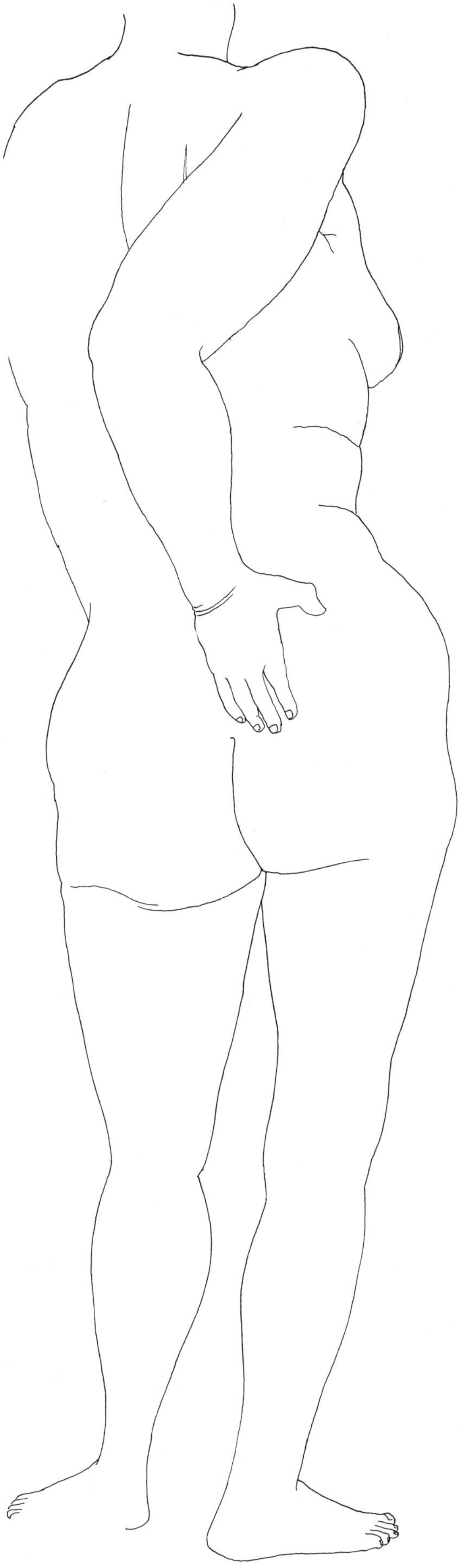

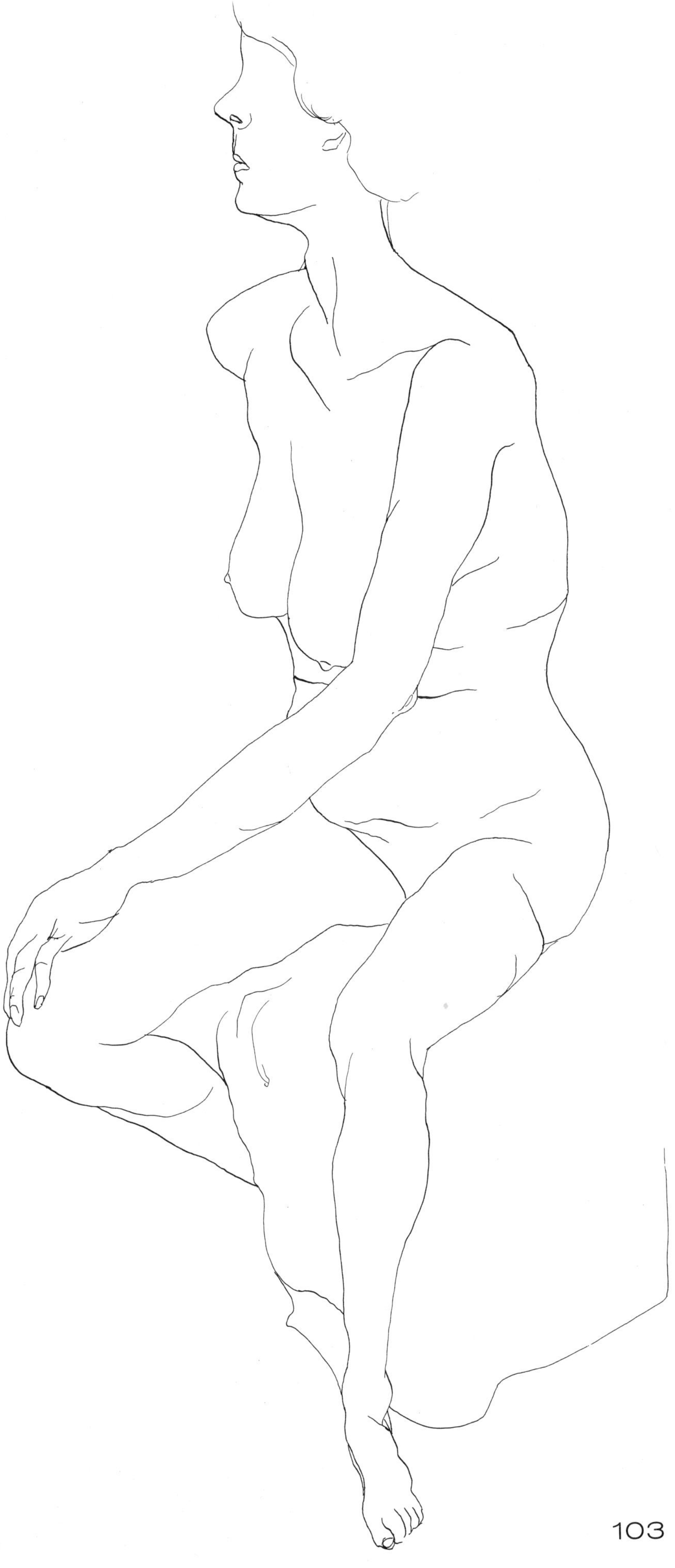

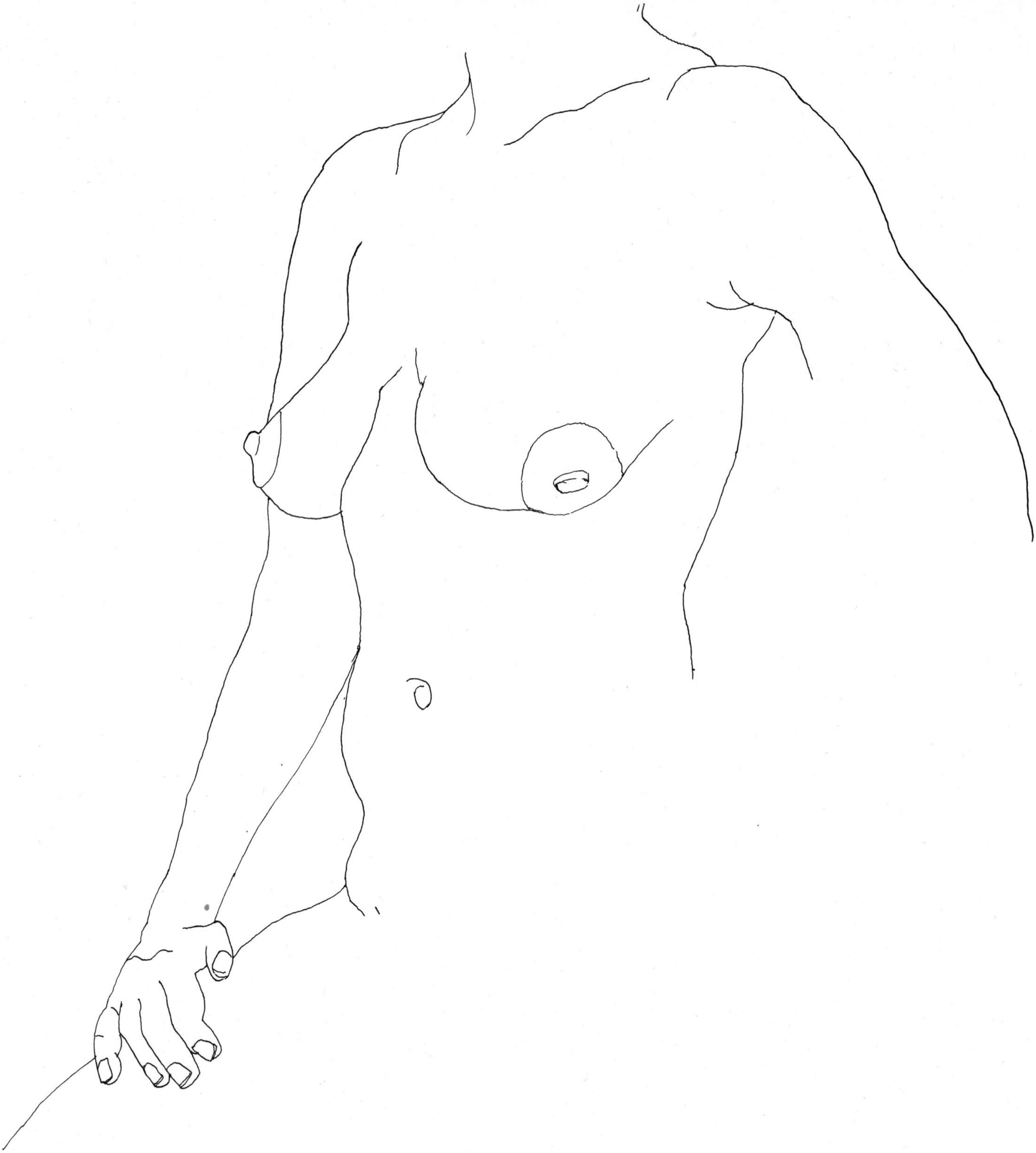

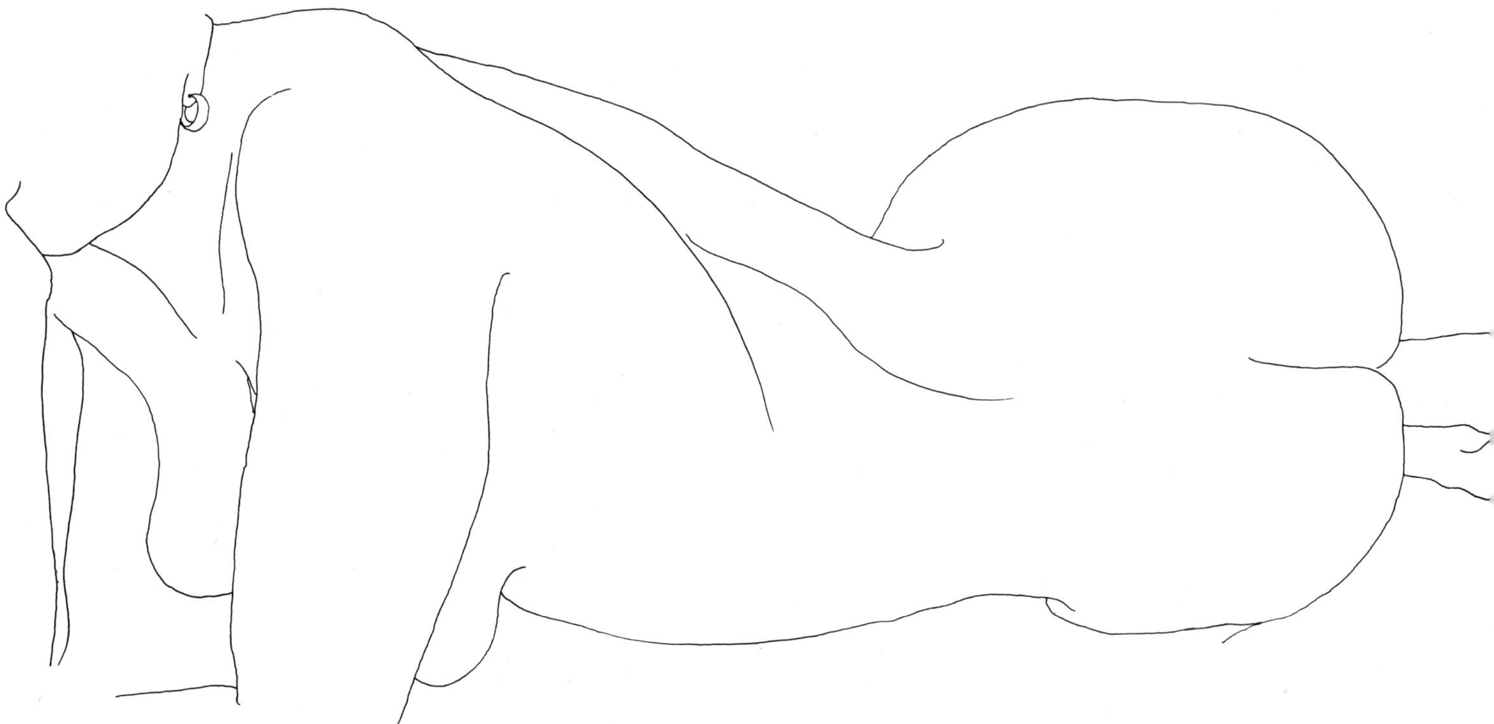

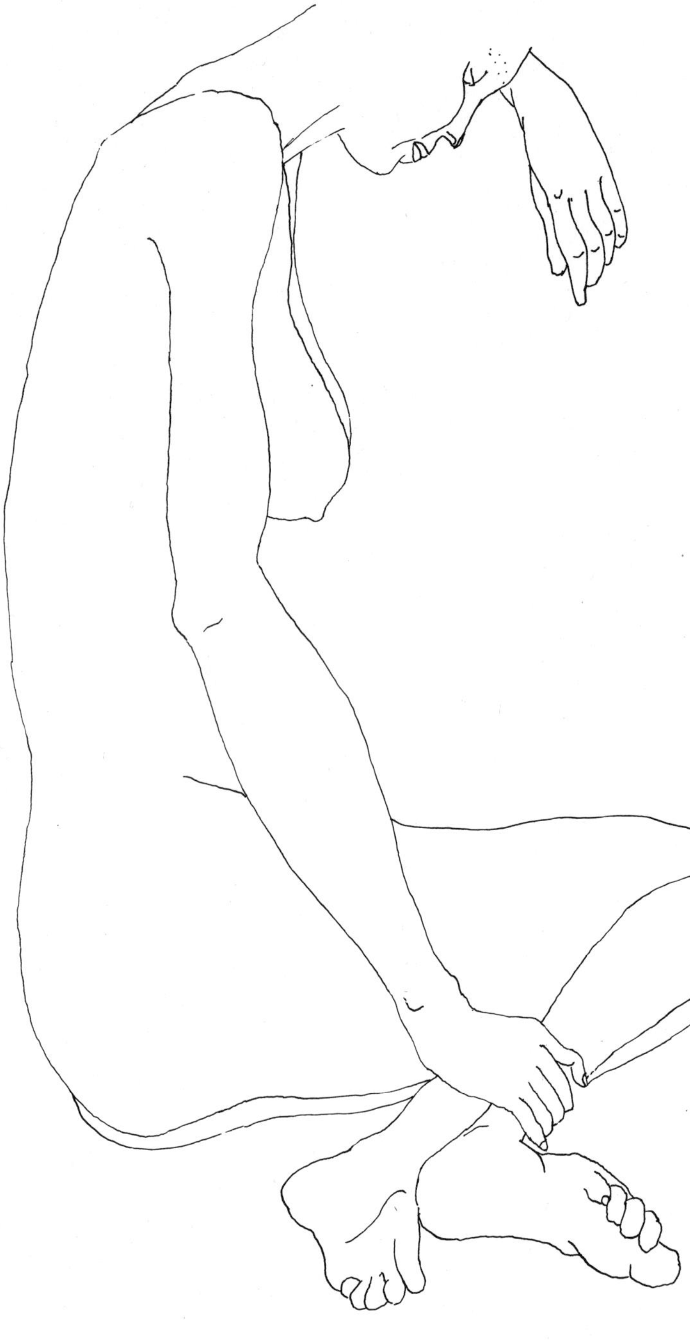

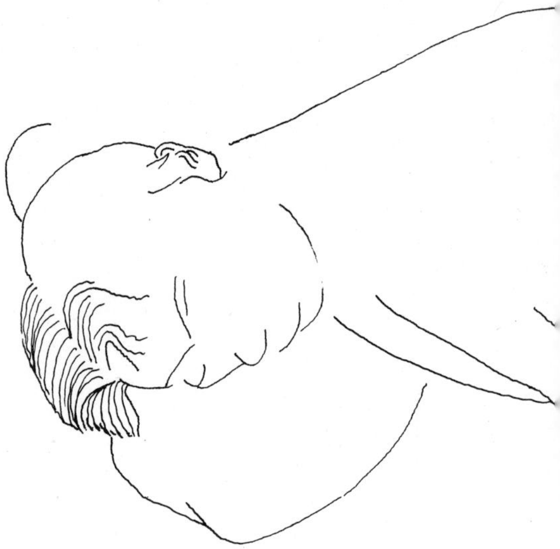

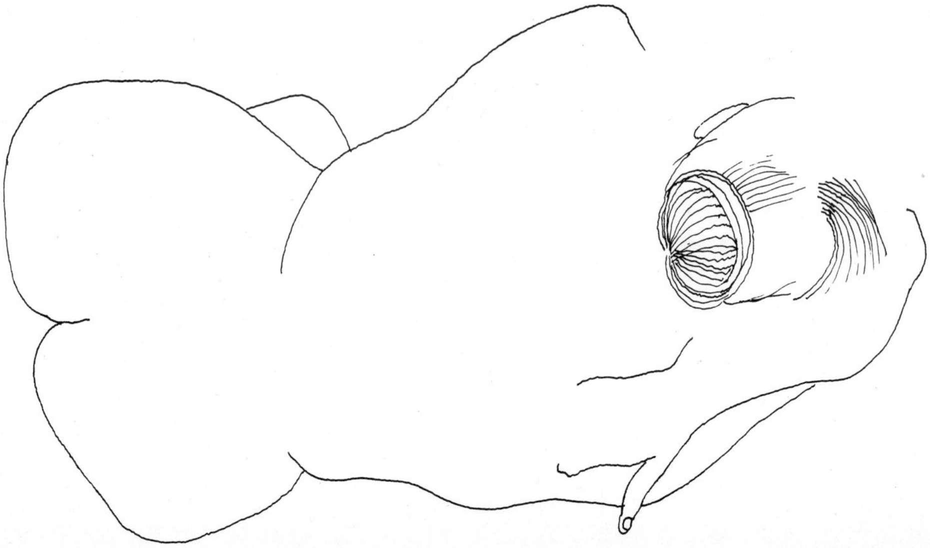

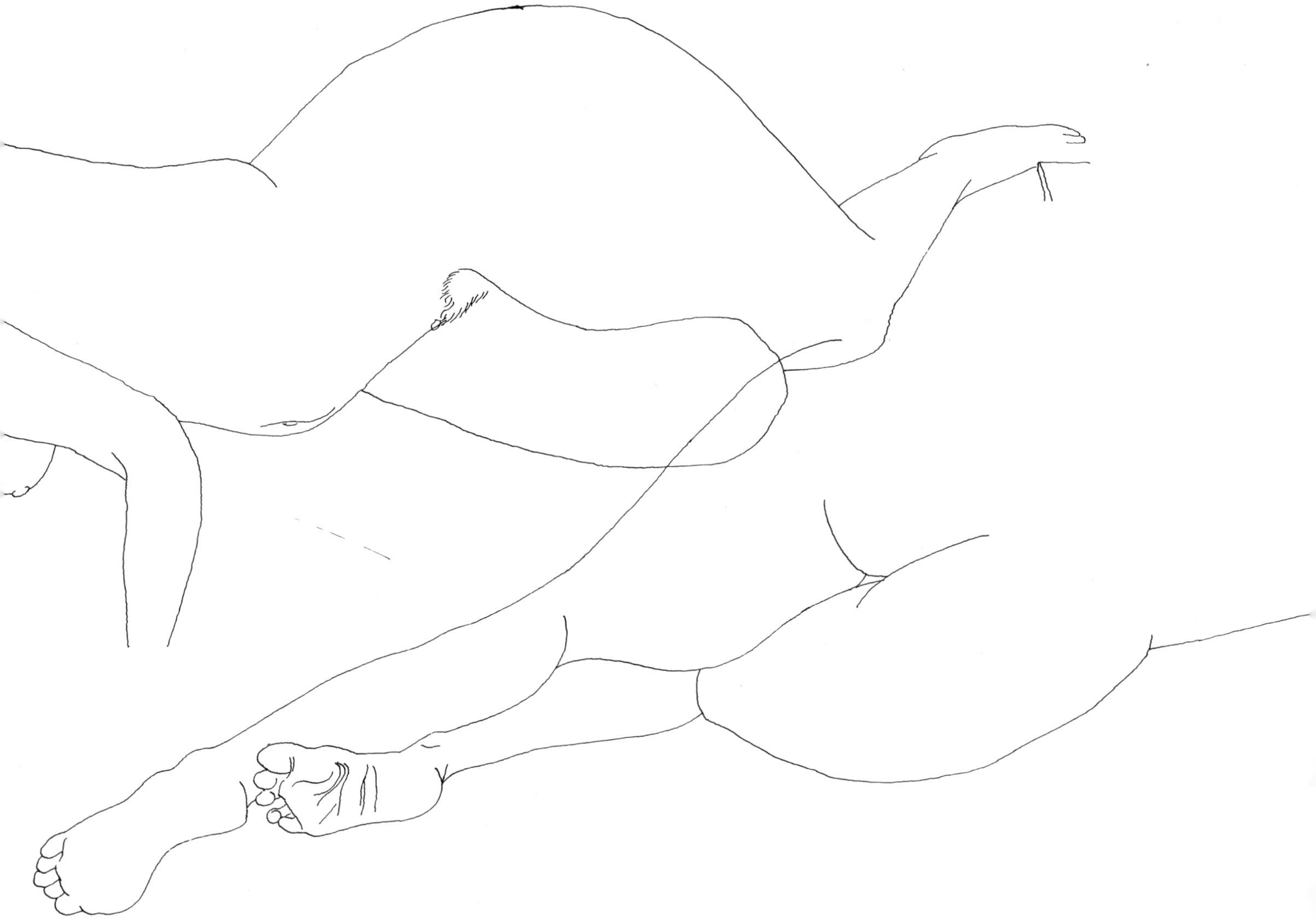

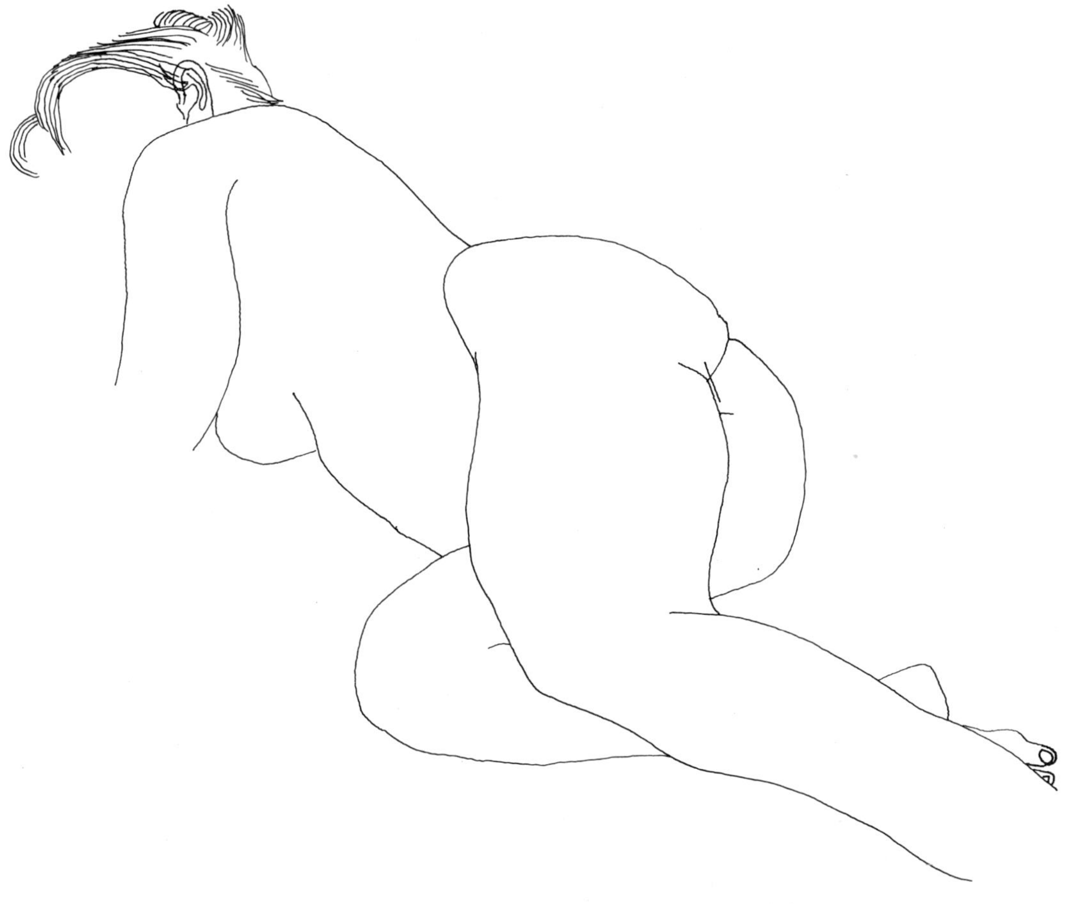

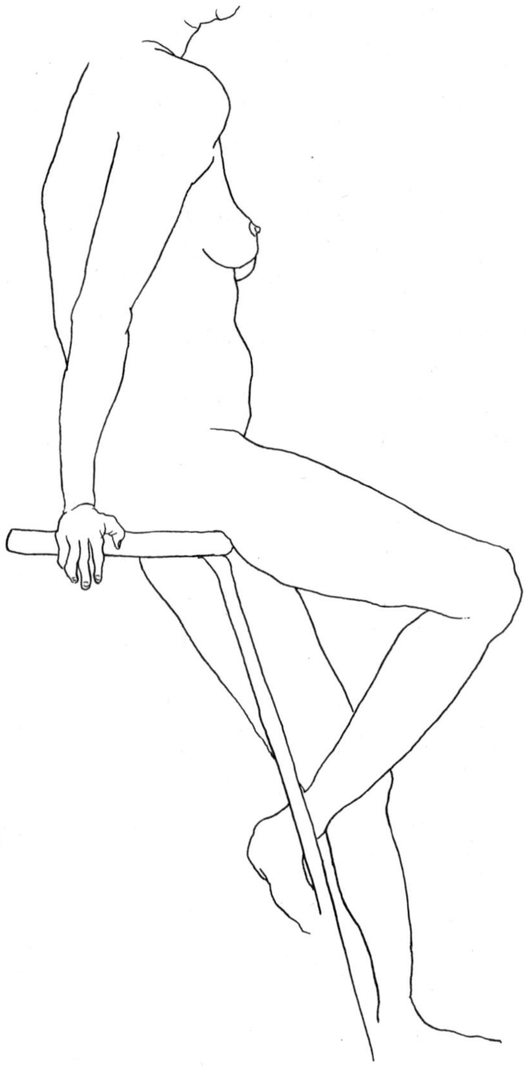

There is one exception to the suggestion that the model should not repeat poses. After a certain amount of experience it will be very worthwhile to draw the same pose from all four sides, in succession. Arrange your paper so that you can get all the four drawings on together, and at the same scale. This will insure that the best comparison will be made of the way the form varies with the point of view.

A study that follows from the above is to look at one side of the figure for a given pose, and draw what you would see if you were looking from the opposite side. Finally, have the model take one pose for the full pose period. Do not draw the model during this period, but look most intently so that after the model steps down, you can draw the entire pose from memory. When you are finished, have the model take the same pose again so you can compare your drawing with the original.

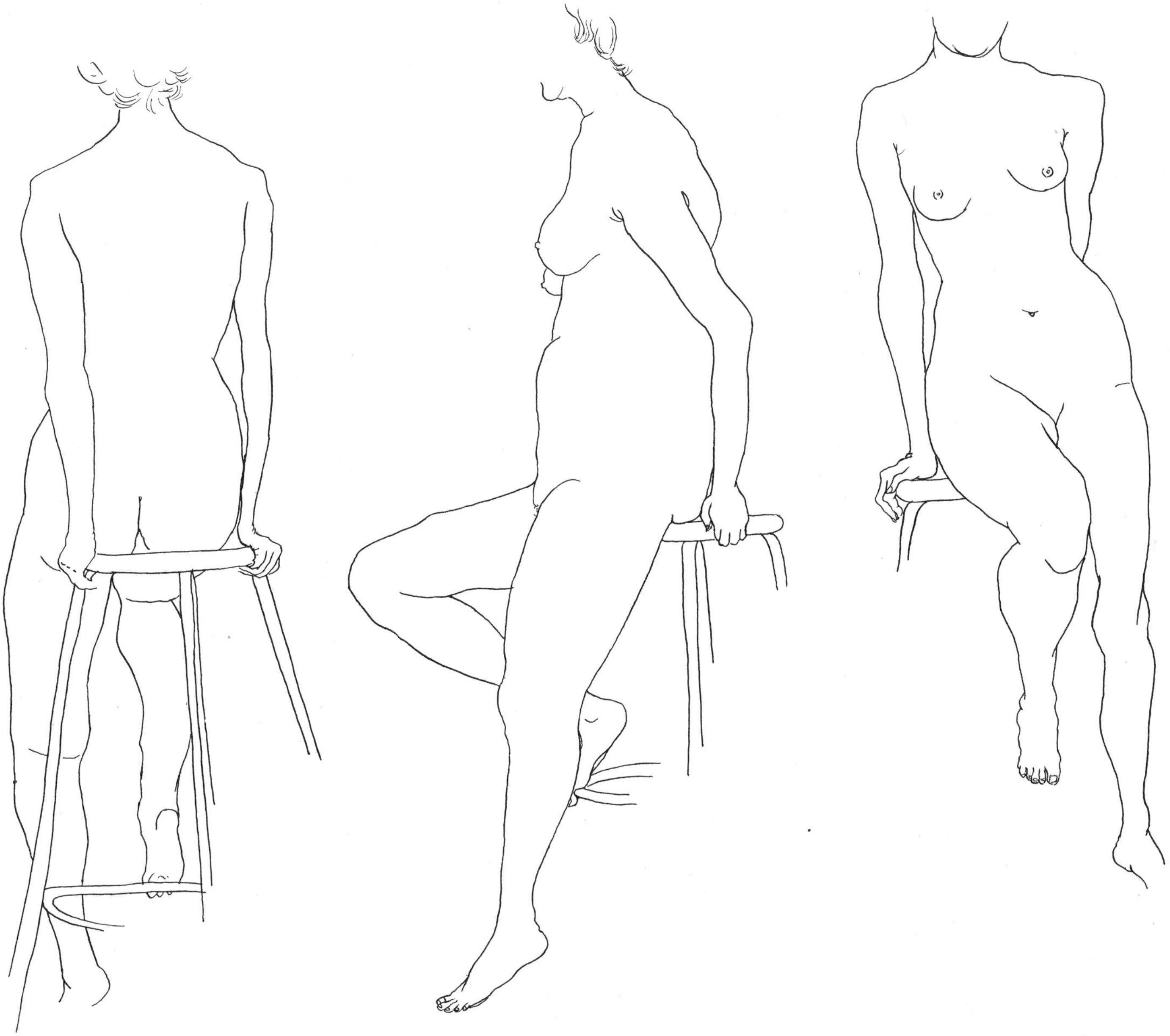

24

BICYCLES *six hours*

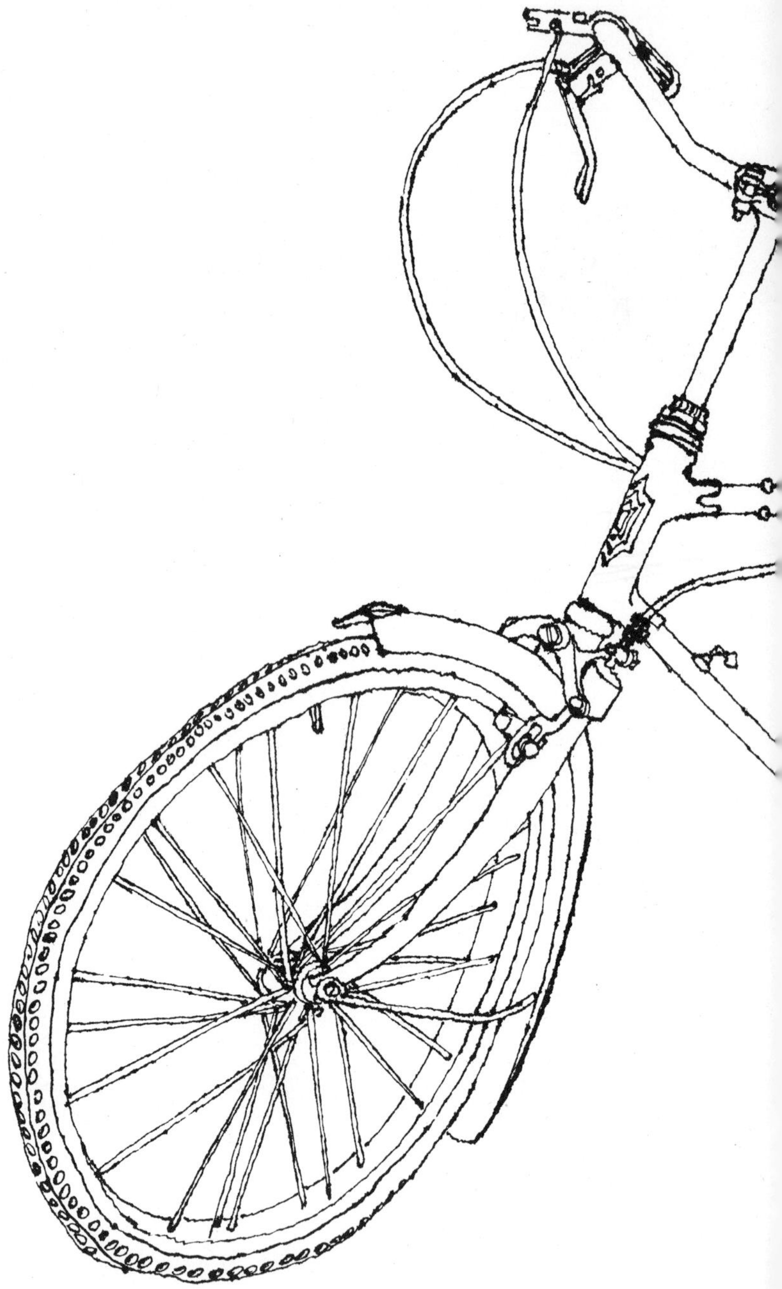

One of the most challenging things to draw, and one that you are now ready to tackle, is that special, precise, elegant, man-made object called the bicycle. This problem will demand of you all your control and the sense of proportion you have by now developed.

Pay close attention to the details of the joints: of the spokes with the hub and the rim, the axles at the forks, and so on. Draw as large as you can on your sheet, and perhaps do some larger studies of the parts before you get into the whole assemblage. Your lines should reflect the exactness and precision of these delicate tubes, wires, and light, circular rims.

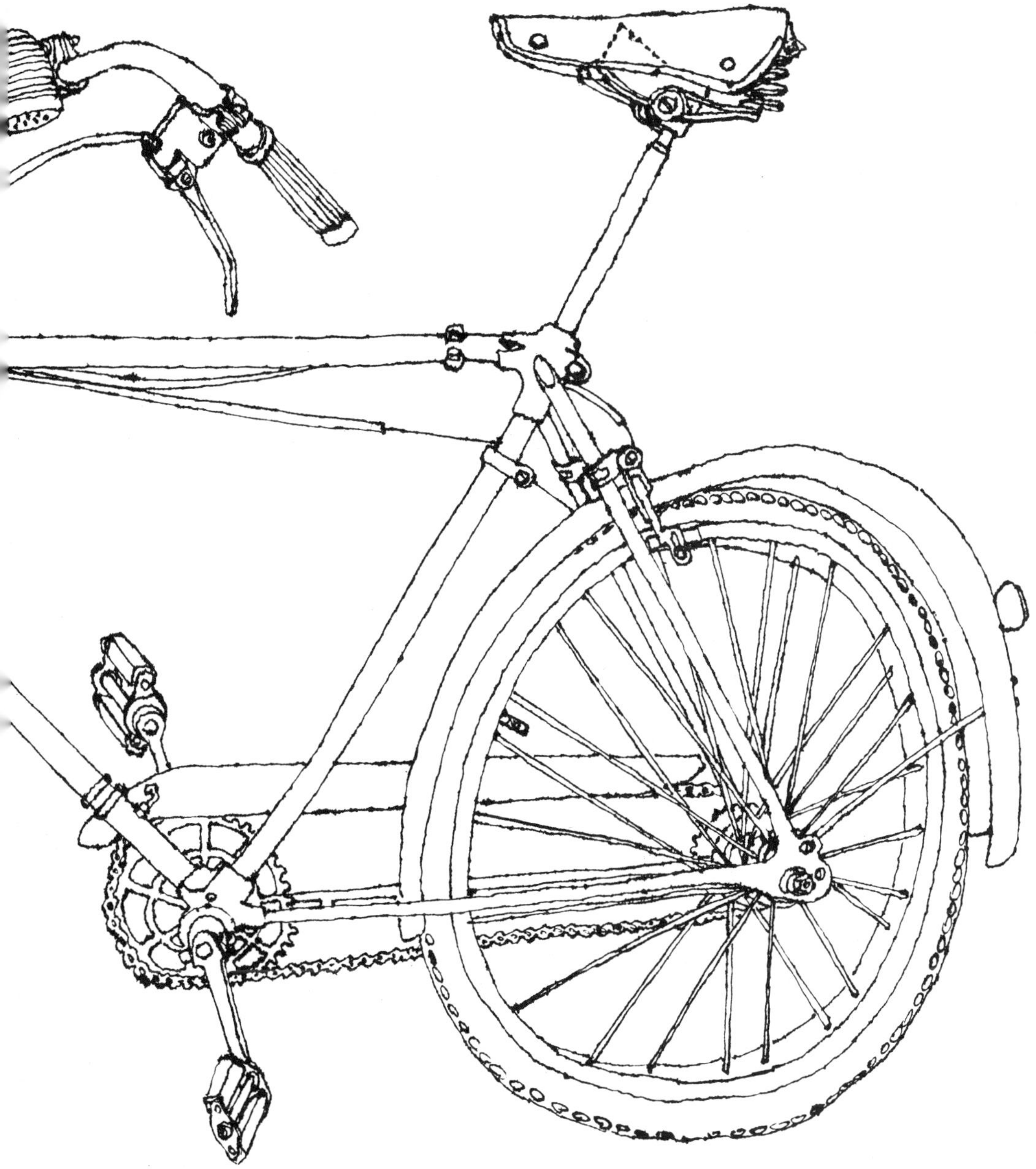

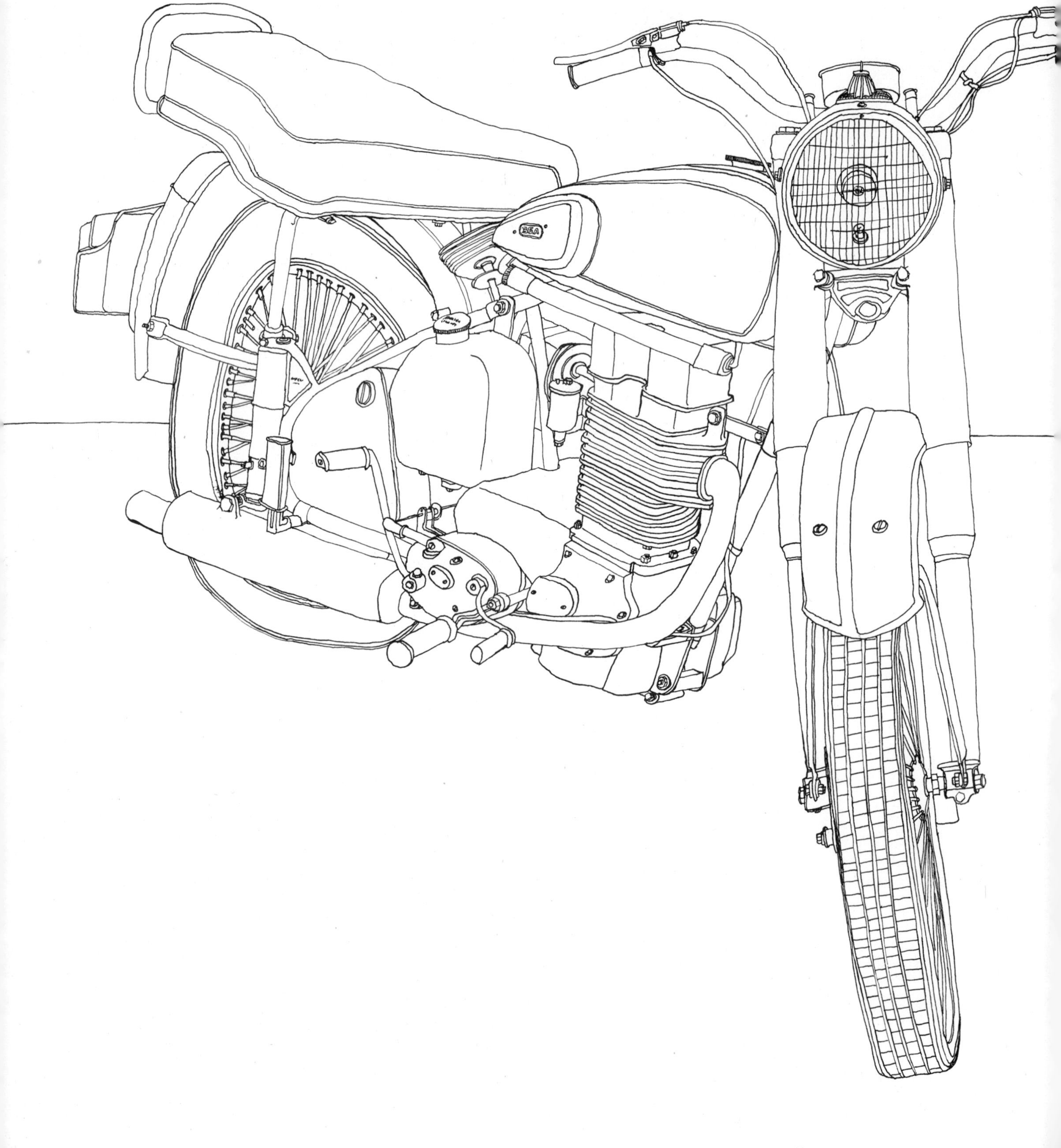

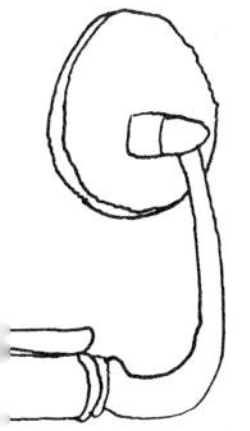

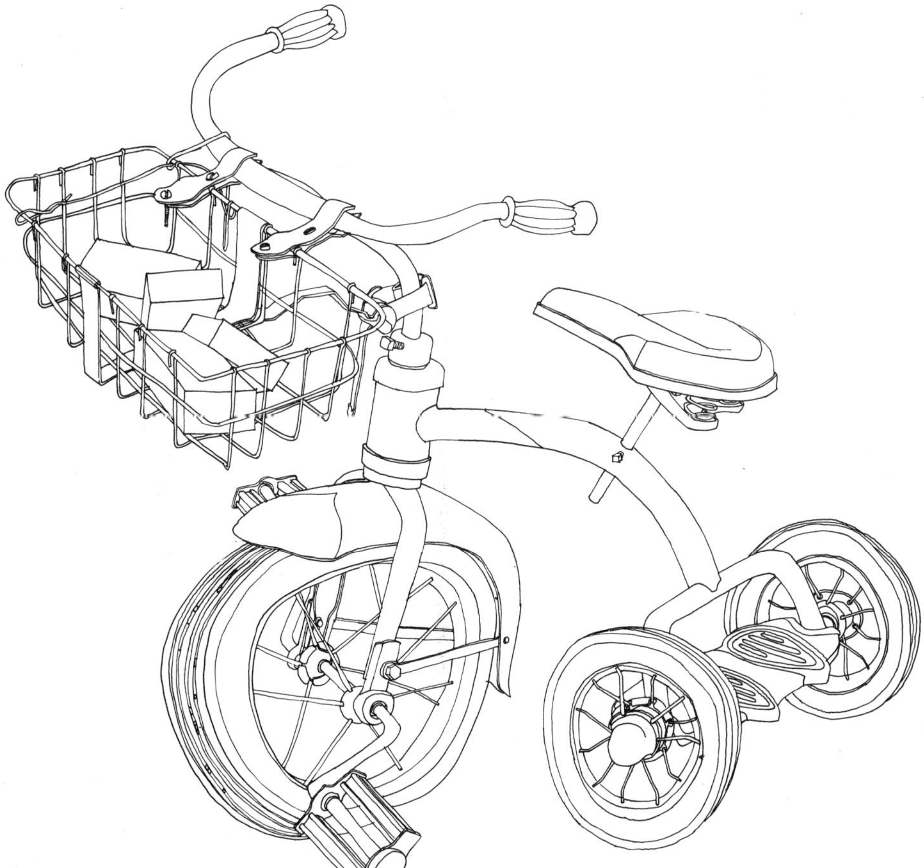

25

MOVING FIGURES *six hours*

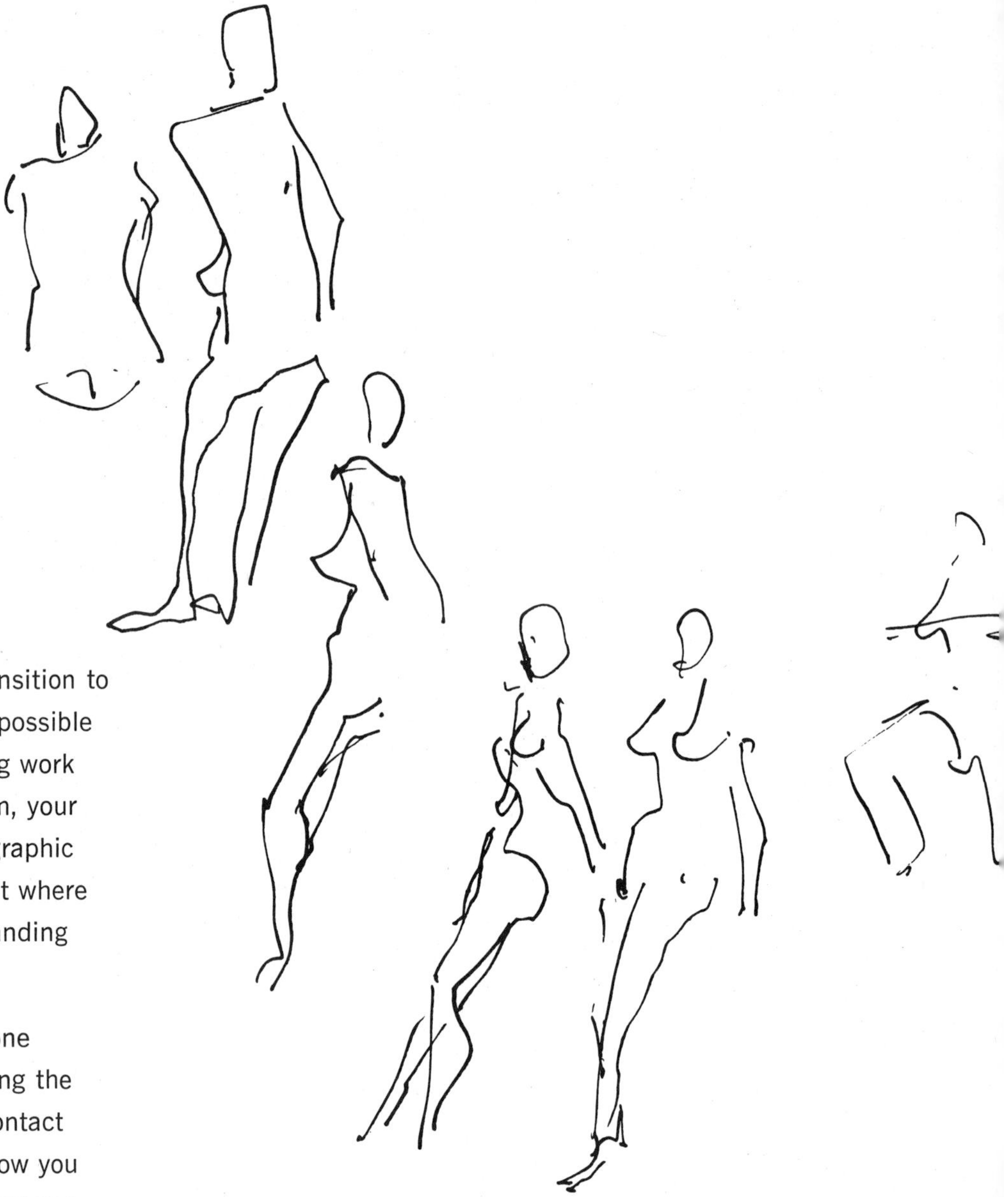

With this problem we will start a transition to a more rapid procedure. This is now possible because the regimen of the preceding work has developed your sensitivity to form, your feeling for the significant, and your graphic inventiveness and control to the point where you are able to work on a more demanding level.

Up to now all your work was to be done slowly, slowly and deliberately, keeping the pen, in your imagination, lightly in contact with the form you are drawing. But now you are asked to stroke the paper with your pen, to let it slide and glide smoothly over the surface while you feel the essence of the moving configuration before you. The model should be instructed to take a variety of poses, as before, but she should move continuously and slowly from position to position, standing upright with arms upraised, then leaning, twisting downward to sitting, kneeling, reclining, and back again, continuously moving, in five minutes or more. The motion should be **very** slow, so slow that you cannot see it if you glance at the model superficially.

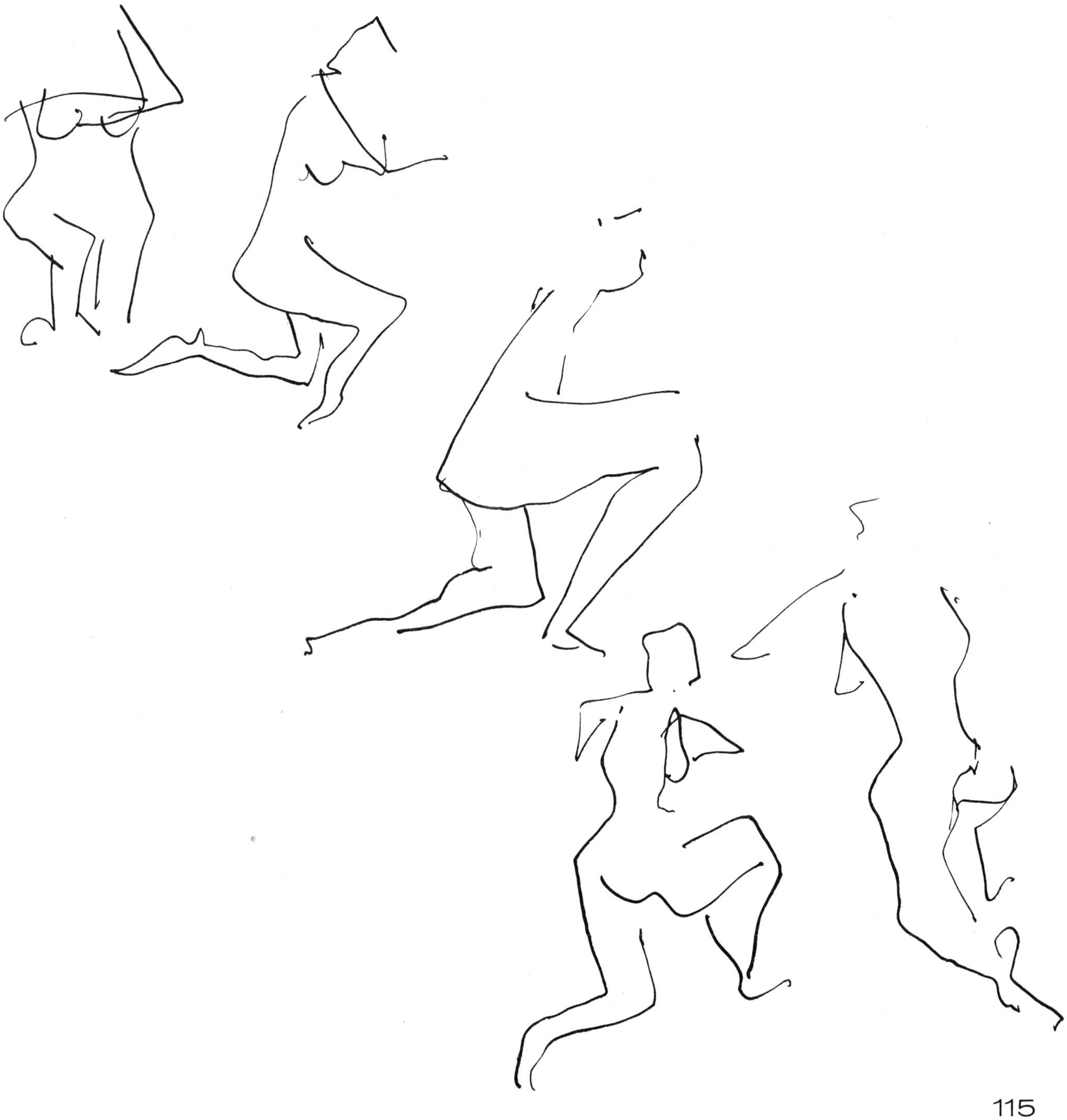

Your paper should be positioned horizontally. Starting at the upper left, start making loose line drawings about 6 to 8 inches high (or long) of the moving model. You will be able to put down quite a bit before you become aware that the pose is radically different: the fact that you know the model is continually moving will spur you to constant quick decisions, and that is the point of this study. When you realize that the drawing you have started no longer relates to the "new" position of the model, abandon the fragment instantly and start a new one of about the same size right alongside the old. Keep up this procedure until you run out of paper.

After many pages of this, and a period of time, go back and look at your work. You will probably be startled to see how well you have done, to have said so much with so few lines.

It will be very helpful if you will count aloud (or have someone count for you) a series of numbers at a slow, even cadence of about a one-second interval. For the first hour allow about twenty seconds for each successive sketch. Shorten this to ten for the second hour, and after that to five. Counting helps you to measure progress, to judge when each sketch should be three-quarters, one-half, and one-quarter complete. Counting also helps to keep you from thinking; you should become completely a transcribing machine with no volition of your own.

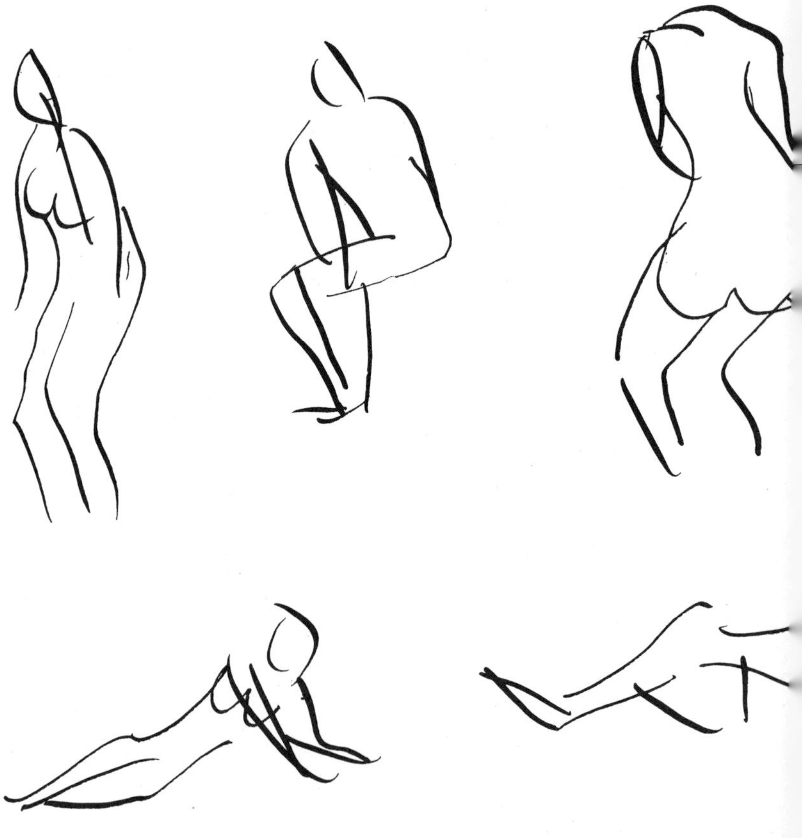

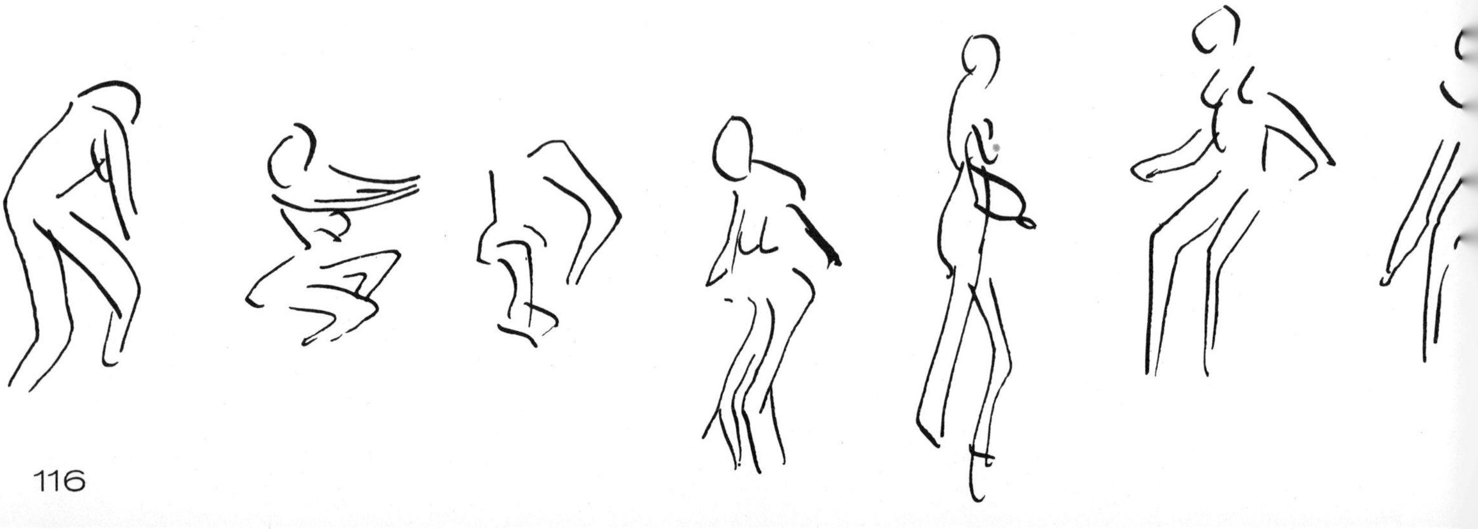

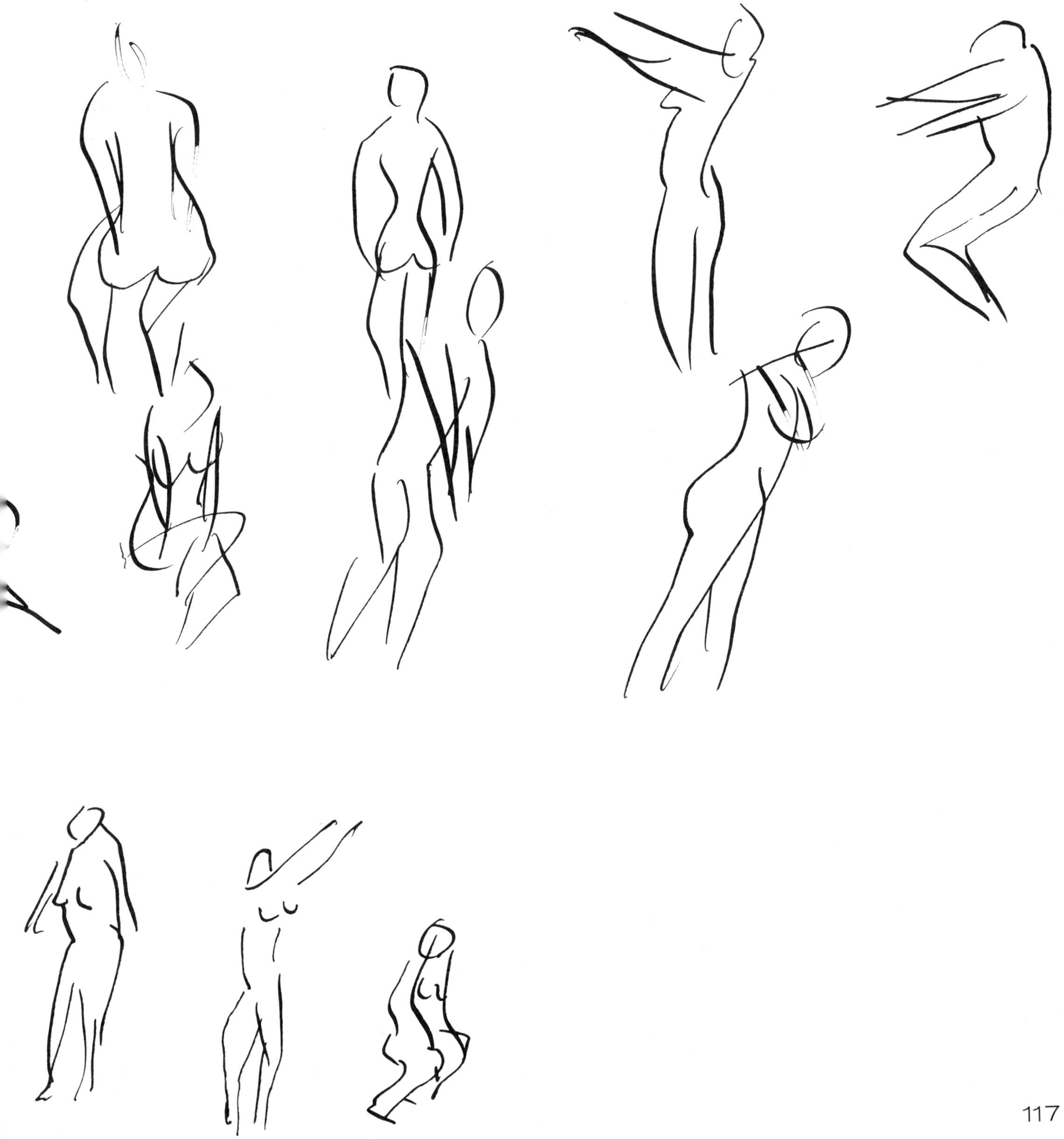

26

CROQUIS *six hours*

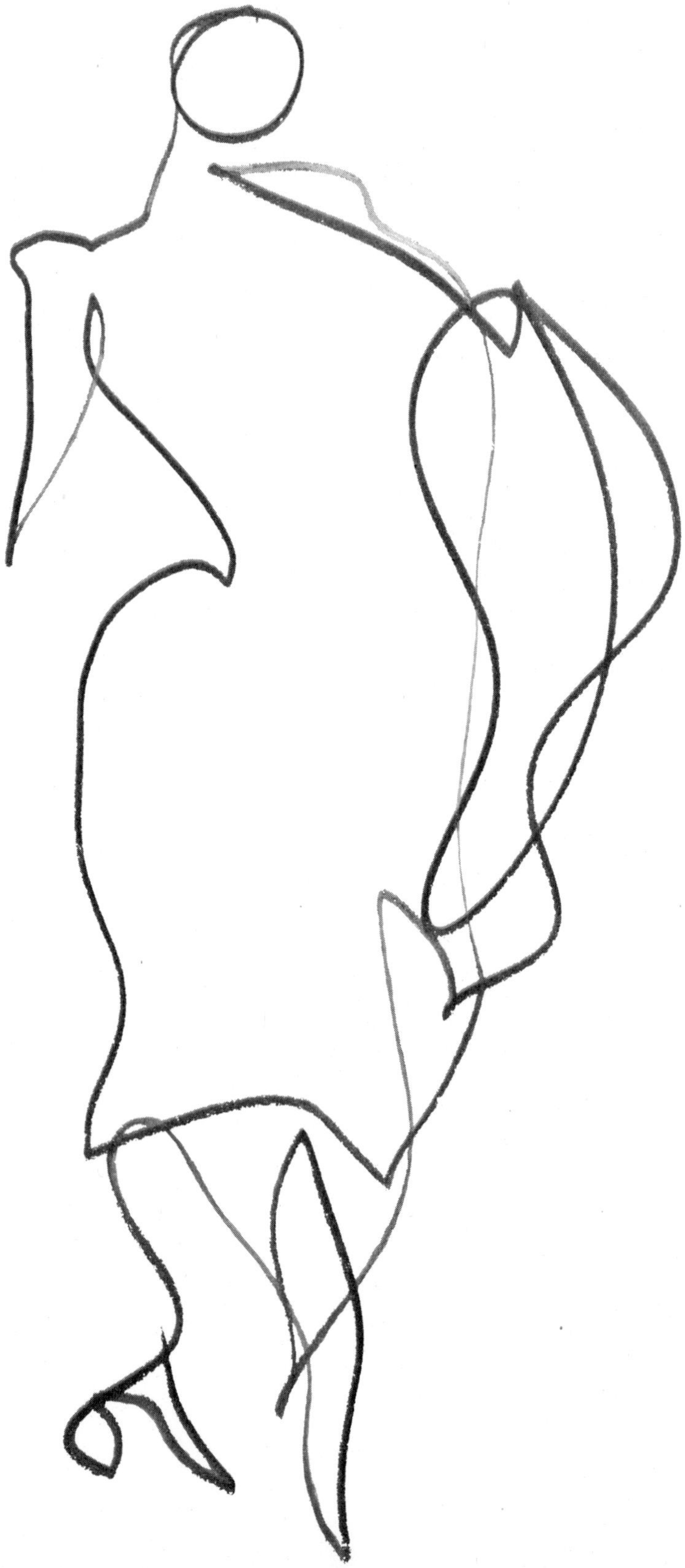

Now we come to the ultimate in quick sketches. Station yourself at some vantage point—a street-level window or someplace where you can draw people strolling about, standing and talking, or working. If possible, use your large-size sheet of paper.

The idea is to make hundreds of small, quick drawings of a wide variety of people and groups of people. Each figure should be not more than 2 inches high and should take not more than 3 seconds. As you can see they really are action scribbles. You will have to keep your pen constantly in motion on the surface of the paper; you must not pause an instant while you are drawing. Work from left to right, from top to bottom, and look at your sheet after you have it half filled up. You will be amazed to see how good most of these scribbles are—made spontaneously and fluently (but based on many hours of patient observation and critical experimentation), and speaking so eloquently of the essence of gesture and character.

Count to yourself as you make your pen fly over the paper; count quite fast—say to six—in order to suggest a rapid pace to yourself.

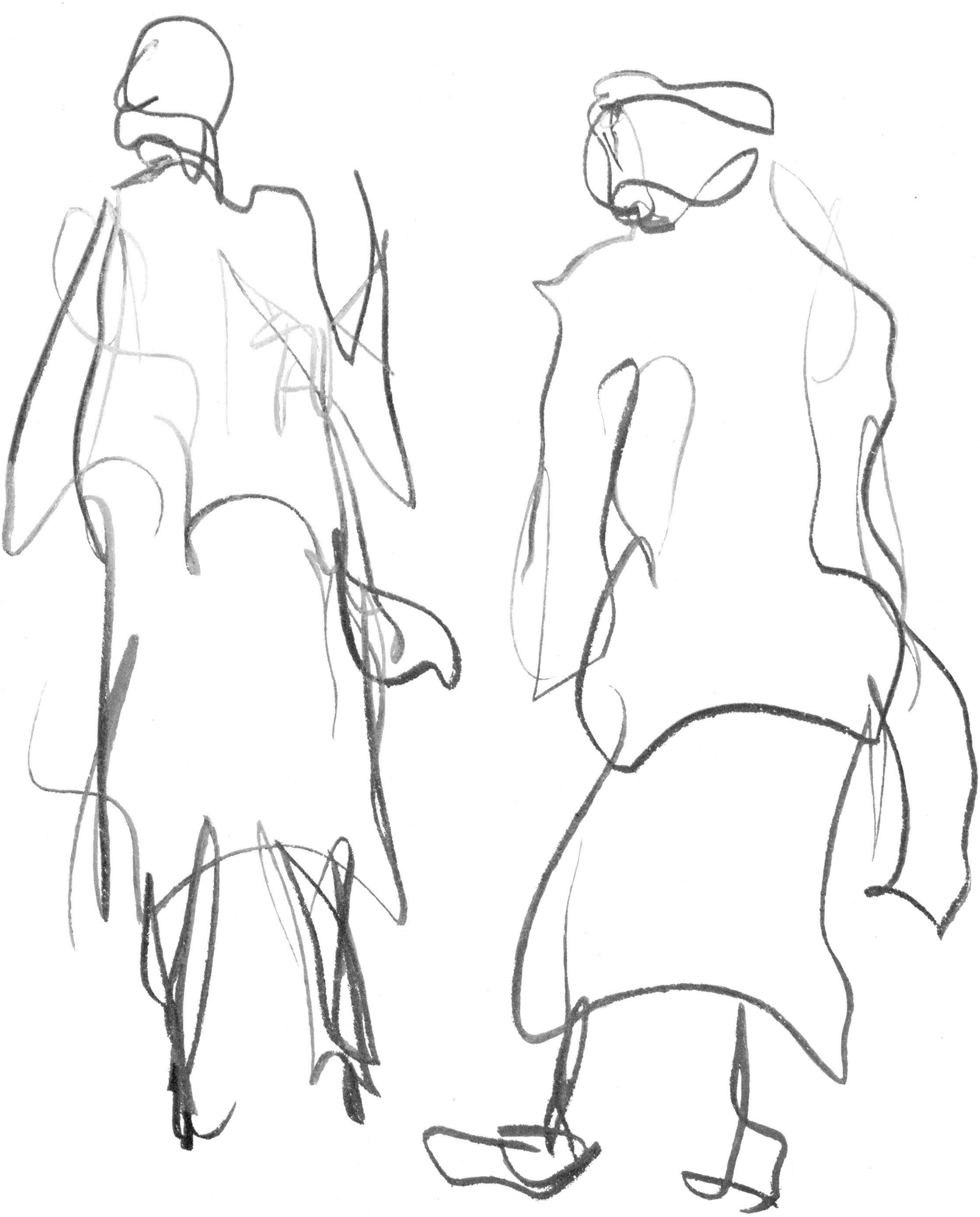

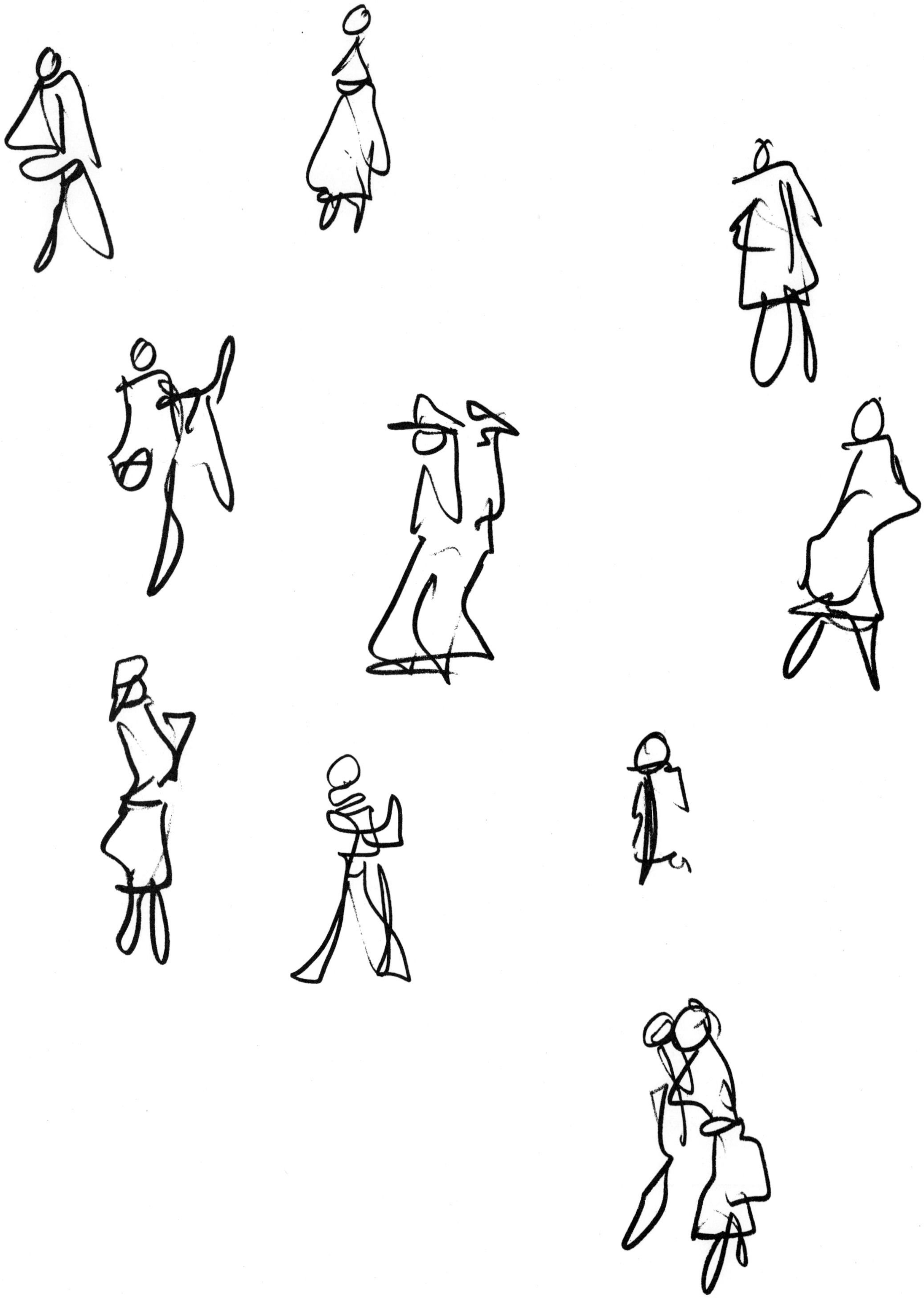

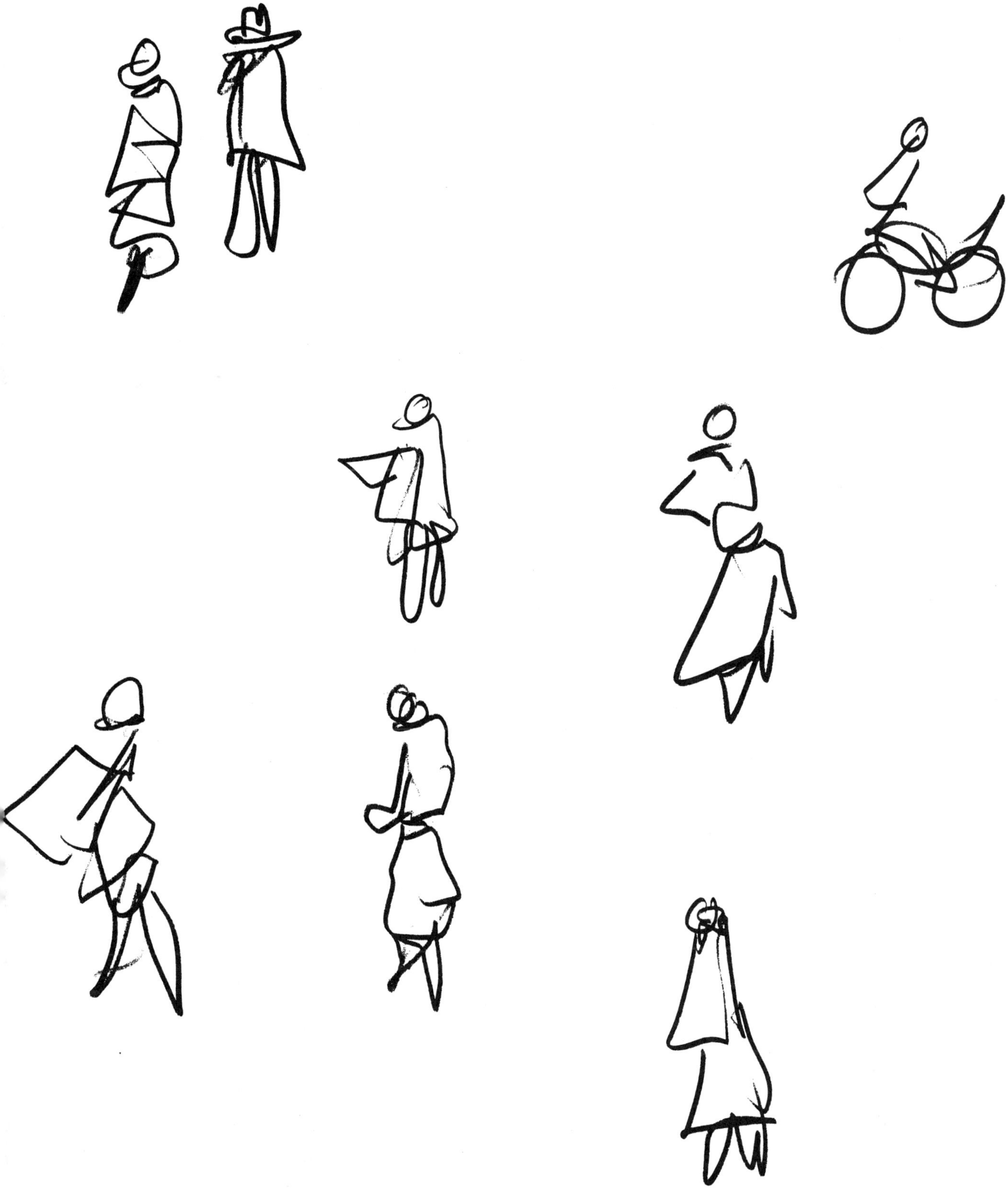

27

SYNTHESIS *six hours*

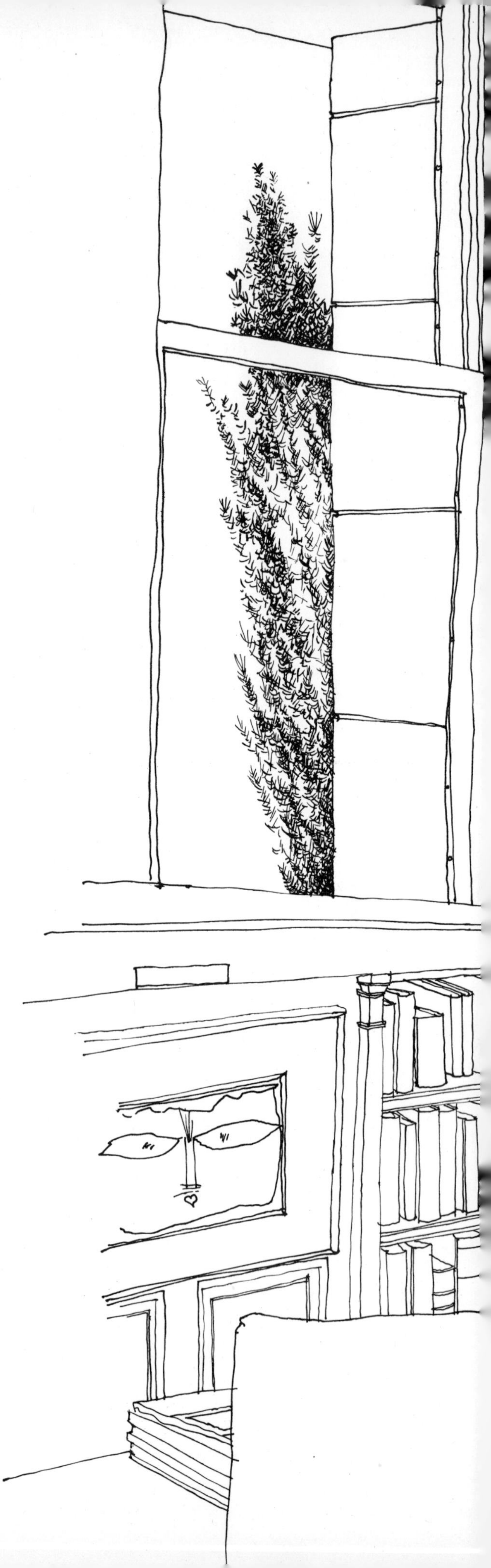

This will be the last problem set for you here. After this, the entire world is your challenge and delight. But now, as a sort of final review, locate some indoor or outdoor scene you enjoy—one that contains walls, doors, and windows; furniture, plants, and people—and draw the whole thing on a large piece of paper, carefully, slowly, and, as always, conscientiously.

Quite possibly some of the people will move or leave. No matter, leave that part of the drawing as it was. There is no law that a drawing must be complete—at least not here! Perhaps it will be best to draw the people first. If they get up and leave, or move, just carry on. There is no reason for any of these drawings to be "complete."

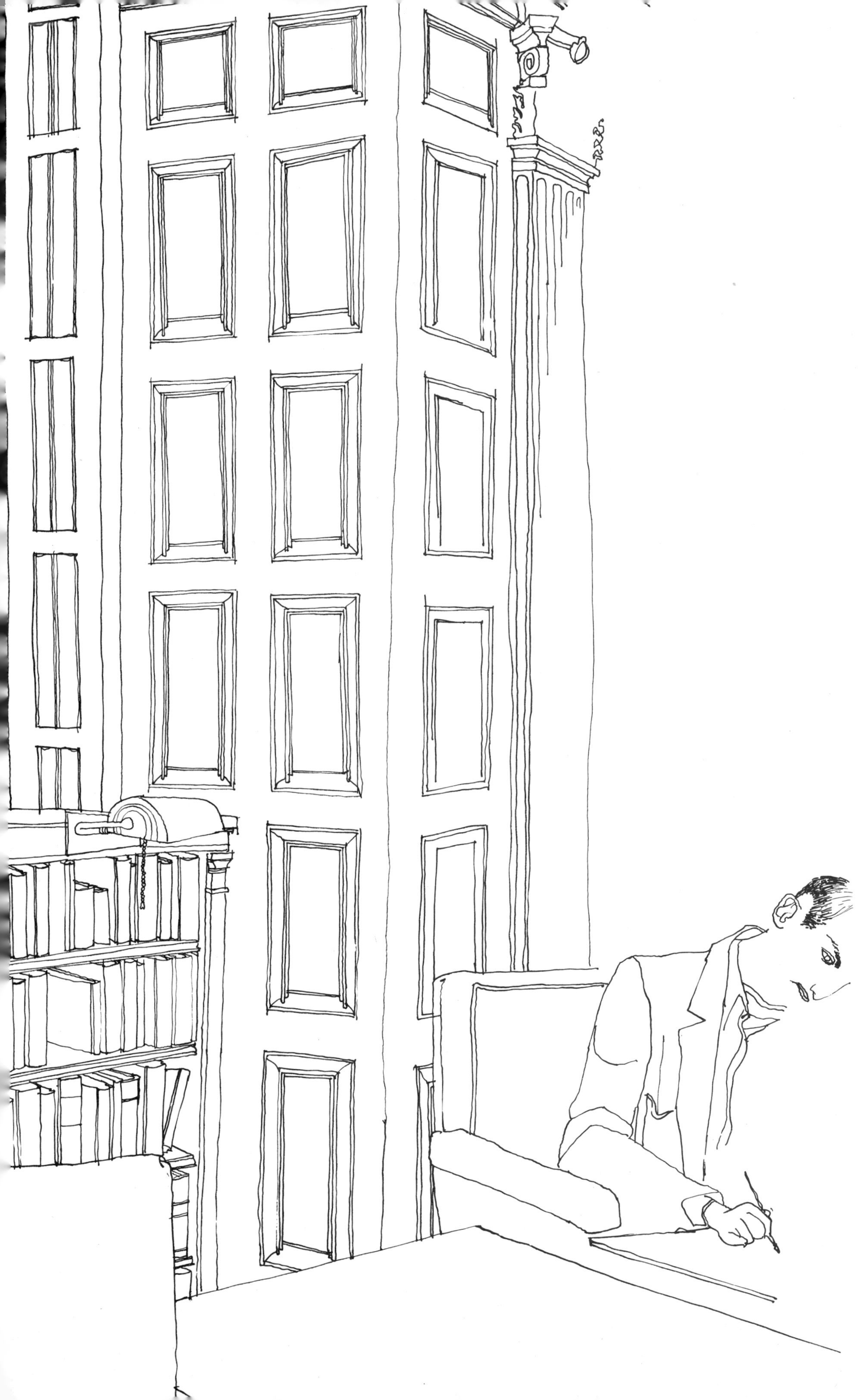

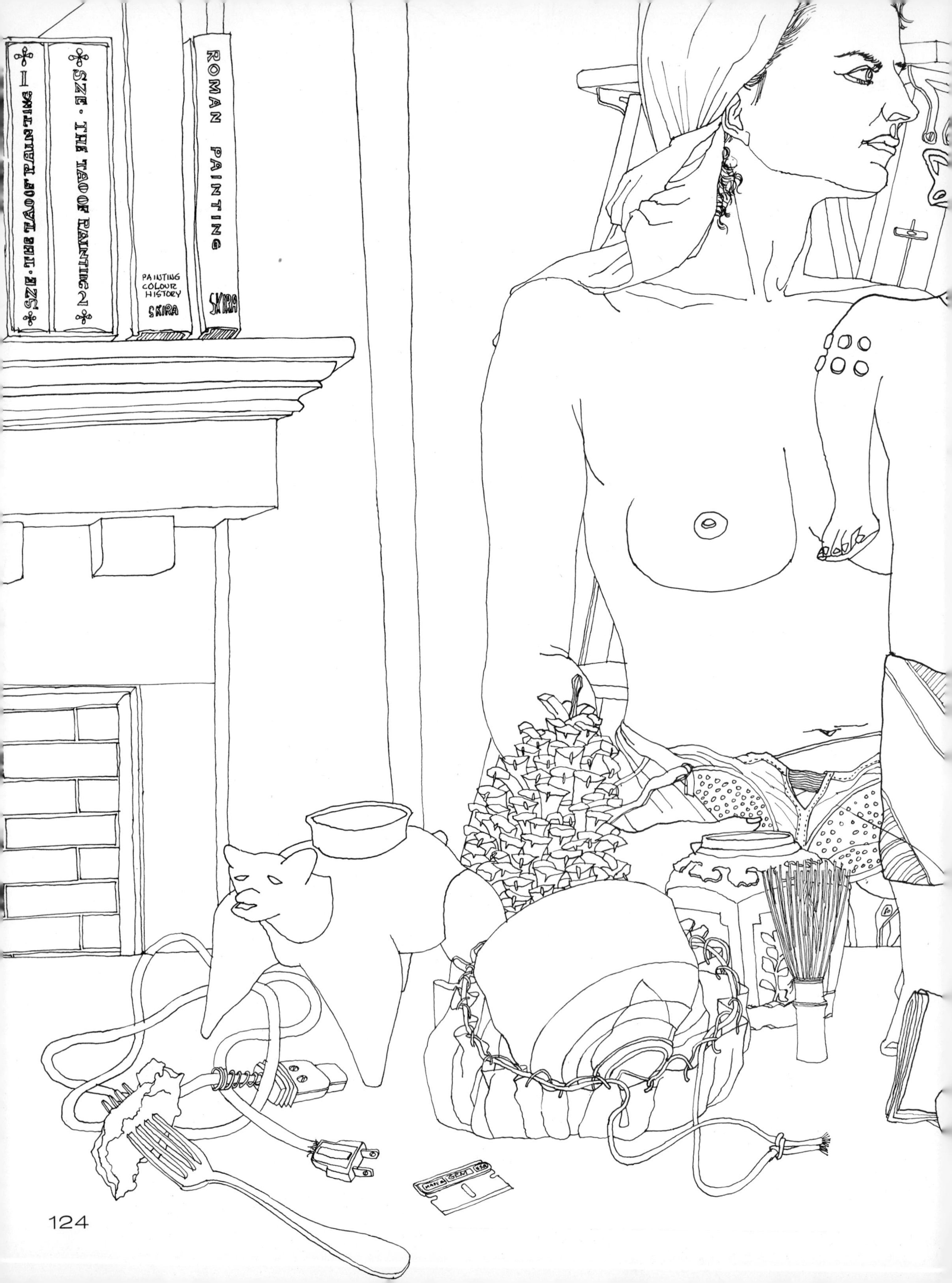
SZE · THE TAO OF PAINTING 1
SZE · THE TAO OF PAINTING 2
PAINTING COLOUR HISTORY
SKIRA
ROMAN PAINTING
SKIRA
GEM

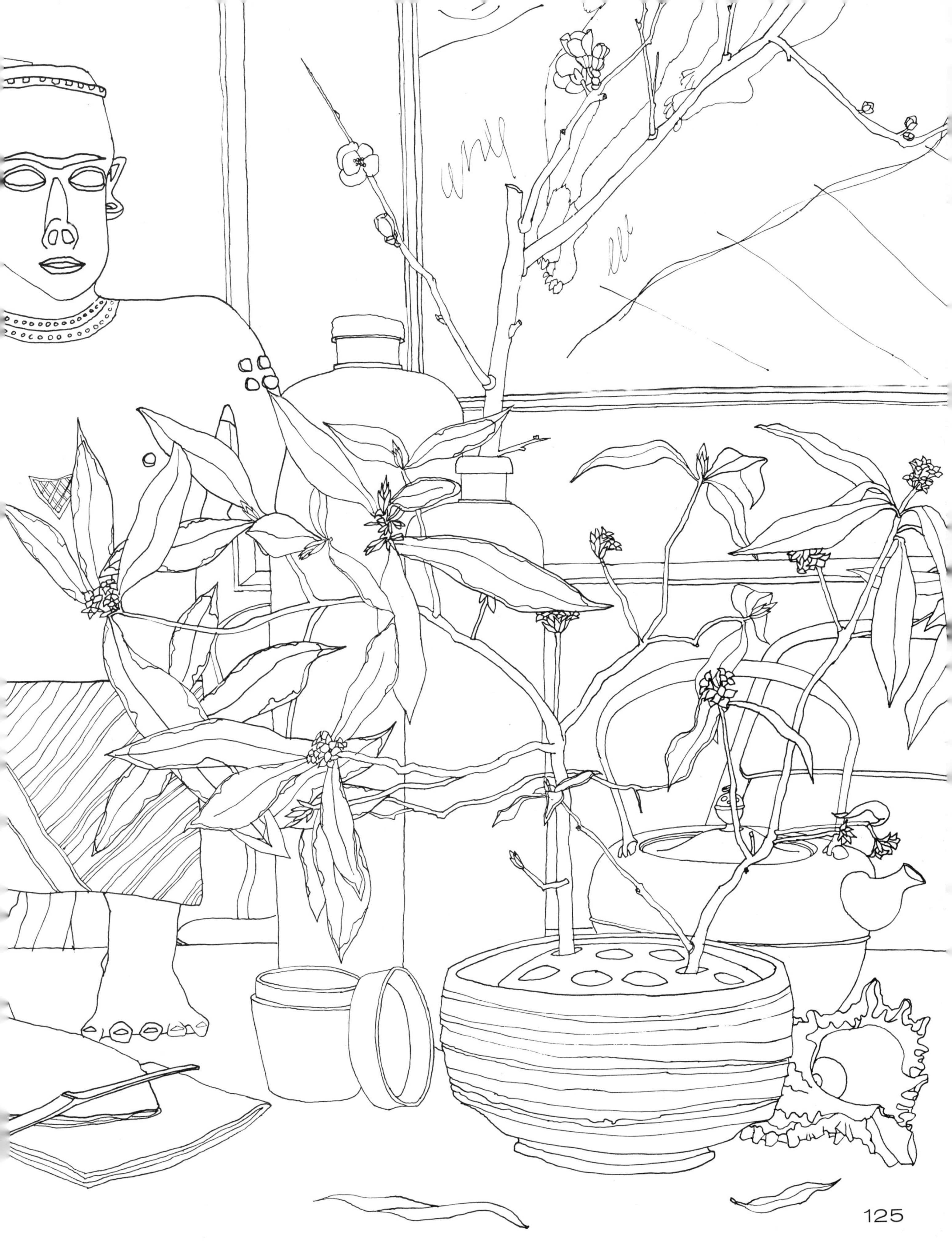

EPILOGUE

At this point, after at least ninety hours of blood, sweat, and tears (as promised you, if you have been conscientious), you are quite a different person from the one who started this primer. Hundreds of sheets of paper give evidence of your growth in sensitivity and competence. The visual world is of much more interest to you now than it was when you started, because you see it now on a new plane of greater awareness, and you can now express yourself graphically with confidence.

So, you have taken the first step of a thousand-mile trip: like Hokusai, you are on your way. But the next step is up to you. You now have the challenge of enriching your means of graphic expression by experimenting with other media than those used here, and of broadening your terms of reference in order to deepen the scope and significance of what you have to say about what you see.

From this present vantage point you will find increased value and pleasure in the drawings of the great masters, old and new, because you are now a junior member of their fraternity. Their achievements will have a new interest for you, not only because you have shared a little of their struggle, but because you can now better appreciate the significance of their achievements.